JAPAN'S FOREIGN POLICY

This book has been published with the
help of a grant from the Social Science
Research Council of Canada using funds
provided by the Canada Council.

JAPAN'S FOREIGN POLICY

F. C. LANGDON

University of British Columbia Press
Vancouver

JAPAN'S FOREIGN POLICY

International Standard Book Number 0-7748-0044-5
Library of Congress Catalog Card Number   73-78894

Printed in the United States of America

To my parents

TABLE OF CONTENTS

List of Tables and Maps

ix

Preface

THE CHANGES TAKING PLACE in the early 1970s in Japan's external relations are providing Japan with unique opportunities for new policy initiatives. Indeed, these new opportunities are forcing Japan to adopt new directions in its foreign policy. A knowledge of its past policies is not sufficient by itself to explain adequately the current trends and alternatives for Japan. Now that Japan has become a leading economic power in the world, it has the potential for a more active foreign policy, and by taking advantage of this economic strength Japan can exercise more influence in world affairs. This increased influence is facilitated by the new and more friendly relations of the major powers. As signified by President Nixon's visits to Peking and Moscow in 1972, the major states are moving towards a balance of power in which the United States is not as vigorously opposed to China and the Soviet Union, nor as closely supportive of Japan and Taiwan. By examining the recent changes in Japan's international environment, this book attempts to provide the basis for understanding the likely impact of those changes in its foreign policy.

I have attempted to select the most important objectives of the Japanese government leaders and to describe the policies of Japan which are designed to achieve these objectives. To permit a better coverage of recent policy developments, I have concentrated on the period since 1960 when the security treaty with the United States was revised amid great controversy and dissent over the alliance policy involved in it. Most of the policy developments which are described occurred during the cabinets of Prime Ministers Ikeda and Sato, but earlier policy decisions are also provided when it is felt that they are necessary for a clearer understanding of the situation.

This book is not a record of Japan's foreign relations, nor is it a compendium of its foreign relations with each country. It concentrates rather on certain goals and objectives of Japan in an attempt to discover why the government made the decisions it did. In the course of considering policy from the point of view of goals, many of Japan's important relations and problems are revealed. The material is not organized by countries but rather it is organized around Japan's goals of prosperity, security, and international recognition. The same country may be treated under one of the goals or it may be treated under all of these, depending on the country's importance to the particular goal. The treatment of goals and policies follows to a considerable extent the handling of them in Wolfram F. Hanrieder's *West German Foreign Policy, 1949-1963*

(Stanford: Stanford University Press, 1967). The postwar external environment of Japan led to many internal political developments and foreign policies similar to those of Germany and encouraged me to adopt a like treatment. In both cases the international pressures determined the type of regime and much of the foreign policy followed. However, Japan was not integrated in multilateral military alliances and economic blocs to the same extent as Germany; therefore, its foreign initiatives have been less and its attention has been absorbed by its superpower ally, the United States, which has also become its chief economic rival.

Japan's foreign economic policies are given unusually extensive treatment because Japan's prosperity goal has tended to dominate the Japanese government's concern during this period. This economically oriented treatment constitutes a new emphasis as most current writing on Japan's foreign affairs tends to emphasize matters of defense and armament as though these were the main concern of Japan's leaders. Hitherto, Japanese leaders have not sufficiently appreciated the role Japan can play in a world which is hesitating on the threshold of forming a more successful trading and investing community and which may not be able to achieve sufficient cooperation among industrialized countries as well as between them and the less developed economies. Japan's difficulty in responding more positively to world economic problems occurs like a leitmotiv throughout the book. However, in success and failure Japanese leaders have given precedence in their foreign policies to economic objectives.

Japan's comparatively small defense effort contrasts with its concentration on economic objectives. Japan's defense policies as well as the fears and misunderstandings by other countries of these policies are examined. Although Japan has yet to increase its armament on a scale comparable to that of countries with the same economic potential, it does face the need to reassess its defense policies because of changing strategic relations in the Asian area. It must decide whether to continue to rely on the United States, to rely more on itself, or to adopt a more neutralist defense policy.

In addition to Japan's goals of prosperity and security, its ambition to acquire greater international status seems to be leading it in the direction of more active influence in world affairs. This is especially true of the East Asian area where it may have to take a more active and less aligned position in the struggles for influence in the region along with the major states, such as the United States, the Sovi . Union, and China. Therefore, aside from the introductory chapters and the concluding chapter, the book is divided into separate sections on foreign economic, defense, and Asian policies for the Ikeda Cabinet and again for the Sato Cabinet.

The cabinets of Ikeda and Sato are treated separately in each of the three major policy areas because each prime minister put his own stamp on policy. Ikeda was more cautious and conciliatory in avoiding the same sort of foreign policy confrontation which had brought about the downfall of his predecessor, Kishi, attempting to satisfy the demands of the American ally while also asserting a more nationalistic and less interventionist policy to satisfy his domestic and foreign critics. In contrast, Sato—like his brother, Kishi—was willing to brush aside the objections of the opposition parties and of the minority in his own party to show his solidarity with the United States and his willingness to stand by South Korea and Taiwan. But he was ineffective in coming to grips with the sharp economic clash that developed with the United States and unable to effect normalization of relations with China. Tanaka shows some of the flexibility and conciliatory character of Ikeda in his quick resolution of the problem of normalizing relations with China and his move toward a more independent nationalist and less interventionist policy. He also has some of the resoluteness of Sato in standing by the security treaty with the United States, although it will probably have to be modified to release Japan from its Far Eastern commitments. The great task of Tanaka is to stop the economic collision with the United States and salvage Japan's most important foreign relationship through a modified security or friendship treaty. If he can master the good points of both Ikeda's and Sato's cabinet leadership, he should succeed.

The crisis year of 1960 is treated extensively in chapter 2 because it was the time of the greatest consideration of Japan's most basic foreign policy of alliance with the United States. Debate and political agitation was much greater even than during the period of 1950 to 1951 when the policy was worked out in the midst of the Korean War. This basic policy consideration will have to be undertaken again in the mid-1970s to arrive at a new equilibrium appropriate to the needs and goals of both Japan and the United States in the international politics of a more fluid "multipolar" world. Chapter 2 also starkly illustrates all the important features of Japan's foreign policy-making process: the external pressures and the domestic response in terms of the struggle with the opposition parties, the struggle within the governing Liberal Democratic party, the role of the government ministries and agencies, the role of business leaders and private organizations, the part of unionists and students, and not least, that of public opinion. Nevertheless, this account is not a systematic analysis of Japan's foreign policy-making because that has already been done in a thorough manner in Donald C. Hellmann's *Japanese Domestic Politics and Foreign Policy* (Berkeley: University of California Press, 1969)—an analysis of foreign policy-making in the mid-1950s which is still applicable. I have also briefly covered the same subject under the title of "Japan's Foreign Policy-Making Process" in the collection, *Japan in World Politics,* edited by Young C. Kim (Washington, D.C.: Institute for Asian Studies, 1972).

The term "Far East," which is purposely vague as used in the Japan-United States Security Treaty, is usually equivalent to the term "East Asia," which is preferred in the text. This latter term is used increasingly outside Japan for the region from Burma and Malaysia in the west to Japan in the east, including China, Korea, and the Soviet Far East. However, the term "East Asia" tends to be avoided in Japan because it was widely used during the Second World War for Japan's sphere of influence and thus has an undesirable connotation of military expansionism in the Japanese language. Instead, it is common in Japan to use the terms "Southeast Asia" or "Asia" rather imprecisely for much of this region.

I have followed the practice of preferring the term "East Asia" except where the term "Far East," as used in the security treaty, is being referred to. During the Ikeda and Sato Cabinets, the term "Far East," as referred to in the security treaty, was understood to mean primarily Korea and Taiwan. At times the Philippines was included in the reference and during the Vietnam War, Indochina was also included. Under the terms of the security treaty, Japan had only the obligation to permit American forces based in Japan to operate freely in the Far East. The Sato-Nixon communique of November 1969 more specifically reaffirmed that South Korea (the Republic of Korea) and Taiwan (the Republic of China) were included under this provision. Among government leaders, the special meaning of "Far East" to designate at least South Korea and Taiwan has been fully understood throughout the period covered by this book.

I would like to acknowledge fully the help of many people too numerous to mention individually by name who have helped me in the preparation of this book over the past five years. They include friends, scholars, and government officials in Japan, Canada, Australia, and the United States. I would particularly like to thank Professor Donald C. Hellmann of the University of Washington, who helped immeasurably with his many suggestions and criticisms.

University of British Columbia
January 1973

F. C. LANGDON

1

Goals and Constraints

PRIME MINISTER TANAKA'S signing of the agreement to establish diplomatic relations with China on 29 September 1972 was one of the most important moves by Japan since it achieved its independence twenty years earlier. Thus, only two months after taking office the new prime minister opened the way to a peace treaty and the end of the hostility with Japan's huge neighbor which had reached a postwar peak under his predecessor. That the year 1972 was a major turning point in Asian and world affairs was further indicated by the unprecedented visit of President Richard Nixon to Peking in February and his virtual agreement that the problem of the rival regime in Taiwan was an internal one for China in which the United States no longer wished to intervene. The meeting of President Nixon with the Japanese prime minister in Hawaii just before Tanaka's historic visit to Peking and the reopening of discussions on a peace treaty with the Soviet Union in Moscow afterward indicate Japan's unaccustomed position of being sought after by all the other major powers. This was a dramatic change from only a year before when Japan was the principal object of American trade and currency sanctions and accused by China of imperialistic aggression.

Is Japan on the threshhold of a new era in Asian international relations in which it is more able than formerly to take initiatives in what is a more fluid external and internal political environment? Not only are the other great powers seeking Japan's favor but Vietnam hostilities have halted once more, thus further promoting relaxation of tensions in the region. However, the Tanaka Cabinet faces intractable problems of inflation and a dangerous trade gap with the United States which are likely to absorb most of its attention. Also, Tanaka has already shown close adherence to previous security policies.

Since the end of the postwar occupation, Japan's principal goals have been to promote its prosperity, insure its security, and gain recognition as a leading world power. It has substantially achieved the first two of these goals, and Japan now has the potential for exercising much greater influence in the world and winning its place as a leading world power. It could utilize its technology and industry to acquire the military strength traditionally associated with major powers, but it would be very difficult to equal the United States or the Soviet Union in this sphere. Besides this, it would also be very desirable if Japan's security and influence could be sufficiently assured without such power.

The great problem for Japan now is to decide the direction it should take in its future development: whether Japan should rearm on a vast scale, and possibly even include nuclear arms; or whether it should continue with its present policy of a limited defense force and augment its role as an economic great power by more extensively assisting the poorer countries, particularly those in Asia. It is evident that Japan's leaders now desire to achieve the status of a leading power without the necessity for nuclear arms and without any large-scale armament. Foreign Minister Fukuda came closest to expressing this goal when he said, "We wish to employ our economic strength to gain an increasing voice in the international community. The tradition once was that a nation used its economic power to become a military power, but that is not the case with us today."[1]

Because of the Japanese people's disillusionment with imperialism and an awareness of the fears of other countries of a revival of Japanese militarism, the government leaders of Japan scrupulously have avoided vainglorious ambitions and they have followed largely non-military and non-interventionist policies. Instead, they have relied upon the peaceful means of trade and economic aid to win both influence and recognition.

For the important goal of security or defense, Japan relies partly upon its own so-called Self-Defense Forces which it has developed slowly and moderately over the years at the urging of the United States. In addition, it relies upon the United States to protect it from any threats or attacks from either nuclear or large conventional forces. Under the terms of the security treaty, Japan receives this cooperation from its great power ally, the United States, and in return Japan lends military bases in Japan to American forces to assist in defending Japan and neighboring countries, such as South Korea and Taiwan. The Nixon Doctrine, which calls for greater independence and self-defense by its allies, provides the challenge for Japan to emerge from its semi-isolationist

[1]C. L. Sulzberger, "Japan's Sun Also Rises," *New York Times*, 10 March 1972, p. 37.

policy and to play a greater role in the Asian region, perhaps even to add a greater modicum of military influence to its foreign policies, which have been so commercially orientated.

Because all of Japan's neighbors fear the possibility of strong Japanese military forces, Japan has tried not to provoke nations in East Asia by avoiding any direct intervention or threat of intervention outside its own territory.[2] It has complemented this passive role with the more constructive one of promoting trade with those countries with which it does not have any formal diplomatic relations, as with China until 1972.

It is the goal of promoting its own prosperity in which Japan has displayed the greatest initiative in its foreign policy. Through reparations, credits, and loans it has gradually re-established diplomatic relations with its non-communist neighbors and built a prosperous trade with a large number of these countries. Through its global commerce especially with the developed countries of the Pacific rim, it has obtained raw materials and, in return, has sold its manufactured goods to them. These economic policies have enabled Japan to recover from wartime damage and to experience unprecedented economic growth and prosperity while bringing its standard of living to a par with some of the advanced countries of Western Europe. In contrast to the period before the Second World War, Japan's trade and investment is now concentrated with its Pacific rim partners, the United States, Canada, and Australia rather than with its Asian neighbors. This concentration of trade with its Pacific rim partners has resulted in a greater interdependence with the developed industrialized countries, although its Asian neighbors continue to be important not only for Japan's prosperity but also for its security. However, it still has not restored completely normal relations with China and the Soviet Union.

Japan cannot pursue its goals exactly as it might wish. Instead, Japan must operate within the framework of constraints both external and internal. The major external constraints are Japan's relations with the major powers and their relations with each other. The pattern of foreign relations in the world since 1949 has been the confrontation of alliances of the Communist states against some of the non-Communist ones. This confrontation reached its peak at the outbreak of the Korean War in 1950 just at the time the United States was sponsoring the return of Japan's independence and the end of its occupation. With the choice of continuing the occupation or achieving independence as an ally of the United States, Japan chose the latter which consequently pitted

---

[2] In this book, China is used to refer to the People's Republic under the Chinese Communists with the capital in Peking. Taiwan is used to refer to the Republic of China under the Chinese nationalists with the capital in Taipei on the island of Taiwan.

it against the Communist states, especially China and the Soviet Union. As American relations have gradually improved with China and the Soviet Union, the cold war confrontation has been reduced. However, Japan's relations with the Communist bloc have been complicated by the hostility of China and Russia, with each other as well as toward Japan.

It is precisely these relations, which have changed with the waning of the cold war to offer more freedom to Japan, which have alarmed many outside of Japan. Combined with Japan's growing economic power this new freedom has given rise to widespread fears of a revival of Japanese militarism. What is not yet understood abroad is that the internal domestic constraints in Japan will probably prevent such a development. It is the purpose of chapter 2 which deals with the 1960 foreign policy crisis, to explain the constraints on Japanese policy, especially as they are manifested in inter-party and intra-party rivalry. While these internal factors will undoubtedly encourage Japan to take a more independent foreign policy, the one policy course least likely to be pursued is military expansionism. In fact, among the Japanese public, dislike of anything smacking of militarism has continued to be a potent internal constraint and has fueled the deep domestic division over Japan's policy of military cooperation with the United States that erupted in 1960.

Whether Japan, in fact, decides upon some new policy initiatives depends a great deal on the internal political constraints from inter-party and intra-party rivalries. These may be as confining as the external constraints from great power rivalry, which are usually more intractable. Probably the most confining restraint on Japan is the very nature of its political party system and its decision-making process. The Liberal Democratic party has continued to maintain unshaken control of the government even though there has been an extraordinary difference of opinion in foreign policy matters with opposition parties. Despite the Liberal Democratic party's majority of seats in the Diet since 1955, it has been inhibited in its defense policies by the opposition. The opposition, led by the Japan Socialist party, has vigorously opposed Japan's defense policy of close cooperation with the United States. Its strong objections to the Japan-United States Security Treaty, the American military bases, and even to expansion of Japan's own armed forces, reflect a deep division in Japanese politics. Its opposition to government policy is shared by most of its supporters—trade unionists, students, and intellectuals. Such inter-party rivalry over defense questions has given rise to street demonstrations and to obstruction and violence in the Diet. As a result it has not been possible, even, to consider conscription, despite the rapid dwindling in the number of young men eligible for military training under voluntary recruitment; the composition and mission of Japanese defense forces have remained limited in scope.

Intra-party rivalry is keen and highly organized. Although there is general agreement on basic defense policy within the ruling party, allegiances can shift in the course of intra-party disputes. The rapid return to normal relations with China and the severing of diplomatic ties with Taiwan in 1972, for example, resulted from the accession of Kakuei Tanaka to party and government leadership and the eclipse of the more vocal anti-Communist members of the Liberal Democratic party.

The conservative politicians united in the Liberal Democratic party have been organized into tight factions in the Diet under the leadership of a dozen prominent leaders. In the competition within the party for the office of party president, the factions have balanced each other in such a way that major policy changes are very difficult to make without disturbing the inner-party equilibrium. Since the president of the majority party is automatically prime minister, it is obvious how important the maintenance of equilibrium becomes. Foreign policy is just one of the areas in which this faction struggle can lead to the downfall of the cabinet and change the leadership within the party. Particularly under Prime Ministers Ikeda and Sato there was a strong tendency to postpone new initiatives and avoid inner-party disturbances. Their predecessors, Kishi and Hatoyama, both fell from grace because of foreign policy decisions which resulted in conflict, not only between parties but also within the ruling party itself. While public opinion, big business, bureaucracy, and opposition parties are important influences on foreign policy, it is this internal equilibrium within the ruling party which represents a great constraint in foreign policy-making.

The national genius for group decision or avoidance of a clear-cut decision is given much scope. This style of behavior militates against decisive leadership, but it is not only the ruling party leaders who suffer from indecision. The bureaucracy, too, suffers from this characteristic. Big business was very critical of the finance ministry officials who tried vainly to keep the yen at its old value for two weeks after the shock of Nixon's economic policy of 15 August 1971 when he levied a surcharge on Japanese imports and forced Japan to revalue its currency. Business leaders were both admiring and envious of the incisiveness of President Nixon, who had been advised by men such as Secretary of the Treasury Connolly and Henry Kissinger,[3] but the Japanese bureaucracy and cabinet could not provide comparable leadership. It was only under Prime Minister Yoshida that the Japanese prime minister showed the decisiveness of an American president. Significantly, Yoshida was relatively unrestrained by strong party factions when he was making the far-reaching decisions in foreign policy which guide Japan to this

---

[3] *Japan Times Weekly*, International Edition, Vol. XII, No. 1 (1 January 1972), p. 12.

day. Even with expert assistants in foreign affairs or decisive cabinet ministers, such as an American president has, the balance of party factions and their supporting groups would still inhibit the Japanese government leader to a great extent.

However, a new party president and prime minister enjoys a short honeymoon period when he is consolidating his position, and he may be able to maintain the momentum he develops as a critic of the preceding leadership. Thus, changes in ruling party leadership will facilitate new foreign policy initiatives. If these occur in a fairly fluid internal and external environment as in 1972, they may permit considerable change. If Japan's leadership continues to seize the initiative during the balance of the seventies Japan will begin to act more like a leading world power.

Unlike other important powers, with the exception of Britain, Japan is handicapped by an unusually extreme degree of dependence upon distant global sources of raw materials at the same time that fear of Japanese economic power or military revival is easily aroused against it. Even if Japan were able to increase its military potential, it is doubtful that this alone would make Japan a great power. The path of economic leadership in Asia and in the world economy, which Japan has been following, is probably the best way it can play the role of a leading power. The danger in this course of action is that the global impact of Japan's economy needs to be controlled more carefully to minimize the clash with its major trading partners and to persuade them to cooperate with Japan.

Japan is poised on the verge of acceptance as a leading world power—by virtue of its economic strength alone. While the other major powers achieve their stature by a combination of economic strength *and* nuclear weaponry, Japan's unique position conveys to it an attractive and enviable basis for world leadership. It may require the toleration of the great military powers, but it has obvious mutual advantages if Japan is encouraged to be less aligned but committed to a policy of cooperation and assistance in solving the problems of countries, rich and poor alike. The disarmament thrust upon Japan after the Second World War followed by the concept of limited self-defense, which it has chosen for itself since that time, may yet prove to be the way to win distinction and the status of a leading world power to which Japan rather idealistically has aspired since that war.

To understand present policy and likely future trends thoroughly, it is essential to go back to the political agitation and reconsideration of Japan's basic policy of alliance with the United States which took place in the crisis year of 1960. This issue—and the way it was handled—will be considered next.

2

The 1960 Crisis

FOR JAPAN, the year 1960 was the most critical of any since the Second World War. It was in that year that the Japanese people saw most clearly the deep and emotional divisions which separated them. The issue was the revision of defense policy. The inter-party and intra-party confrontations were extreme and public participation was greater than it had ever been before—or has been since. Perhaps most important was the nature and scope of the constraints operating in Japan both during the crisis over the passage of the Mutual Security Treaty with the United States and afterward when Prime Minister Ikeda restored stability.

The ratification of the treaty in 1960 offered an opportunity to reconsider Japan's policy of depending on an American security guarantee and permitting American bases in Japan to be used for protecting South Korea and Taiwan. The antagonism between the United States and the Soviet Union in 1960 seemed to reconfirm the danger from the Soviet Union if Japan continued to provoke it by lending bases to the United States. However, the manner in which Prime Minister Kishi pushed the treaty bills through the Diet aroused the indignation of parliament and public alike and diverted attention from the improved terms of the treaty. The basic revision of policy, in fact, was overlooked. The treaty was ratified only by a parliamentary strategem and evoked continued opposition from a vocal segment of the population which has been able to check any extensive military commitments on the Japanese side. The treaty became law but the passions it aroused were sufficient to cause the ruling party to change leaders.

For a long time, Japan had recognized the importance of economic growth as a basis for achieving its other goals. The economic dependence

7

which grew up with the United States was greatly facilitated by the prior conditions of the Allied occupation. When the United States found itself continuing to occupy the two former enemy states of Germany and Japan and compelled to give them emergency aid, it feared this would turn out to be an unreasonable financial burden. Instead, it decided to extend rehabilitation aid to these countries similar to the Marshall Plan, which had been intended to assist its wartime allies to recover from both economic and political setbacks. By giving rehabilitation aid to Japan, the United States became its sponsor among the other Western countries and ensured Japan's entre to Western markets and resources, thereby ensuring that it would be self-sufficient.

After the war, with the Communist control of mainland China and the isolation of Japan from many of its Asian neighbors, Japan was even more dependent on the United States as a source of supply and as a market for its exports. This situation was further magnified by the American disposal of surplus agricultural commodities through Japan to supply the initial lack of food and raw materials for processing. Even after Japanese independence in 1952, American surpluses continued to be sold to Japan so that a considerable degree of economic interdependence was created which helped to fuel the growth of trade that became so great in the 1960s.

Despite his long resistence to rearmament, Prime Minister Yoshida had felt compelled in the 1950s to yield to American pressure for Japanese rearmament, which involved the receipt of surplus and even obsolescent military equipment of which the United States wanted to dispose. Military interdependence paralleled economic interdependence, although the Japanese prime minister and his successors never armed to the extent urged by the United States. They gave priority to the civilian economic recovery and growth and only diverted to military defense the minimum effort necessary to win American cooperation and economic support. In fact, Japan's stance on its armed forces seemed to be more of a concession to ensure economic assistance, whereas American economic assistance tended to be a concession to ensure Japanese military cooperation.

In 1950, Ikeda, who was then finance minister, was selected by Prime Minister Yoshida to go to Washington as his envoy to offer the use of military bases in Japan in exchange for a security arrangement with the United States in connection with a peace treaty.[1] The more immediate purpose of the visit was to get the Japanese austerity budget, which had been imposed by the occupation headquarters, modified to ease the business depression in Japan. As the trip would have been disallowed

---

[1] Kiichi Miyazawa, *Tokyo—Washinton no Mitsudan* (Tokyo: Jitsugyo no Nihon Sha, 1956), pp. 47-52.

by General Douglas MacArthur's staff for its real purpose, it was represented as an inspection tour for the finance minister to familiarize himself with the latest techniques abroad and thus enable him to evade the eye of the military headquarters.[2]

Ikeda's discussions in May 1950 in Washington laid the foundations for both the peace and security treaties by providing for "temporary" American protection of Japan in exchange for military bases in Japan being provided for the American forces. These bases were intended to defend Japan as well as South Korea and Taiwan, ensuring American domination of the area.[3] Official negotiations were broken off just as they began when the Korean War broke out. Upon resumption, the negotiations did, however, confirm the military cooperation which had been secretly contemplated in May by Japan and the United States. A security treaty was finally signed in San Francisco in September 1951, on the same day as the peace treaty, which provided military bases in Japan in return for a guarantee of Japan's defense by the United States.

Ikeda thus was a participant in the first negotiations which led to the military alliance between the countries that was later to be the greatest cause of division in Japanese politics. Ikeda, as Yoshida's representative, was also seeking economic assistance at the expense of concession in the defense sphere. This was destined to be the kind of formula in both international and domestic politics followed by him and by his successor, Sato.

Again, in 1953, on Yoshida's behalf, Ikeda went to the United States to discuss economic and military matters.[4] At these meetings, the American Secretary of State, John Foster Dulles, pressed for repayment of the aid given by the United States during the occupation and also for the creation of a Japanese military force of more than 300,000 men, which would be similar to that later to be created by West Germany. Ikeda pressed Yoshida's long-standing objections to such a force. Nevertheless, he agreed to a gradual increase of 20,000 men to bring the Japanese Land Self-Defense Force to a total of 180,000 men—a goal still not fully reached even by the early 1970s.

From 1954 to 1960, the Japanese government was not led by Yoshida's proteges, but mainly by his two chief rivals among the conservative politicians, Hatoyama and Kishi. However, upon assuming the office of the prime minister they quickly adopted most of Yoshida's foreign policies. In doing so they aspired to less dependence upon the United States. Hatoyama restored diplomatic relations with the Soviet Union,

[2] Ibid., pp. 39–46.
[3] Ibid., p. 59.
[4] Ibid., pp. 167–280.

and Kishi restored trade and established more friendly relations with the Asian non-Communist neighbors and sought greater influence for Japan in the defense cooperation with the United States.

In late 1958, the opposition political parties and their supporters—chiefly trade unions and some university student leaders—had already led a successful campaign against the government.The cause was a bill to increase the powers of the police. The ruling party was deeply split over the bill and rather than risk further fragmentation of his government, Kishi, the prime minister of the time, withdrew the bill. However, the student leaders thought their violent protests had frightened the government into submission.

The opposition parties had opposed the original security treaty in 1951 and had hoped to use the joint protest approach, which had been so successful in 1958, to arouse irresistible opposition to the new security treaty in favor of having no security treaty and as a result, no foreign military bases. In particular, the Socialists criticized and opposed the new security treaty from the time of its introduction into the Diet. Ouside the Diet, the opposition to the new treaty was coordinated by the People's Council to Prevent Revision of the Security Treaty in which the General Council of Trade Unions (Sohyo) and the Japan Socialist party were the most important participating organizations. The Japan Communist party and the National Federation of Student Self-Government Associations (Zengakuren) some of whose leaders had become enamored of violence were denied full sponsorship status but managed to participate in planning and carrying out anti-treaty demonstrations anyway.

On 27 November 1959, the council conducted a petition march on the Diet with the participation of about 25,000 people. Nearly 5,000 rioting young workers and students broke into the Diet compound under radical student leaders with the largely unwitting assistance of the Socialist Diet leaders who intended that only a few people were to be admitted to peacefully present petitions to the government. On 16 January 1960, a student group struggled with the police to obtain control of Haneda Airport in a vain attempt to prevent Prime Minister Kishi from flying to Washington to sign the security treaty. The police prevailed and Kishi proceeded to Washington where he signed the treaty on 19 January 1960.

Within the Diet, the opposition Socialists were vigorous in their criticism of the treaty bills which had to be passed to constitute ratification of the treaty. They demanded a dissolution of the House of Representatives and the calling of a new election which, in effect, would act as a referendum on the treaty. Unprecedentedly long hearings were held in the Special Committee on the Security Treaty in the House of Representatives. The opposition speakers seized upon every point that could be used to embarrass the government spokesmen who felt compelled mainly to reiterate the government's support of the agreement.

If the government had disregarded the opposition and brought the treaty to a vote on 26 April 1960, there would have been thirty days left in the session. According to the Constitution, if the second house, the House of Councillors, had failed to approve the treaty within the thirty days, the treaty would automatically have taken effect on 26 May. However, on 26 April, an even larger demonstration than that of November was held near the Diet by the council which had planned it in expectation of the government forcing a vote. The Liberal Democratic leaders permitted debate to proceed and wished to extend the session to insure time for discussion and passage.

In the meantime, the international situation had deteriorated as the cold war had flared up under President Eisenhower and Prime Minister Krushchev. President Eisenhower was due to go to the Soviet Union and visit with Prime Minister Krushchev and then return to the United States via the Far East and Japan on a mission of friendship and peace. Unfortunately, almost the opposite occurred. On 1 May, an American reconnaissance plane, a U-2, was shot down over the Soviet Union but the United States initially denied even having a plane in the area. Prime Minister Khrushchev then announced that the pilot, Francis Gary Powers of the American Central Intelligence Agency, had been captured. This led to his trial and imprisonment in the Soviet Union and to the admission by the American president of American responsibility for the spy flights. At the summit meeting in Paris between the two leaders, Krushchev denounced Eisenhower. A "friendly" visit to the Soviet Union was clearly impossible and the president replaced it with an inspection tour of military bases in the Far East, including Japan. The president's visit to Japan therefore assumed a military character in contrast to the original plan.

Earlier, similar U-2 reconnaissance planes were discovered to be based in Japan, and the Japanese Socialists claimed they were for sinister missions despite American disclaimers that they were only used for high-altitude weather observation. The Socialists insisted that such planes were contrary to Japanese-American security arrangements and that these "black jets" were an example of American bad faith under the current security treaty. The admission that these planes were indeed used for reconnaissance of the Soviet Union was a severe blow to the Japanese government leaders and its advocacy of the new security treaty. Japan was further agitated by the claim of the Soviet Defense Minister

Malinovsky that he had ordered Soviet rocket commanders to strike back at military bases from which any planes took off to violate Soviet air space.[5]

The Japanese government's sudden passage of the treaty on the night of 19 May amid great opposition and confusion produced a serious crisis in Japan. Normally, when a matter has not been settled in Diet proceedings on the last day or two of a session, the session can be extended, although the opposition may attempt to filibuster to prevent it and thus cancel any pending legislation. However, on 19 May, well before the scheduled end of the session on 26 May the government party leaders had their members of the Steering Committee for the House of Representatives ask to extend the session for fifty days to give time for deliberation on the treaty. The party leaders had their members on the executive of the Special Committee on the Security Treaty take the contradictory tactic of proposing that the treaty discussion be ended in that committee, presumably so that it could be taken up in the house plenary session. This maneuver disregarded the requirement of examining all petitions in committee before ending consideration of a matter.

The opposition members of the steering committee objected to the extension request and then refused to attend any further meetings. In their absence the government members voted in favor of extension. The Socialists who attended the special treaty committee meeting submitted a motion of non-confidence in the government, which according to the rules of the Diet took precedence over the other business. However, there was a great deal of shouting and confusion during which the chairman declared that the motion of the government party members to discharge the bills had been passed. In protest, most of the Socialist Diet members and their secretaries sat down in the corridor leading to the chamber of the House of Representatives to prevent the speaker from opening the meeting. The speaker repeatedly asked the Socialists to leave the corridor, but they refused. Finally he called in 500 policemen to carry the Socialists out of the building. The Socialist Diet members refused to re-enter the House of Representatives and boycotted the plenary session. When the plenary session finally opened just after midnight there were no opposition members present. Members of some government party factions were not informed that the treaty itself would be voted on, and some of them had left while some of those who remained refused to cast a vote. The remaining Liberal Democrats passed the motion to extend the session and then passed the treaty bills which had been discharged from the treaty committee even though only the extension of the session to permit further consideration had been announced earlier.

[5]George R. Packard, *Protest in Tokyo, The Security Treaty Crisis of 1960* (Princeton: Princeton University Press, 1966), p. 233.

The Socialists refused to attend any other Diet meeting for the remainder of the session and claimed that the two committee meetings and the plenary session were improper and that the actions taken were invalid. However, the government had the majority of votes in the committees and the house and was able to pass its bills. The Socialists even considered carrying the Diet boycott further by resigning en masse. They hoped that this might force a dissolution and a new election which would nullify the unilateral treaty passage. This tactic was not resorted to because it was doubted that it would deter the conservatives.

The reason for the sudden approval of the treaty, which had not been announced openly beforehand, gradually became evident. The passage at that time would result in ratification thirty days later, on 19 June when President Eisenhower was scheduled to arrive in Japan—to inspect American Far Eastern defenses and not as an envoy of peace. The government was therefore denounced as being subservient and irresponsible.

Prime Minister Kishi and his close advisors were surprised at the force of the reaction to the tactics of 19 May. Virtually every major newspaper condemned the government's arbitrary manner in pushing through the treaty and called for the resignation of the cabinet and a general election. Massive demonstrations organized by the left-wing parties and unions attracted hundreds of thousands who marched in the vicinity of the Diet to protest. Thirteen million signatures were obtained on petitions demanding that the Diet not ratify the treaty. These demonstrations continued until ratification became automatic thirty days after it had passed the House of Representatives on 19 May.

The huge well-organized demonstrations and strikes were peaceful except for a few outbreaks led by ultra-radical students. One group of students under Communist leaders of the National Student Federation detained Eisenhower's press secretary, James Hagerty, and the American Ambassador to Japan, Douglas MacArthur, General MacArthur's nephew, on 10 June while they were riding in their car from the Tokyo airport. However, they were finally rescued by an army helicopter. The worst rioting, at the Diet took place on 15 June, and was apparently precipitated by a group of rightist youths who drove a truck into some protesting students. Students under ultra-radical leaders expelled from the Communist party broke into the Diet compound and fought with police. A woman student was trampled to death in the melee. Some students also attacked the prime minister's residence.

In response to the student violence of 15 June, Prime Minister Kishi announced the next day that he had asked President Eisenhower to postpone, (that is, cancel) his visit as Kishi could not guarantee a safe reception. Kishi's leadership had aroused an unprecedented degree of protest which made him a liability to the ruling Liberal Democratic party. Due to his relatively arbitrary Diet tactics and his record as a pre-war nationalist, Kishi was more vulnerable than most prime ministers to criticism from his rivals within the party. The crisis provided considerable advantage to the dissident factions of his party to call for his resignation and to condemn his handling of the ratification of the treaty.[6] Kishi announced that he would accept responsibility for the crisis by resigning after the treaty went into effect. He thus bowed to the agitation against him among the opposition and dissident factions in his own party. But he did not agree to dissolve the Diet and call for elections, which would have annulled the treaty. He thus held firm to the policy of defense cooperation with the United States and passed the revised security treaty. Although Kishi risked adverse American reaction by cancelling the president's visit, he avoided an unpleasant international incident.

Within the dominant coalition, the faction chiefs, Ikeda, Ono, and Ishii all hoped to succeed Kishi as party president and prime minister. Each favored continued American defense cooperation but voiced disapproval of the arbitrary passage of the treaty. When Kishi announced his intention of resigning, the way was opened for one of these rivals to succeed him. The outcome was finally determined by the decision of Kishi to throw support of his faction, together with that of his brother, Eisaku Sato, to Hayato Ikeda. On 14 July, Ikeda obtained the necessary majority of votes at the Liberal Democratic convention, and he was designated prime minister on 18 July at an extraordinary session of the Diet. He was formally appointed with his cabinet by the emperor on the following day.

Big business leaders, such as those at the head of the Federation of Economic Organizations, feared repercussions from the crisis in business relations with the United States. They therefore strongly supported the change of leadership in the Liberal Democratic party and its new president, Ikeda. They also sent representatives to the United States to reassure American businessmen of the continued goodwill on the part of the Japanese and to allay any misapprehension of hostility for the United States which might have been caused by the agitation over the treaty crises.

Ikeda's main task when he took office was formidable and, perhaps, even impossible. On the one hand he had to restore domestic tranquility and reassure his people—and his parliamentary opposition—that the new treaties did not mean increased subservience to the United States. On the other hand he was confronted with the necessity of placating the

---

[6]The dissident coalition of factions *(han shuryu ha)* consisted of Miki-Matsumura, Ishibashi, and Kono factions.

United States and assuring that powerful ally of Japan's continued goodwill and support.

Ikeda articulated his somewhat contradictory mandate in these words:

> I will cooperate with friendly parties in the opposition as well as the governing party to restore political confidence both at home and abroad. I am determined to strive for stable parliamentary politics.
>
> Despite the difficulties since the war the maintenance of peace and the greater cultural and economic development evidence the achievement of the Japanese people.
>
> I would like to correct the government's political approach to undertake practical policies, and properly develop the characteristics in which our people excel. Thus, if we avoid future unrest and restore order and common sense, we can hope for advancement in people's livelihood, prosperity, and welfare. I believe we will heighten the respect and confidence of friendly foreign countries, and stop threats from abroad as well as contribute to the peace and welfare of all mankind.[7]

The objectives of restoring parliamentary politics to normal, preserving order, and developing the domestic economy were repeated a few days later in a meeting with foreign correspondents.[8] The phrase, "correct the government's political approach" *(seiji no shisei o tadasu)*, was a pledge to avoid the provocative tactics of the Kishi Cabinet in confrontation with the opposition parties as well as an attempt to reassure both the general public and the opposition parties.

The agreement to dissolve the House of Representatives and call for a general election on 20 November of that year finally induced the opposition parties to end their boycott and return to participation in Diet proceedings. This did not prevent all Socialist boycotts thereafter, but the Ikeda Cabinets were relatively free of the type of confrontation that had been so common in the previous three years.

To restore foreign confidence in Japan, Ikeda set about putting the Japanese house in order. To assert greater independence for Japan, he also explained to foreign newsmen that it was necessary to place more emphasis on Japan's relations with Southeast Asia and with Europe than had been the case in the past. This meant departing from Japan's excessive emphasis upon the United States, something which was later carried out through aid schemes in the Asian area and improved commercial agreements with the European countries.[9]

[7] Yoshio Miyamoto, *Shin Hoshu To Shi* (Tokyo: Jiji Tsushin Sha, 1962), p. 614.
[8] *Asahi Shimbun*, 23 July 1960, p. 1.
[9] Ibid.

Reverberations from the security treaty crisis of 1960 continued to trouble the domestic political scene, especially during the preparations for the general election which was to be held in November. An effort was made to build a consensus around economic policy in both its domestic and international aspects. Ikeda exerted considerable influence upon the Liberal Democratic party policy which was put together with great care for the election as the party leaders felt this was a turning point for which policy needed to be thoroughly relevant. The resultant policy was also significant as a guideline for later governments.[10]

An effort was made to popularize a policy of doubling the national income in the coming decade. The main political association of the Ikeda faction was the Kochikai, which provided political contributions for its members. When the Kochikai met to discuss the economic growth rate the country should aim for, the members favored the relatively conservative figure of 7.2 percent per annum.[11] Ikeda's economic adviser, Osamu Shimomura, urged that the policy be based on plans for an assumed rate of 11 percent per year. The resultant figure of 9 percent, which was decided upon by Ikeda, was a compromise between the two proposed rates, and would permit a doubling of national income in the following ten years. This objective became the slogan for the election campaign. However, it was not particularly adventuresome when it is realized that the national income had doubled in the previous five years.

Strictly speaking the doubling of income was a reference to the nation's income rather than to personal incomes, although it was taken to apply to the average voter. It was undoubtedly a popular approach as it appealed to the self-interest of the public. It was to be given concrete content by the events which produced a consumption boom. The party policy was phrased as follows:

> For three years starting next year 1961 we will continue growth at 9 percent per year so that in 1963 the gross national product will be 17.6 trillion yen, an increase of over 30 percent and our aim will be to attain a national income increase of over 26 percent at approximately 150,000 yen per capita.
>
> By thus appropriately inducing and extending economic growth, we will reach a level of income of over twice as much in approximately ten years. We will achieve full employment. We will plan a balanced income in agriculture, forestry, and fishing industries, medium and small as well as large industries, in different regions,

[10] Miyamoto, *Shin Hoshu To Shi*, pp. 616–17.
[11] Masaya Ito, *Ikeda Hayato: Sono Sei to Shi* (Tokyo: Shiseido, 1966) p. 84.

and so on. We aim to guarantee the livelihood of those too weak to maintain themselves.[12]

The opposition parties were surprised by the new Liberal Democratic party's policy which broke precedent by actually quoting firm figures. The Socialists proposed a four-year plan for an economic growth rate of 10 percent as part of their long-range plan. The Democratic Socialists, on the other hand, offered an eight-year plan for an increase in employment of ten million people and a doubling of national consumption.

The foreign policy portion of the Liberal Democratic party's election policy resembled its domestic program with its emphasis on peace in international relations and its economic approach to Asia, particularly its relations with the communist states. It, however, rejected neutralism and reaffirmed the security cooperation with the United States.

> To achieve harmony and unity among our people and to mobilize their full potential, we shall independently and positively push on with a peaceful foreign policy that meshes with our nationally determined objectives.
>
> We intend to decide all our problems through discussion and through peaceful methods centering on the United Nations. We shall cooperate fully in strengthening the functions and actions of the United Nations.
>
> We reject neutralism and we shall greatly expand our collaboration and cooperation as far as possible as a member of the Free World with all free countries alike, starting with the United States.
>
> For the sake of our country's security until the functioning of the United Nations is sufficient, we shall firmly support the Japan-United States security system and provide the necessary minimum of our own self-defense forces.
>
> For the economic development of Asia and Africa we shall strengthen our cooperation and set up such things as an overseas economic development fund and by planning such policies to expand friendly relations.
>
> We expect exchanges with the Soviet Union and Communist China through economic and cultural contacts on the basis of the principles of non-interference in internal affairs and respect for each other's political and social systems. We shall further strive for return of the Northern Territories (the Southern Kuriles,

---

[12]Miyamoto, *Shin Hoshu To Shi*, pp. 618–19. See also *Asahi Shimbun* for 5 and 6 September 1960, morning and evening editions, for texts of party policy. The increase in national income per capita was from $1,600 to approximately $2,000.

Shikotan, and the Habomai Islands) taken by the Soviet Union at the end of the Second World War.[13]

This contrasted with the Socialist's confrontation tactics with its capitalist opponents at home and in conjunction with its ideological comrades abroad.

An emergency Diet session was called on 17 October to enable the prime minister to dissolve the Diet and call for an election. In Prime Minister Ikeda's policy speech to the opening session he attacked the Socialist party's neutralism and emphasized that Japan's prosperity rested on its good relations with the Western bloc and economic and security relations with the United States:

> Because we have trusted in the United Nations and the Japan-United States Security Treaty and taken the policy of a gradual increase in our own defense forces, we have been able to maintain peace and security effectively with a minimum of expense relative to today's world and carry out a striking economic growth. Recently, among part of our people can be seen a line of thinking insisting that neutralism is an effective means to guarantee our security. First, this kind of insistence neglects a careful look at the international environment of our country. Second, it overlooks the fact that our country's national strength has considerable weight in the balance of power between East and West. Third, it lacks consideration of the position we are in where cooperation with the group of free countries is the first basic principle of our high degree of economic growth and of our prosperity. I think it is a kind of illusion, something we certainly cannot accept.[14]

The three leading parties passed a resolution at this Diet condemning the use of violence in politics. The parties were subsequently anxious to pass legislation to deal with violence but they could not agree on details. The conservatives feared excesses by mobs or protesters such as the left-wing parties had been involved in, and the opposition parties wanted to take steps to curb rightist groups and individuals with whom some conservatives were thought to be connected. Despite these differences the disposition of party leaders was strengthened in their effort to check each party's more volatile followers.

[13] Miyamoto, *Shin Hoshu To Shi*, pp. 617–18. Note that there is no mention of asking for the return of the Ryukyu (Okinawa) or Bonin Islands held by the United States since the Second World War.

[14] Miyamoto, *Shin Hoshu To Shi*, p. 625; for both the prime minister's and the foreign minister's policy speeches, see evening editions of the *Asahi Shimbun* and *Nihon Keizai Shimbun*, 21 October 1960.

Unfortunately, this agreement did not prevent violence and the most serious act of terrorism that followed was the killing of the new Socialist party Chairman, Inejiro Asanuma. This particularly atrocious act occurred during a debate by the leaders of the three principal political parties at Hibiya Hall in Tokyo before a large audience as well as before millions of television viewers. The debate was sponsored by the League for a Clean Election Campaign and was presented along the lines of the Kennedy-Nixon debates. Asanuma was stabbed by a young fanatic who had been incited by an extreme rightist group led by a prewar ultranationalist, Bin Akao.

The results of the election on 20 November were a surprisingly large vote of confidence for the conservatives, increasing the number of seats of the Liberal Democrats by 13 to a total of 296.[15] This constituted a majority in the house which then had a total of 467 seats. After the election, four independents also joined the party. This was the largest number of seats won by any party since the war and the second highest in the history of the Diet. Despite the victory in terms of parliamentary strength the Liberal Democrats experienced a slight decrease in the percentage of the total popular vote. The Socialist party won an additional 23 seats to bring their total to 145 seats, about half those of the Liberal Democrats. This increase was largely at the expense of the Democratic Socialists which had broken away from the Socialist party in 1959. They lost 23 seats. This represented the growth of left wing preponderance within the Socialist ranks by the more Marxist factions, which gained strength at the expense of the more moderate socialists. If the total popular vote of the two Socialist parties had been combined, it would have shown an increase of a small amount over that of the previous general election. The Communist party increased its parliamentary strength from one to three seats, but this was insufficient to give it status as a negotiating body in the Diet.

The election was not held sufficiently close to the treaty crisis to be interpreted as a treaty referendum, nor did the outcome suggest a repudiation of the policy of either the conservatives or the progressives. The government claimed a more independent role in military matters but one which preserved cooperation with the United States. The election results could be interpreted as a popular mandate to a moderate conservative leadership to emphasize an economic policy of growth at home in cooperation with trade and economic collaboration with the industrialized nations, especially the United States. The defense cooperation was only tolerated by the major portion of the public as long as it

[15]The popular vote of the LDP was only 0.2 percent less than in 1958: Robert A. Scalapino and Junnosuke Masumi, *Parties and Politics in Contemporary Japan* (Berkeley and Los Angeles: University of Caifornia Press, 1962, chart 2, p. 158.

did not involve Japan in hostilities or unnecessary confrontation with its neighbors. [16]

Fortunately for Ikeda, the security treaty was signed and operative for its ten-year term when he took office. The great furor over arbitrary ratification of the treaty had distracted attention from the merits or demerits of the treaty provisions, and the antagonism, which had been concentrated on Kishi, tended to drain away once he had resigned as prime minister. When Ikeda took office, there was a strong desire on the part of the Japanese people to return to normal conditions as well as a feeling by many of the participants in the crisis that they may have gone too far and have been caught up in more than they felt committed to later. General support was given to Ikeda and even the newspapers formerly extremely critical of Kishi altered their editorial slant in favor of the new cabinet.

The new prime minister played down the divisive policy of military alignment reaffirmed in the new security treaty, although he acknowledged the government's adherence to the policy it contained, as did he and his successor in virtually every major foreign policy speech in the Diet during the following decade. To distract attention from military affairs he emphasized domestic economic growth and the concomitant growth of foreign trade and other economic relations, particularly with the United States. This policy was aimed at reducing economic discontent and was capable of attracting support right across the political spectrum. It was, in short, the same consensual policy of putting economic affairs first which had been so successful under other conservative leaders like Prime Minister Yoshida. By seeking to ameliorate economic discontent at home and increase trade and friendly relations with the United States as well as with other countries, the conservative leader tried to outbid the progressive group in seeking popular consensus on its foreign policy.

The methods used by Ikeda in 1960 to ameliorate the domestic division were very similar to those used by both him and Yoshida in the previous decade. Both leaders designed a foreign policy program by which Japanese security was purchased by permitting American strategic dominance in the area through the loan of military bases and the provision of supporting services so vital to that dominance. The security cooperation with the United States was then sold to a pacifist-minded nation thoroughly disillusioned with warfare and armaments by obtaining American economic cooperation, the foundation upon which Japan's extraordinary postwar growth and prosperity has been built. Japanese opposition to

[16] Douglas H. Mendel Jr., *The Japanese People and Foreign Policy* (Berkeley and Los Angeles: University of California Press, 1961), pp. 42-59.

involvement in the cold war was partially appeased by a plentitude of economic benefits under which Japan waxed stronger until it became ready for great power status in the 1970s in all respects except armaments.

The dramatic clash over security policies in 1960 was greatly aggravated by an unusually well-organized and cohesive campaign by opponents of the Japanese government leaders including those in the dissident factions of the governing Liberal Democrats. To this was added newspaper criticism and an unusually sharp confrontation within the Diet as well as outside it. The breakdown of the first American-Soviet detente and the spy plane incidents affecting Japan added fuel to the flames of conflict.

In the revision of the security treaty in 1960 both the government and opposition aimed at the primary goal of achieving greater international status through greater independence of the United States. The Liberal Democrats sought it by a treaty giving more participation and control over defense arrangements and over American forces in Japan. This recognized Japan's increased status by acknowledging greater participation in a vague manner but still within a cooperative framework. The opposition parties and groups sought increased status by abrogation of the treaty and expulsion of the United States from military bases to assert Japan's independence.

Prime Minister Kishi used the Liberal Democratic control of the government to ratify the treaty in the face of the stiffest opposition including a petition from nearly a third of the electorate against the treaty. The new prime minister adopted more conciliatory measures in the Diet and made the decision more palatable, at least to those who were less opposed, by emphasizing the economic benefits that flowed from security cooperation with the United States. By encouraging unofficial contacts and trade relations with China, he tried to reduce the hostility of Japan's Communist neighbor as well as to show some greater independence of the United States as desired by the domestic and foreign opposition to the Liberal Democrats. By reaffirming Japan's non-intervention in her neighbors' affairs and retaining Japan's defense forces at a minimum level, he catered to the pacifist mood of the nation as well as to the neutralism of the opposition forces.

The conflict of goals and policies could not be eliminated but they were balanced against each other to mitigate the clash. Cooperation with a great power ally was balanced against friendly gentures to Communist neighbors, and military risks were offset by economic benefits.

Fig. 1 Japan and Neighboring Countries.

3

Minimum Defense

JAPAN HAS PURSUED its security goal chiefly through cooperation with its great power ally, the United States, ever since the signing of the peace treaty in 1951. This policy of cooperation has been given implementation through the security treaties of 1951 and 1960, which lent military bases to the United States in return for American guarantee of Japan's defense.

To further demonstrate its spirit of cooperation with the United States, Japan undertook to create a defense force of modest size. When it was first planned, the force was conceived by Prime Minister Yoshida as a peace-keeping unit to maintain civil order in the face of expected Communist-led demonstrations or rebellions. In time, however, the force grew in size and its duties were expanded. Today the Japanese armed forces are large enough and well enough equipped to withstand a conventional attack from an enemy until United States' forces can come to their aid.

As Japan's defense forces grow in technical effectiveness, they offer the means by which Japan can approach closer to its goal of greater international status by reducing its dependence upon the United States in defense matters. They also permit Japan to have a freer hand in determining its own foreign policy decisions in relation to its smaller neighbors and the major powers of the world. Despite public acquiescence in the creation of a modest defense, the main opposition party has unsuccessfully pressured the government to eliminate the defense forces and to abrogate the security treaty. There has also been criticism of this policy from other countries in the region, particularly from the communist countries.

In 1960, Prime Minister Ikeda reacted to this opposition by appealing to nationalist sentiment, urging greater self-reliance in defense to rally support behind the military forces. He wished to keep these in existence and to have them continue their auxiliary role which was necessary for the mutual cooperation with the United States. However, he was clearly forced by the opposition parties into a position of only mild support for this policy of Japanese cooperation. That effort he himself called "a minimum."

Even the minimum defense forces desired by Ikeda were substantial compared with the small National Police Reserve with which Japan began to rearm in 1950. Before that time Japan was completely disarmed following her defeat in the Pacific War. The defeat brought strong popular disillusionment in Japan toward the military leaders and a strong opposition to rearmament and any form of military intervention in the affairs of other countries. Nevertheless, there was considerable fear and suspicion of the Soviet Union in a disarmed Japan, especially if the sheltering American occupation troops were withdrawn as a result of peace negotiations.

Background to Japan's Defense Policy

After the Pacific War, Japan was expected to be neutralized and placed under the supervision of either the major allied powers or the United Nations, although the country was occupied almost exclusively by American forces. In the chill of the cold war the possibility arose that a separate peace might be made with the United States and Britain without the participation of the Soviet Union. Prime Minister Yoshida and his successor, Prime Minister Katayama, both made approaches to American officials in 1947 to ask if the United States would be willing to protect Japan against its traditional enemy, the Soviet Union.[1]

The United States agreed to provide protection later but protection that had been intended to be only temporary. At the same time that Japan obtained an American security guarantee, it promised increasingly to take on the task of self-defense. This policy has encountered serious obstacles because of the limitations imposed by the peace clause of the Constitution of 1947, which outlawed the possession of land, sea and air forces, as well as other war potential in accord with the allied postwar disarmament policy for Japan. Prior to the Korean War, the Japanese government argued that no armed forces were permitted by the Constitution and this position is still maintained by the leading opposition party, the Japan Socialist party. When Yoshida first confronted Dulles on rearmament, the prime minister argued that the Constitution,

---

[1]The most complete account is in Martin E. Weinstein, *Japan's Postwar Defense Policy, 1947-1968* (New York: Columbia University Press, 1971), pp. 12-42.

popular sentiment, and the economic weakness of Japan made Japanese rearmament impracticable.

Article IX of the Constitution reads:

> Aspiring sincerely to an international peace based on justice and order, the Japanese people forever renounce war as a sovereign right of the nation and the threat or use of force as a means of settling international disputes.
>
> In order to accomplish the aim of the preceding paragraph, land, sea, and air forces, as well as other war potential, will never be maintained. The right of belligerency of the state will never be recognized.[2]

Hitoshi Ashida, who later became prime minister, was chairman of the constitutional committee of the House of Representatives at the time of the passage of the new Constitution. He claimed responsibility for inserting the key phrase, "in order to accomplish the aim of the preceding paragraph" at the beginning of the second paragraph of article IX. This phrase made the following statement that "land, sea, and air forces would never be maintained" apply only to the purpose of the first paragraph.[3] And the first paragraph only mentioned war and the threat or use of force to settle international disputes. That is, it referred to threats and attacks of an aggressive nature. It did not forbid armed forces maintained only for defensive purposes—provided they were not used to attack or threaten others or the arms were too modest to constitute "war potential."

Later, Ashida said that defensive forces were not forbidden and article IX did not constitute any military prohibition in the case of national defense or international sanctions. Not only could Japan have armed forces, but it could engage in international peace-keeping operations. It was only after the outbreak of the Korean War and the agreement to rearm that the Japanese government accepted the Ashida argument as to the meaning of the second paragraph of the peace clause. It then argued that only limited forces for self-defense were constitutional. This permitted the government to carry out its second objective of maintaining a modest Japanese defense force in addition to the first objective of obtaining and keeping the American guarantee. Indeed,

---

[2] Supreme Commander for the Allied Powers, Government Section, *Political Reorientation of Japan, September 1946 to September 1948* (Washington, D.C.: U.S. Government Printing Office, 1949), p. 102.

[3] D. C. S. Sissons, "The Pacifist Clause of the Japanese Constitution, Legal and Political Problems of Rearmament," *International Affairs*, Vol. XXXVII, No. 1 (January 1961), pp. 48–49. The idea expressed by "never" does not appear in the Japanese text of paragraph 2, Article IX. (Hereafter, this work is cited as "Pacifist Clause.")

the first objective was made dependent upon the promise to carry out the second.

Thus it was that the allied wartime and immediate postwar objective of disarming Japan, which was enshrined in the allied-sponsored Constitution in its article IX, was overcome by pressure for rearmament. The result was not, however, to simply reverse the disarmament policy and permit Japan to rearm freely. In the later reinterpretation of article IX, which amounted to an amendment to the Constitution, the Japanese government argued it could have a modest defense force only—one which ideally would be capable of protecting Japan to at least a reasonable degree but not capable of attacking other countries. In this way, the essential idea behind the allied policy and article IX of preventing Japanese aggression was retained. The interesting aspect of Japan's limited armament objective was that it was self-enforcing. It is Japanese public opinion, opposition parties, and dominant political leadership which insist upon and enforce limitations on Japanese rearmament. These have proved to be very potent forces indeed.

The early plans for the peace treaty were dropped because of disagreement between the United States and the Soviet Union over the matter of permitting a four-power veto of the peace terms and the fear of jeopardizing the settlement of a German peace treaty. After the cold war reached its climax with the formation of the NATO alliance and after the United States took the initiative to resume Japanese peace negotiations in 1949, it became even more likely that the Soviet Union would not participate in a Japanese peace treaty, especially if such a treaty included retention of American military bases in Japan. Japanese conservative leaders including Yoshida, who had again become prime minister in 1948, wished not only to protect Japan from Russian threats and attack but also to preserve the Liberal Democratic parliamentary regime against Communism whether from abroad or in combination with radical Socialists within Japan itself.

In the negotiations, John Foster Dulles, who became the chief American peace negotiator, pressed for complete political and economic freedom for Japan in the face of opposition from the other allies who wanted limitations placed on Japanese competitive industries. Dulles also wanted Japan to rearm. With the outbreak of the Korean War in June 1950, the American leaders were confirmed in their conviction that they must retain military bases in Japan as well as win Japanese cooperation by obtaining its freedom from occupation control, freedom to trade at will, and freedom to rearm. The other allies were dismayed at the possible revival of Japanese economic and military power and had to be persuaded, through concessions, to sign the peace treaty.

In the substantive negotiations of 1951, Dulles proposed a NATO-like multilateral collective defense arrangement with the United States to include Japan, the Philippines, and Australia. As with West Germany included in Western European and Atlantic alliances, Japan would have been given its independence subject to indirect control by virtue of its inclusion in the alliance with its former enemies. However, this American proposal was rejected out of hand by Prime Minister Yoshida who absolutely refused to consider rearmament. Taking advantage of the cold war development, Yoshida invited American forces to remain in Japan by lending bases in exchange for an American guarantee of Japan's defense. This would also obviate the need for Japan to rearm at a time when it was economically prostrate as a result of the Pacific War.

In the meantime, the American military commander, General Douglas MacArthur, who was also allied occupation commander in Japan, ordered the Japanese to create a 75,000-man National Police Reserve to prevent any internal communist rebellion when most of the American forces normally stationed in Japan were fighting in Korea. The prime minister complied promptly with this demand as he felt his government for the first time would have some direct control over its domestic radicals. Yoshida's parliamentary regime thus obtained a substantial guarantee against its internal enemies but still needed to obtain one against its external enemies.

The Japanese prime minister's proposal of offering military bases for a guarantee of security ran counter to the current American policy of making security commitments only to countries prepared to participate actively in their own defense. The two positions were finally compromised to produce the security bargain on which the peace settlement rested and which still governs Japan's defense policy more than twenty years afterward. Yoshida conceded that Japan would undertake gradual rearmament as its economic progress permitted and the United States agreed to defend Japan in the meantime. This security bargain was embodied in a separate security treaty of 1951.

Another treaty of 1951, the peace treaty, between Japan and most of the non-Communist countries at war with Japan, ended the allied occupation of the country and gave Japan its political and economic independence. It included little about security beyond asserting that Japan had the right of self-defense and the right to enter collective security agreements. This was included to make clear that the signatories of the peace treaty understood that the new Constitution of Japan sponsored by the Allied powers did not forbid defensive armament or cooperation with American military forces even though it outlawed war and armed forces of an offensive nature.

It is probably true that the United States could not have agreed to a peace treaty of such a generous nature if it had not also received military bases, but the bases were not given as a necessary condition of Japan's freedom but rather were lent only temporarily in order to obtain the security guarantee. Japanese leaders felt Japan had earned its freedom by good behavior since the end of the war and by the implementation of internal reforms in accord with the wartime and immediate postwar objectives of the Allied powers. The lending of the bases was a sufficient concession on Japan's part to compensate for the security guarantee because the United States received something of value. This seemed to involve another, but not clearly defined, bargain. The United States, by receiving military bases, obtained not only a means to defend Japan but also gained strategic and valuable locations from which it could exercise great military influence in East Asia as well as in Japan itself. Some misunderstanding of this aspect has persisted among those who insist that Japan essentially received American protection at no cost to itself. Not only did the United States gain in regional power and influence but also Japan suffered the consequences of poor relations with the Soviet Union and China—even though it gained inexpensive and generous protection.

To induce countries like the Philippines and Australia to agree to the generous peace treaty with Japan, the United States was compelled to offer security guarantees to these countries against the possible revival of Japanese military threats. The United States did this by signing separate security treaties with each of them. Thus, a series of bilateral interlocking security treaties was begun in the Asian area.

The main security bargain with Japan was spelled out clearly in the preamble of the security treaty of 1951:

> Japan desires, as a provisional arrangement for its defense, that the United States of America should maintain armed forces of its own in and about Japan so as to deter armed attack upon Japan.
>
> The United States of America, in the interest of peace and security, is presently willing to maintain certain of its forces in and about Japan, in the expectation, however, that Japan will increasingly assume responsibility for its own defense against direct and indirect aggression, always avoiding any armament which could be an offensive threat or serve other than to promote peace and security in accordance with the purposes and principles of the United Nations Charter.[4]

This formulation approached very close to the actual policies followed

[4]U.S., Department of State, *United States Treaties and Other International Agreements*, Vol. III, pt. 3, "Security Treaty Between the United States of America and Japan," TIAS 2491, 8 September 1951, p. 3331.

and expressed the nature of the security bargain which the two countries made and have adhered to ever since. Although not constituting a clear guarantee of the defense of Japan, this was implied by the expectation that American forces would deter any potential attacker of Japan. The protection was provisional until Japan could build its own military forces to a strength sufficient to defend the country from internal and external attack.

The security bargain was given even clearer formulation as subsequent events unfolded. In 1952, when the Japanese were troubled by Soviet Sabrejet flights over Hokkaido during the Korean War, an exchange of notes between the American ambassador and the Japanese foreign minister was made public. These notes stated that the United States would take "all possible measures necessary and proper under terms of the Security Treaty . . . to repel all such violations of Japan's territorial air." [5] The Japanese government considered this to be an implementation of the guarantee against direct attack although, in general, American military action to defend Japan from bases there was limited to requests from the Japanese government. After one Russian plane was shot down by American forces over Japan, the trespasses over Hokkaido ceased.

The security bargain also involved a temporary loss of Japanese territory. Japan, in effect, lent not only bases but also territory to the United States. The southern islands (principally the Ogasawara Islands, which include the Bonin Islands and Volcano Islands) and the south-western islands (the Ryukyu Islands, including the large island of Okinawa and other nearby groups of islands constituting the former Okinawa Prefecture) were placed under American jurisdiction by article III of the peace treaty. [6] The American forces assumed civilian as well as military control of the islands. In effect, the islands became American colonies. In the southern islands, most of the Japanese residents were banished to Japan; only a few Japanese of American ancestry were permitted to remain. On Okinawa the nearly one million Japanese residents were subject to American regulations.

The Japanese leaders were prepared to accept a temporary continuation of the occupation of these islands under American jurisdiction as a part of the security bargain. Their retention under American military rule was deemed essential by American officials to give full scope to military operations and to insure their strategic dominance in the maritime areas of East Asia. During the Pacific War, these occupied islands had been captured only after bloody fighting by American forces

---

[5] Weinstein, *Japan's Postwar Defense Policy, 1947-1968*, pp. 70–74.

[6] U.S., Department of State, *United States Treaties*, Vol. III, pt. 3, "Treaty of Peace with Japan, Declarations by Japan, and Exchange of Notes," TIAS 2490, 8 September 1951, pp. 3169–3328.

so that military leaders were reluctant to relinquish their absolute control if they were required to defend the region again.[7] The military leaders were not overruled until the United States presidents gradually came to agree to return control of the occupied islands between 1967 and 1972, putting the bases under the same restrictions as those in Japan proper.

The security treaty with the United States dealt with more than the security of Japan. For the Japanese leaders its purpose was to gain American protection: for the American leaders it was to insure strategic dominance of the maritime areas in East Asia including Japan. Article I of the security treaty of 1951 stated that American garrison forces "may be utilized to contribute to the maintenance of international peace and security in the Far East." Significantly, the statement that the forces may be used to contribute to the security of Japan was indicated after the mention of security of the Far East. Also, it should be noted that the phrase "may be utilized" is permissive. It implied that the United States may not so act at its own discretion.

By lending bases not only for its defense but for American strategic influence in East Asia, Japan was indirectly responsible for the exercise of American influence and power in the region. The most important part of that activity, from the American standpoint, was the responsibility to permit American forces to operate effectively in the region. However, Japan gradually applied limitations on the operation and armament of American forces while at the same time retaining American protection. Nuclear weapons were forbidden and the Japanese government was to be consulted and be in agreement before troops could be dispatched from the bases. It was principally to escape such restrictions that the American military leaders demanded territorial jurisdiction in the islands of the south and southwest. During and after the Korean War, bases in these areas had been and were used by the United States to protect South Korea and Taiwan as well as Japan. For Japan's neighbors, Japanese responsibility was even more important as it enabled the United States either to protect these countries, as in the case of South Korea or Taiwan, or else to threaten them, as in the case of the People's Republic, North Korea, or the Soviet Union. The former countries wished for unrestricted American military use of Japanese bases and the latter countries wanted to have military bases and forces entirely removed.[8]

[7] Japan, Ministry of Foreign Affairs, Public Information Bureau, *Okinawa, Some Basic Facts*, Japan Reference Series, No. 2-69, 1969, p. 4.

[8] Chinese People's Institute of Foreign Affairs, "Foreign Minister Chou En-lai's Statement on the Announcement by the United States of America of the Coming into Effect of the Illegal Separate Peace Treaty with Japan," *Oppose the Revival of Japanese Militarism* (Peking: Foreign Languages Press, 1960), pp. 18–25.

This situation is still a major factor in Japan's position today. The indirect regional responsibility is a disadvantage to the extent that it embroils Japan in quarrels with its neighbors or involves Japan in American quarrels which may place Japan in jeopardy. It does, in fact, have a two-fold character which constitutes contradictions in Japan's security policy and is a chief source of political strain in the form of foreign policy disputes with its neighbors and arguments between government and opposition parties in Japan. Part of the price Japan pays for its own protection is indirect responsibility for the way the United States chooses to protect or threaten other countries in the region.

The United States was anxious to persuade Japan to make a greater military effort, and the opportunity to press the point presented itself when the Japanese came to ask for economic assistance. In 1953, on Ikeda's second mission to Washington for Prime Minister Yoshida, he resisted pressure from both the pentagon and Secretary of State Dulles who asked for nearly double the forces that Japan's leaders would agree to.[9] It was the promise of economic assistance that had persuaded the Japanese to increase their land force from 160,000 to 180,000 men. It is significant that even the top priority of economic assistance could not compel the Japanese to extend the limits of their military cooperation.

The American planners thought a Japanese land force was necessary in anticipation that Japanese forces could be used for a regional defense role. But Japanese leaders have not been willing to extend the scope of the direct defense idea outside their own territory. The complacency of the pentagon at contemplating re-creation of Japanese overseas forces may have rested on the mistaken assumptions that the American military power in the postwar period would always be great enough to command obedience from smaller powers, or that Japan would always agree with American foreign policy, or that the objectives of the two countries would always be the same. The very fact that Japan refused to rearm as the United States wished and that it refused to accept any external military role should have been ample proof that its military objectives were not the same as the United States considered they should be.

But not everyone in Japan agreed to limited defense and there was some demand for a defense buildup at least on the scale contemplated by American planners. The defense industries in Japan favored a land force of fifteen divisions comprising 300,000 men, a maritime force of 70,000 men and 290,000 tons of shipping, and an air force of 130,000 men and 3,750 planes.[10] In February 1953, a six-year plan was proposed

[9] Kiichi Miyazawa, *Tokyo-Washinton no Mitsudan* (Tokyo: Jitsugyo no Nihon Sha, 1956), pp. 167-280.

[10] Asahi Shimbun Anzen Hosho Mondai Chosa Kai, *Nihon no Boei to Keizai*, Vol. IX of *Nihon no Anzen Hosho* (Tokyo: Asahi Shimbun Sha, 1967), p. 173.

by the Defense Production Committee *(Boei Seisan Iin Kai)* of the Federation of Economic Organizations *(Keizai Dantai Rengo Kai* or *Keidanren),* the chief big business association, to meet these requirements. It was expected that the fifteen divisions would be expanded later to thirty with double the number of men. But, to judge from the lack of results, the Defense Production Committee's proposals have carried little weight in either government or business circles.

Not only did the government leaders' priorities not accord with such a buildup but the opposition political parties and public opinion were also opposed to the plans for defense forces capable of meeting external attack. Simultaneously with the Washington negotiations for the Mutual Defense Assistance Agreement, Prime Minister Yoshida succeeded in getting the support of the second largest party in the Diet, the Progressive party, which had hitherto rejected rearmament as unconstitutional. Despite continued opposition the government managed to pass the Self-Defense Forces Law. On 1 July 1954, Japanese forces were given the mission of "defending the country against both direct and indirect aggression."[11] Thus they were to have the mission of repelling direct external attack similar to a conventional military force.

The objective of limited armament was emphasized by avoiding the use of regular military terminology. The Self-Defense Forces limitation to self-defense of Japan was partially suggested by the names given to the various services. The components were a Ground Self-Defense Force, a Maritime Self-Defense Force, and an Air Self-Defense Force. Even the designations of ranks and ratings were different from those used in the prewar period to distinguish the services from the old Imperial army and navy. The intention of the use of these names was also to make the new defense forces more acceptable to the public, as well as to emphasize their limited nature in accord with constitutional interpretation.

Prime Minister Yoshida not only insisted on limited armament but rejected conscription also. This contrasted with Chancellor Konrad Adenauer of West Germany, who readily agreed to conscription in order to win allied agreement to independence, even though the measure was unpopular with the public. In Japan, voluntary enlistment has consistently failed to fill the authorized quota of men, small though the quota is. Nevertheless, no Japanese political leader of importance has urged conscription, such is its unpopularity.

To insure that the limited defense interpretation did not include expeditionary forces, the House of Councillors managed to pass a

---

[11] Article III of the Self-Defense Forces Law. Asahi Shimbun Anzen Hosho Mondai Chosa Kai, *Ampo Mondai Yogo: Shiryo Shu,* First Supplement to *Nihon no Anzen Hosho* (Tokyo: Asahi Shimbun Sha, 1967), p. 227.

resolution in June 1954 affirming that "the Self-Defense Forces will not be sent overseas."[12] Attempts of the opposition parties to pass similar self-denying resolutions in the House of Representatives had been frustrated by the government, which was reluctant to commit itself in advance. However, the government did present the view that in case of attack by an aggressor, it would be justified in undertaking naval bombardment. Yoshida said that to obtain and utilize fully modern armament would be to acquire the sort of war potential forbidden by article IX of the Constitution.[13] This apparently ruled out nuclear arms.

The constitutionally permissible type of defense forces and their mission were therefore narrowly interpreted even though the conception of "defense" can be subject to an enormous breadth of interpretation. The agreement to rearm in the peace settlement of 1951 gave rise to two movements in Japan. One was among the conservatives, who aimed at amending the Constitution to authorize clearly defensive rearmament. The other was a movement led by the Socialists, who aimed at preventing any kind of conservative revision likely to alter article IX or to bring other changes.

Yoshida belonged to the group which opposed any kind of amendment even though he was otherwise relatively conservative. He believed that the limited defense interpretation of article IX was sufficient for Japan's security needs, and he feared the political confusion which would likely accompany premature attempts to alter the Constitution. As one of its chief protagonists at the time of adoption, he was opposed to any tampering with the written document.[14]

Nobusuke Kishi, later secretary general of the Liberal party, who was never on cordial terms with Yoshida although accepted by him as a member of the Liberal party, headed that party's committee on the revision of the Constitution. This committee was forced on Yoshida by conservative revisionists. Kishi's committee recommended that article IX be modified to authorize clearly defense forces and actions. However, these recommendations were not acted upon and the wording of the Constitution was not changed.

The basic security policies of Japan, worked out under the leadership of Prime Minister Yoshida, remain in effect to this day. The elaboration and modification under subsequent cabinets have not changed the essential character of the security bargain or the means chosen to implement it. The defense guarantee was obtained in a security treaty; Japanese claims to return of its occupied islands were made and a basis laid

[12] Ibid., p. 98.
[13] Sissons, "Pacifist Clause," p. 54.
[14] Shigeru Yoshida, *The Yoshida Memoirs, the Story of Japan in Crisis*, translated by Kenichi Yoshida (London: Heinemann, 1961), p. 146.

for their reversion; modest defense forces were created; reduction or prevention of international tensions were attempted by avoiding regional defense participation; and efforts were made to establish or maintain friendly relations with other states. This last objective of reducing tensions involves definite security aspects. By avoiding a large-scale military buildup, Japan can head off antagonism and reduce the fear of a revival of Japanese imperialism. By attempting to establish peaceful economic relations with virtually all other important states, Japan protects itself by preventing or reducing hostility and any likely attack or threat.

Other countries' fear of revival of militarism and Japanese attempts to dispel this fear constitute an important external check on Japanese rearmament and extension of military influence. Such fear supplements the internal check involved in the constitutional limitations arising under article IX. The persistent fear of other countries of Japanese militarism indicates that the rather extensive Japanese efforts to avoid it and genuinely effect a constructive peaceful diplomacy have not been understood or fully appreciated. Unfortunately, constructive efforts of this type seldom earn headlines to the same extent as suspicion or warlike deeds. On the other hand, the suspicion of other countries does goad Japanese leaders to greater constructive and peaceful efforts as does the similar type of internal political opposition led by the Japan Socialist party. The insistence of the Socialists upon complete disarmament and appeal to the original meaning of the article IX supported by pacifist sentiment in Japan has probably been the chief goad in enforcing the narrow interpretation given to permissible Japanese defense efforts.

Prime Minister Ichiro Hatoyama, who succeeded Yoshida in 1954, accepted the revisionist philosophy of the conservatives. Moreover, he agreed with the Socialists that the defense forces did indeed violate the Constitution. As a private member of the Diet he advocated amendment of the Constitution to clearly permit defense forces. This was a position which proved to be extremely awkward when he later became prime minister. In taking this position he had temporary support from the Socialists but was opposed by the Yoshida Liberals. Even in 1955, when the conservatives formed one party, the Liberal Democrats, he could not obtain the required two-thirds majority vote in the Diet to inititate the amendment. Since he could not change the Constitution, even Prime Minister Hatoyama was obliged to accept the limited defense reinterpretation of article IX. He therefore concluded that some rearmament was not unconstitutional, provided it was limited.

As befitted a revisionist in favor of a substantial self-reliant defense effort, Hatoyama thought even modern military forces would be constitutional provided they were for the purposes of self-defense. Like those before and after him, he considered that expeditionary forces were not permitted under the terms of the Constitution. During the early part of his prime ministership he thought Japan could not have nuclear weapons without an amendment to the Constitution. However, to avoid surrendering the nuclear option when the question of American introduction of Honest John tactical nuclear missiles came up, he decided that nuclear warheads might be permissible if absolutely necessary. Fortunately, they were not required. [15]

His successors were to follow this interpretation that nuclear weapons were permissible for defense, but were not needed yet, and no subsequent prime minister has been willing to receive or permit the United States to introduce such weapons into the American military bases in Japan. The United States did install nuclear weapons on its Okinawa base, but as previously noted, the island was practically an American colony. Again, the Japanese attitude to nuclear weapons contrasts with that of West Germany where the United States not only brought in nuclear warheads, but the West German forces provided the missiles in which they were housed—an American serviceman was needed only to activate the warhead. In Japan, Honest John missiles were brought into Japan proper, and fitted with conventional explosives. However, they were designed so that they could be fitted with nuclear warheads if Japanese leaders ever agreed to this. Hatoyama did establish the important precedent, which still governs, that no nuclear weapons would be brought into Japan without his government's agreement. [16]

With the conclusion of the Korean War, American forces in Japan were reduced just when the Japanese forces were being increased. Thus, conditions moved toward a greater balance of responsibility for Japan's defense cooperation. The Eisenhower administration was soon to depend on the threat of massive retaliation by nuclear weapons and was eager to shift the burden of military manpower to its allies, thus anticipating the Nixon Doctrine by fifteen years.

The Japanese obligation to rearm was further clarified by article VII of the Mutual Defense Assistance Agreement of 8 March 1954, which was negotiated between the countries to enable the United States to furnish military equipment to Japan. In this agreement, Japan agreed to fulfill its military obligations under the security treaty as permitted by political and economic stability with manpower, resources, and facilities. [17] Japan thus began to assume part of the burden of its own

[15] Sissons, "Pacifist Clause," p. 55.

[16] Weinstein, *Japan's Postwar Defense Policy, 1947-1968*, p. 80.

[17] U.S., Department of State, *United States Treaties*, Vol. V. pt. 1, "Mutual Defense Assistance Agreement, with Annexes, Between the United States of America and Japan," TIAS 2957, 8 March 1954, p. 668. See also Weinstein, *Japan's Postwar Defense Policy, 1947-1968*, pp. 74-76.

defense, as Yoshida had agreed in 1951.

On signing the Mutual Defense Assistance Agreement in 1954, American Ambassador John Allison said: "This agreement takes us one step nearer to the time when the Japanese people will not need to rely on American forces for protection. It takes us one step nearer the time when the United States can withdraw its forces from Japan." [18] Prime Minister Hatoyama wished to negotiate a new security treaty providing for greater equality for Japan and hence greater independence in its foreign policy. The greater flexibility of the Hatoyama Cabinet and its willingness to accept some greater rearmament provided scope for this ambition.

In August 1955, Prime Minister Hatoyama sent Foreign Minister Shigemitsu to Washington to discuss revision of the security treaty. At the meetings, Secretary of State John Foster Dulles demanded, in return for a more equal treaty, that Japan rearm to the extent that it could defend itself from a Soviet attack and participate with the United States in the defense of South Korea and Taiwan. Shigemitsu told Dulles that Japanese ground forces were about 150,000 and would be increased to 180,000 by 1958; total armed forces were to reach 260,000 in 1960 and on this basis he asked for a new security treaty. In the meantime, American planners had reduced their estimates of requirements of Japanese forces from 350,000—which Dulles had demanded in 1951—to 200,000 well-equipped ground forces which would be sufficient as a result of lessening tensions in the area. But Dulles still wanted regional defense participation by Japan.

At first, Shigemitsu said the overseas dispatch of forces was out of the question until article IX was amended. When he returned to Tokyo and hinted that Japan might consider sharing in the defense of the western Pacific including Guam, he raised a political storm. [19] Even rival conservative party leaders seized on the issue to criticize the prime minister and the government, and Japanese government leaders quickly repudiated a policy of military participation outside Japan proper in the face of the adverse reaction. Again, the force of Japanese popular opinion foiled the American plans to enlarge Japan's defense force and increase its responsibilities.

In 1956, the Twenty-Fourth Diet provided for a National Defense Council, which included the prime minister and the ministers concerned with defense, and the purpose of the council was to advise the cabinet on security policy. It established a Basic National Defense Policy and the First Defense Buildup Plan which went into effect in 1957 and was

[18] U.S., Department of State, "Statement by Ambassador to Japan Allison on Signing the Mutual Defense Assistance Agreement," *Department of State Bulletin*, Vol. XXX (5 April 1954), p. 519.

[19] Weinstein, *Japan's Postwar Defense Policy, 1947-1968*, p. 80.

to be completed in 1960. The basic policy read:

> The goal of national defense is to prevent direct and indirect aggression in the future; and, if by chance aggression occurs, to repel it; and thereby to preserve our country's independence and peace which takes as its basis the principles of democracy. To achieve this goal, the basic policy is as follows:
>
> 1. To support the action of the United Nations, to promote international cooperation, and to achieve world peace.
> 2. To firmly establish the necessary basis to stabilize people's livelihood, increase their patriotism, and guarantee the security of the state.
> 3. To gradually build up effective forces to provide the minimum degree of defense necessary in accord with national strength and national sentiment.
> 4. Until the United Nations is able to acquire the ability to effectively stop external aggression, to deal with it on the basis of the security system with the United States. [20]

The First Defense Buildup Plan aimed at a Ground Self-Defense Force of 180,000 men, which would approach the American estimated requirement of 200,000 men, a Maritime Self-Defense Force of 124,000 tons of shipping and 200 aircraft, and an Air Self-Defense Force of 1,300 aircraft. The annual defense budget was about 463,000 million yen (about $1.25 billion) for equipment, personnel, and training. This plan was intended to fulfill the obligations under the Mutual Defense Assistance Agreement of 1954. However, reliance still would be necessary on American equipment, some of which was obsolete.

In June 1957, Prime Minister Kishi, who had become prime minister in February of that year, went to Washington to ask for a security treaty of greater mutuality or at least one that would be less unequal. He found Eisenhower and Dulles less concerned than previously at Japan's failure to rearm to a greater degree. The European allies had also failed to rearm on the scale hoped by the United States, which meanwhile had come to rely increasingly on the concept of massive nuclear retaliation and was beguiled by the more conciliatory attitude of the Russian leaders who had succeeded Stalin. The Japanese leader wanted a treaty which reflected the fact that Japan was no longer defenseless under the rearmament already achieved, the projected First Defense Buildup Plan, and his government's willingness to take on more of the burden of its own defense with respect to its own territory. Kishi also wished to have a stronger voice in the choice of equipment and deployment

[20] Asahi, *Ampo Mondai Yogo*, p. 121.

of American forces at the military bases in order to give Japan a greater role in its own defense and involvement in the Far East. This change of course greatly pleased the American officials.

In the joint communique of 21 June 1957, signed by Kishi and Eisenhower, it was agreed to establish a joint intergovernmental security consultative committee. [21] The intention of withdrawing all ground forces of the United States within a year was also indicated. As public dissatisfaction over security cooperation had focused on the American military bases, this proved to be a popular agreement. The scaling down of American forces abroad was not due to this agreement alone; it was mainly the result of a reduction of American troops following the Korean War and the Radford plan, which reduced American troops overseas by 800,000. The communique also indicated that Prime Minister

TABLE 3.1
AMERICAN AND JAPANESE MILITARY PERSONNEL LEVELS IN JAPAN,
1954–59
(THOUSANDS)

Year	United States	Japanese	Total Forces
1954	210	111	321
1955	150	157	307
1956	117	181	298
1957	87	192	279
1958	65	208	273
1959	58	215	273

SOURCE: Based on Tomohisa Sakanaka, "Boei Ryoku Seibi no Hoko to Mondai Ten," Asahi Shimbun Anzen Hosho Mondai Chosa Kai, *Nihon no Jiei Ryoku*, Vol. VIII of *Nihon no Anzen Hosho* (Tokyo: Asahi Shimbun Sha, 1967), p. 90, *Nihon no Anzen Hosho* (Tokyo: Anzen Hosho Chosakai 1968), pp. 366–67.

Kishi had requested the return of jurisdiction over the southern islands (Bonins) and the southwestern islands (Okinawa). President Eisenhower reaffirmed Japan's residual sovereignty over the islands, but he considered continued American military control necessary because of threats to security in the region. As a result of these threats, the United States was unwilling to weaken its strategic position in the region by limiting or sharing its control over those island bases as it already had in Japan proper.

Within three months of the meeting a joint Japanese-American Committee on Security was established to provide regular security consultations between the two countries. It consisted of the Japanese foreign

[21] U.S., Department of State, "Visit of Prime Minister Nobusuke Kishi of Japan: Joint Communique," *State Department Bulletin*, Vol. XXXVII, (8 July 1954), p. 52.

minister, the director general of the defense agency, the United States ambassador to Japan, and the commander in chief Pacific or the commander United States Forces Pacific as his alternate. The remaining American ground forces were removed quickly thereafter leaving only air and naval units in the military bases in Japan. In 1958, negotiations to revise the security treaty were begun.

The Security Treaty of 1960

The resulting Treaty of Mutual Cooperation and Security between the United States of America and Japan was signed 19 January 1960.[22] This new security treaty changed virtually nothing in the way of basic Japanese defense policies, but it was of considerable value to Japan in gaining formal recognition of participation in control of American garrison forces—something already gradually conceded in practice. The United States failed to attain its objective of Japanese participation in regional defense; therefore it refused to surrender territorial jurisdiction of the outlying occupied islands and retained unfettered use of the military bases.

Insofar as Japan succeeded in resisting pressure to share in regional defense to obligate its forces to overseas service and attained consultative curbs over the military bases within Japan proper, it more or less wrote its limited or minimal defense concept into the treaty relationship. This considerable achievement was not appreciated by domestic and foreign treaty opponents who continued to take the extreme position that the Japanese government violated the Constitution even with its minimal armament concept and that American bases and Japanese forces should be eliminated entirely. Many opponents believed that bases, far from deterring attack, invited aggression which might drag Japan into an unwanted war with enemies of the United States, and the renewed anxieties of the cold war of 1960 did much to stimulate such fears.

For Japanese leaders, such as Prime Minister Kishi, an important gain was making explicit the previously implied security guarantee of the earlier treaty. The chief purpose of the revised security treaty was still to deter attack on Japan by the Soviet Union. Article V of the new treaty provided: "Each Party recognizes that an armed attack against either party in the territories under the administration of Japan would be dangerous to its own peace and safety and declares that it would act to meet the common danger in accordance with its constitutional provisions and processes."[23] Japanese leaders felt the more explicit

---

[22] U.S., Department of State, *United States Treaties,* Vol. IX, pt. 2, "Treaty of Mutual Cooperation and Security Between the United States of America and Japan," TIAS 4509, 19 January 1960, pp. 1632–51.
[23] Ibid., p. 1634.

the guarantee, the more effective the deterrence.

Unlike the North Atlantic treaty, in which an attack on one party is regarded as an attack on all, the parties were only pledged to meet the common danger after regular governmental decision-making processes had taken place. Though weaker than the Atlantic formulation, it was similar to other Pacific security treaties such as the one between the United States and Australia and New Zealand. A loophole might prove to be the lack of the specific pledge by the United States to "maintain armed forces of its own in and about Japan" which was found in the earlier treaty. The United States could thus withdraw all its forces or neglect to deploy them even if this were desired by Japan. On the other hand, as Japanese leaders wished, Japan's responsibility in the matter of direct defense was limited to the home islands. It was not even responsible for outlying occupied territories such as Okinawa until 1972 when the island reverted to Japanese sovereignty.

The greater mutuality mentioned in the treaty title refers to Japan's claim to increased participation in planning, equipment decisions, and deployment conclusions. Article IV of the new treaty provided that "the Parties will consult together from time to time regarding implementation of this Treaty, and, at the request of either Party, whenever the security of Japan or international peace and security in the Far East is threatened." The joint Japanese-American Committee on Security was specifically provided for in the third exchange of notes to the treaty where its name was changed to the Security Consultative Committee. [24] Thus, a regular body to carry on consultations between the countries on defense cooperation at least symbolized the good intentions of the United States to concede some greater measure of participation in defense decisions.

Foreign Minister Aiichiro Fujiyama said the Far East included the area north of the Philippines, the China coast, the offshore islands, and the vicinity of Japan. [25] Prime Minister Kishi then tried to limit this definition by saying it was the Philippines and the vicinity of Japan but not the China mainland or the offshore islands near Taiwan that constituted the Far East. He also included the Soviet-occupied Kurile Islands but later modified this to include only the northern islands which were claimed by Japan. Presumably, Japan-based troops would not go outside the specified areas and therefore Japan would not be implicated in American operations elsewhere. The prime minister wavered over

[24] U.S., Department of State, *United States Treaties,* Vol. XI, pt. 2, (Third) "Exchange of Notes to the Treaty of Mutual Cooperation and Security Between the United States of America and Japan," TIAS 4509, 19 January 1960, pp. 1650-51.

[25] Asahi Shimbun Anzen Hosho Mondai Chosa Kai, *Nichi-Bei Ampo Joyaku no Shoten,* Vol. X of *Nihon no Anzen Hosho* (Tokyo: Asahi Shimbun Sha, 1967), p. 179.

whether the Quemoy and Matsu Islands, where the two Chinese regimes had fought with some American involvement in 1958, should be included. Even the American officials had not made clear the extent to which they regarded themselves bound to defend those islands under their security treaty with Nationalist China.

In the Diet debate on the new treaty, attention was focused on the area of the Far East in which Japan was responsible for permitting garrison forces to operate. The prime minister told the House of Councillors on 10 February 1960 that no agreed definition had been worked out with the United States.[26] His statement casts some doubt on the real desire of either government to take the consultations very seriously.

An authoritative statement issued by the Japanese government on 27 February 1960 said the Far East was, in general, the area north of the Philippines and in the vicinity of Japan as well as areas under the jurisdiction of the Republic of Korea and of the Republic of China. Subsequent debate indicated that the Chinese islands of Matsu and Quemoy as well as the northern occupied islands were included, and American Senate hearings confirmed this.

Japan had the right to prior consultations in case of combat deployment to these areas in order to assess the need for it, but it was committed to permit American defense of the area. The extent to which Japan could check or influence the United States in case of disagreement remained unclear.

In conflict with the impression given by the prime minister of the considerable curbs on the use of the American bases and on the Japanese responsibility for them, the chief of the Foreign Ministry Treaty Bureau, Kumao Nishimura, thought there was nothing to prevent dispatch of those forces to other areas—if it could be deemed to be for "security of the Far East."[27] It therefore could be deduced that such a course would extend rather than reduce Japanese responsibility. In such a case, the Japanese government would not even have the right to consultation. In the case of the important Okinawan bases the Japanese government could do nothing. It did manage to have an agreed minute attached to the treaty in which the United States promised to consult it should Okinawa or any occupied territory actually be attacked.

Prior consultations were promised in case of American combat operations in Taiwan, Korea, and neighboring Russian territory from bases

[26] Ibid., p. 181.

[27] Japan, Kokkai, Shugi In, "Fujiyama Gaimu Daijin no Nichi-Bei Anzen Hosho Joyaku Kaitei ni Kan Suru Kosho no Keii ni Tsuite no Enzetsu ni Tai Suru Tokano Hisako no Shitsugi," *Kampo Gogai: Shugi In Kaigiroku,* 33rd Diet, 10 November 1959, No. 6, p. 66. See also Hoshino Yasusaburo, "Kokkai Ronso kara Kyokuto, Jizen Kyogi, Kempo," *Sekai,* No. 172 (April 1960), p. 54.

in Japan which Japan was pledged to permit under article VI of the treaty. That article specified that the bases granted by Japan were not only for the purpose of contributing to the security of Japan (against the Soviet Union) but also for the maintenance of international peace and security in the Far East (insuring effectiveness of American military power in South Korea and the Taiwan Straits as well as in Japan). Prior consultations were spelled out in the first exchange of notes to the treaty by which changes in deployment of American forces or equipment were to be discussed:

> Major changes in the deployment into Japan of United States armed forces, major changes in their equipment, and the use of facilities and areas in Japan as bases for military combat operations to be undertaken from Japan other than those conducted under Article V of the said Treaty, shall be subject of prior consultation with the Government of Japan.[28]

The circumstances requiring prior consultation were provided in a "verbal understanding" between the American Ambassador to Japan Douglas MacArthur, who was the nephew of General Douglas MacArthur, and Foreign Minister Fujiyama. The deployment of a division of land or air forces or a task force in the case of the navy would require consultation. Similarly, a change in equipment involving nuclear warheads or medium- and long-range missiles would require consultation. The provision has never been invoked although the opposition parties have raised the question a number of times.[29]

There was no explicit acknowledgment of a Japanese veto over American troop deployment or arms. Still, there was the implication that the United States might or should consult Japan beforehand on important decisions touching their mutual defense interests in East Asia. Subsequently, failure to do this, as in the Nixon visit to China, naturally eroded confidence in the United States, even if it was done on the plea that it was necessary to preserve essential secrecy. However, the refusal of the Hatoyama Cabinet to permit the introduction of tactical nuclear weapons did become a binding precedent as far as nuclear weapons were concerned, at least until 1972. The Eisenhower-Kishi joint communique on the signing of the treaty had come close to agreeing to a Japanese veto on the matters mentioned in the first exchange of notes: ". . . the Prime Minister discussed with the President the question of

[28] U.S., Department of State, *United States Treaties*, Vol. XI, pt. 2, (First) "Exchange of Notes to Treaty of Mutual Cooperation and Security Between the United States of America and Japan," pp. 1646–47.

[29] *Japan Times Weekly*, International Edition, Vol. XII, No. 18 (29 April 1972), p. 1.

prior consultation under the new Treaty. The President assured him that the United States Government has no intention of acting in a manner contrary to the wishes of the Japanese Government with respect to the matters involving prior consultation under the Treaty.''[30]

Such an assurance could only bind those who made it, but it seems to have set a precedent for Eisenhower's successors. The American refusal to surrender Okinawan territorial jurisdiction for nearly twenty years from 1952 was due to the fear of curbs on the use of bases by the Japanese government under pressure of public opinion. When the United States finally agreed in 1969 to return Okinawan civil jurisdiction, its officials made every effort to extract from Japan an acknowledgment that it would permit the use of the bases in Okinawa to carry out the effective defense of Taiwan and South Korea. Considering nuclear weapons unnecessary under existing conditions, the Japanese leaders extracted promises from the United States to remove them from Okinawa upon reversion, thus extending Japan's nuclear prohibition along with civil jurisdiction to the former occupied territories just as American officials had previously feared. However, the enormous growth of opposition in Okinawa and Japan to unlimited American use of Okinawan bases rendered the American position increasingly difficult.

Prime Minister Kishi's testimony before the Japanese House of Representatives on 11 March 1960 argued that the new treaty gave Japan the necessary curbs on American military operations:

> It is true that under the present Treaty American troops can use Japanese bases and that now the Japanese Government cannot influence the operations of the United States military stationed here. America can operate just as it pleases. Under these circumstances there is a danger that Japan might be involved in a war without its prior knowledge.
>
> But, if such a case should arise under the new Treaty, the American troops would have to get Japan's consent in prior consultations in order to move, and thus a limitation has been imposed. This is one of the points wherein the new Treaty had been improved over the old one with a logical revision.[31]

The Kishi statement exaggerated the degree of freedom enjoyed by the United States under the old treaty. It also claimed Japanese consent to be required for American troop use which was not supported by anything explicit in the treaty or the attached agreements.

[30] U.S., Department of State, *Department of State Bulletin*, Vol. XLII (8 February 1960), pp. 179-81.

[31] George R. Packard, *Protest in Tokyo* (Princeton: Princeton University Press, 1966), p. 202.

The policy on the use of American military bases in Japan touched the quick of Japan's security interests and involved some conflict of purpose. Japan's principal ostensible objective was the defense of its own territory through an American security guarantee with American garrison forces as hostages. The principle objective of the United States was the defense of the Far East by maintaining its powerful military position to prevent extension of the influence of the Soviet Union, the Chinese People's Republic, and the Korean Democratic People's Republic.

The American military influence was not regarded by the Communist states as protection for the region but as a threat to them. For China, the protection of the nationalist regime on Taiwan constituted intervention in its civil war and the preservation of a competing hostile regime within the boundaries of its own country. North Korea took a similar view with regard to American protection of South Korea and North Vietnam subsequently shared this view with respect to South Vietnam. This situation did not reflect Japan's claims that it would seek only friendly relations with all other countries, and the situation naturally made Japan's Communist neighbors hostile to it. It also called into question the Japanese attempt to limit its defense efforts and to avoid antagonizing other states.

The 1960 treaty acknowledged Japan's greater importance by giving it a larger share in altering the security arrangements. The provision for American assistance in suppressing large-scale internal riots or revolts sponsored by Communist states in article I of the 1951 treaty was dropped as it belonged to the time when Japan lacked sufficient armed forces of its own. The ability to handle internal disturbances itself signified greater independence. The earlier treaty also lacked a fixed term, and both parties had to agree that the United Nations or some other collective defense arrangement was sufficient to protect Japan before termination. The 1960 treaty, on the other hand, had a fixed term of ten years. Thereafter, either party could terminate the treaty on one year's notice which again enhanced Japan's voice in defense arrangements. Since its expiration in 1970, no new ten-year term has been agreed upon, as urged by former Prime Minister Kishi, but the countries operate under the terms of the one year's notice arrangement with the expectation that the treaty might be terminated or replaced by new arrangements in a few years.

In order to make the treaty more acceptable to the Japanese public, the government succeeded in having numerous references to the United Nations inserted in the treaty. Article VII made clear that these references in no way modified the obligations both parties already had as members of the United Nations. It merely indicated the professed intention of the two governments to act peacefully and to respect the principles of the international organization.

Ikeda's Minimum Defense Policy

To appeal to nationalist sentiment, conservative politicians in Japan increasingly used the phrase "self-reliant defense" *(jishu boei)* in reference to Japan's defense policy after 1960. This naturally implied some greater independence of the United States in security matters. Prime Minister Ikeda used the term in referring to his policy. When he took office in July 1960 Ikeda told newsmen that he wished to replace the United States as the focus of Japanese foreign policy. Instead, he said, Southeast Asia and Europe would become increasingly important to Japan. [32]

In the prime minister's first major policy speech to the Diet, he used the phrase "self-reliant" to describe his security policy:

> A fully self-reliant buildup of our Self-Defense Forces is our present duty as an independent country, but, of course, it must correspond to our national strength and to national conditions. While continuing to entrust the security basis of our country to the United Nations and to the Japan-United States Security Treaty, we are following a policy of gradual strengthening of our defense forces. I firmly believe that our country has the lowest defense expenditures in the world today with which it has been able to maintain peace and security and the remarkable economic development that is the foundation of the successive conservative party administrations. [33]

A fully self-reliant defense by definition exludes alliances with other powers. Ikeda's reference to Japan's continued reliance on the United Nations was an appeal to pacifist sentiment. However, if Japan was forced to call for United Nations assistance, the assistance would most likely come in the form of United States servicemen. (The United Nations' role in Korea in the early 1950s provided a meaningful precedent.) The gradual but limited defense force buildup would permit a little more independence, but the boast of almost the lowest defense expenditure in the world did not suggest a very self-reliant buildup. As the principal negotiator under Prime Minister Yoshida for moderate defense levels and as one who proclaimed its success in terms of economic and military effectiveness, Ikeda was not one to endorse any greatly increased rearmament. Japan's rearmament was really only the minimum necessary to satisfy the United States so that it could be induced to provide protection if Japan was threatened by external attack.

It was the program of the Liberal Democratic party in the November

[32] *Asahi Shimbun,* 23 July 1960, p. 1.
[33] Japan, Kokkai, Shugi In, "Ikeda Naikaku Sori Daijin no Shisei Hoshin ni Kan Suru Enzetsu (Gaiko ni Kan Suru Bubun)," *Kampo Gogai: Shugi In Kaigiroku,* 36th Diet, No. 3, 21 October 1960, pp. 23–26.

1960 election campaign which more accurately characterized the new government's security policy: "For the sake of our country's security until the functioning of the United Nations is sufficient, we shall firmly support the Japan-United States security system and provide the necessary minimum of our own Self-Defense Forces."[34] Although the United Nations is also mentioned here, its mention in this context is to characterize it correctly as insufficient and emphasize the reliance upon the United States. Japan's own forces are only appropriately mentioned last as a necessary minimum (to induce the United States to protect Japan). There is no pretension to self-reliance. About the only group against whom the Self-Defense Forces were adequate by themselves were domestic opponents such as the Communist party which might have resorted to force under some circumstances.[35]

Unfortunately for Ikeda's hopes of greater independence in defense matters, the comparative peace of the middle and late 1950s was shattered by the renewal of the cold war between the United States and the Soviet Union as well as by local wars in Indochina and in the border areas of India and China. Even when the Cuban missile crisis was over and the two superpowers again moved toward detente, the American leaders continued to fear Chinese expansion in Indochina and India. It was natural in the circumstances for President John F. Kennedy to look for greater military support from Japan.

This probably accounted for the lavish hospitality extended to Ikeda when he again visited Washington in 1961. Ikeda, however, had just passed through the treaty crisis at home and was loath to arouse the passions of 1960 by agreeing to any further security cooperation—certainly not any overseas dispatch of Japanese forces. When the American Secretary of State, Dean Rusk, broached the desirability of permitting nuclear powered submarines to call at Japanese ports for provisioning and rest, he was promptly refused by Foreign Minister Kosaka even though it was in the midst of the friendly discussions in the American capital.

Ikeda did give verbal support to the United States struggle with Communism in the world in his speeches, which were sympathetic to the American position. However, he permitted a year's hiatus to intervene

[34] Yoshio Miyamoto, *Shin Hoshu To Shi* (Tokyo: Jiji Tsushin Sha, 1962), pp. 617-18.

[35] This in fact, was stated by the Communist Party leader in referring to the 1960 Treaty Crises. Later Secretary General Kenji Miyamoto said: "Some say that as hundreds of thousands of people demonstrated, they could have overpowered the police who numbered only 20,000 to 30,000. If only there had been able revolutionaries, a revolution could have been accomplished, they say. . . . To that end, the Japanese people must completely overpower the Self-Defense Forces. . . ." Japan, Ministry of Foreign Affairs, Public Information Bureau, *The Search for National Security*, Japan Reference Series, No. 4-69, p. 21.

TABLE 3.2
AMERICAN AND JAPANESE MILITARY PERSONNEL LEVELS IN JAPAN,
1960-72
(THOUSANDS)

Year	United States	Japanese	Total Forces
1960	48	206	254
1961	45	209	254
1962	45	216	260
1963	46	213	259
1964	46	216	262
1965	40	225	265
1966	35	226	261
1967	39	231	270
1968	39	235	274
1969	40	234	274
1970	40	232	272
1971	36	234	270
1972	24 [a]	232	256

SOURCE: Based on Sakanaka, "Boei Ryoku," p. 90, *Nihon no Anzen Hosho*, 1968, pp. 366-67; *Asahi Nenkm*, 1970-1973, *passim*.
NOTE: [a]This figure should read 66 if Okinawa-based forces are added as a result of the return of the Southwestern Islands 15 May 1972.

before pushing through the Second Defense Buildup Plan. He even let the hard-won right of consultation under the Security Consultative Committee to almost lapse. The first meeting of the committee was called in September 1960 but the second was not convened until a year and a half later. Although consultation was a gain fought for by Kishi to enhance Japan's independence and participation in security cooperation, Ikeda was reluctant to take advantage of it to avoid attracting the criticism of the treaty opponents.

Some of the paralysis in the implementation of building up the defense forces began to wear off as the treaty crisis of 1960 receded. In 1962, agreement was reached in cabinet over a Second Defense Buildup Plan which was to run from 1962 to 1966. Although constant improvement in the forces continued, manpower levels were never to grow much beyond what they had reached under Prime Minister Kishi before 1960.

The prime aim of the Second Defense Buildup Plan was the improvement of existing forces. The Ikeda government found it easier to improve the quality of the forces than the quantity. The Japanese leaders aimed at a greater force mobility, improvement in support and supply capacity, stockpiling of ammunition, and replacing used and obsolete equipment. Even some steps toward underwriting research were begun. For the five year period from 1962 to 1966, a budget of 1,150,000 to 1,180,000 million yen (more than $3 billion) was agreed upon.[36]

[36]Asahi Shimbun Anzen Hosho Mondai Chosa Kai, *Nihon no Boei to Keizai*, Vol. IX of *Nihon no Anzen Hosho* (Tokyo: Asahi Shimbun Sha, 1967), p. 78.

The National Defense Council put its recommendations in surprisingly concrete language in July 1961, "To deal effectively with aggression under the Japan-United States security system in a limited war using conventional weapons."[37] The limitation to local conventional war was a victory for the finance ministry which begrudged every yen spent on military equipment. The defense agency would have preferred vaguer terms that would have permited the largest possible ambitions, making the above formulation more flexible.

As long as Japan restricted its ambitions to its own defense, it was concerned primarily with maritime and air forces rather than with ground troops. Japan's intent was to maintain supremacy of the air and water surrounding the islands, including the Japan Sea. The intention was to be able to close off the Tsushima, Tsugaru, and Soya Straits.[38] However, the self-imposed restrictions under current constitutional interpretation could some day be relaxed to permit Japan to help more directly in the defense of South Korea. On such an assumption, contingency planning was made and military exercises were held in November 1962 and June 1963.[39] The 1962 Three Arrows Study of the Self-Defense Force was premised upon a reinvasion of South Korea by North Korea and China.[40]

Regional Cooperation

Initially, prospects for improving Japan-South Korean relations appeared good. However, the government of Syngman Rhee, president of South Korea, was overthrown by a student revolt assisted by the neutrality of the military forces in 1960 at the time of the treaty crisis in Japan. Rhee had fought Japanese domination of Korea for decades and refused to compromise on South Korea's enormous claims against Japan. The new government soon came under the control of military leaders led by General Chung-hi Pak. Unlike Rhee, Pak was more inclined to forget some of the resentment of past injustice and to compromise for the sake of Japanese economic assistance to the lagging South Korean economy. In November 1961, General Pak visited Japan to see Ikeda and shortly after was visited in turn by Ikeda's representative. As a consequence the often broken-off talks between the two countries were resumed.

[37] Shunsaku Kato, "Postwar Japanese Security and Rearmament; With Special Reference to Japanese-American Relations," *Papers on Modern Japan, 1968*, ed. D. C. S. Sissons (Canberra; Australian National University, 1968), p. 72.

[38] Ibid., p. 73.

[39] Ibid., p. 73 footnote 33.

[40] Japan, Kokkai, Shugi In, Yosan Iinkai. *Yosan Iinkai Giroku*, 48th Diet, 10 February 1965, No. 10, 15 pages including the "very secret" document of 10 June 1962. See also *Chuo Koron*, "Mitsuya Kenkyu Kokkai Gijiroku Shugi In Yosan Iinkai Zembun, 10 February 1965," April 1965, pp. 155–82.

Prime Minister Ikeda did make an effort to respond to the pressure of the American Secretary of State, Dean Rusk, who raised the question of normalizing Japan's relations with South Korea at the joint Japan-United States ministerial conference in November 1961 in Hakone. As the defense of South Korea and Japan was thought to be integral to the anti-communist position in East Asia, the United States desired the two countries to be on friendly terms in order to make a more effective joint contribution to their defense.

In 1962, when Foreign Minister Ohira of Japan went to New York for the United Nations General Assembly session, Secretary of State Rusk urged him to offer the South Koreans at least $300 million in grants to indemnify the South Koreans for the Japanese annexation of their country which had lasted so long. The ruling Liberal Democrats in Japan were divided on the extent to which to meet the South Korean demands. The factions of Kishi, Sato, and Ishii, who were members of the dominant coalition within the ruling party, favored compromise and agreement with South Korea to improve trade. The Ono, Kono, Fujiyama, and Miki factions, most of whom belonged to the dissident group in the party, were much less favorable to meeting the South Korean demands. Finally in December 1962, eight of the factions formed an informal committee to lobby for a South Korean settlement.

Major business leaders in Japan also backed a solution to the problem of restoring relations with South Korea for the sake of trade and investment. Despite the virtually unanimous agreement within Japan that a solution would be good for business, the mutual dislike of the two peoples was deep-seated. The opposition parties were opposed to aiding the South Koreans because it would further divide Korea and prevent eventual unification. The opposition parties also feared that closer relations with South Korea would strengthen anti-Communist military cooperation, as the United States indeed hoped. Perhaps because of fear of a repetition of the 1960 crisis or because of illness, Ikeda did not push negotiations to a conclusion earlier although the solution to be reached by his successor was virtually assured. Efforts to strengthen the cooperation of Japan and South Korea for the sake of greater security thus failed during Ikeda's tenure of the prime ministership.

When the United States, the Soviet Union, and China agreed to a settlement to the crisis in Laos in 1962 at a second Geneva Conference, President Kennedy was compelled to act to prop up Thailand's wavering confidence in American determination to contain communism in that area. He therefore dispatched some American forces to Thailand, mainly for air bases which have been in use ever since.

The opposition parties in Japan complained that some of these American troops had been dispatched from Japan. The Japanese government leaders felt compelled to complain in turn to the United States for failure to consult it, and as a result the United States Ambassador, Edwin O. Reischauer, and Japanese Foreign Minister Kosaka agreed to maintain closer contact on such matters in future to prevent misunderstanding. Ambassador Reischauer admitted this failure to keep the Japanese fully informed but he also chided the Japanese for demanding detailed troop reports in a military emergency which suggested a lack of faith on the part of an ally.

Since Southeast Asia lay outside the Far East, as interpreted under the security treaty, there was apparently no necessity to consult Japan as far as the letter of the treaty agreements was concerned. It was becoming evident to the Ikeda Cabinet, however, that it would be to Japan's advantage to hold regular consultations with the United States, particularly as this point had already been won in principle by Prime Minister Kishi. Defense agency officials asked for regular discussions; they pointed out that if they were forwarned of likely developments, they might be able to offer constructive suggestions. On the other hand, they said, if they were called in only when an emergency arose, their role was likely to be nothing more than a rubber stamp of approval for already-determined American policy. [41]

As the leader of the Western bloc and a nuclear superpower which bore the greatest burden in the common defense, the United States has usually been unwilling or unable to consult its major allies fully in important military decisions until it has already decided what it would do. This was a precipitating reason for France's defection from NATO and to disappointment of the Japanese leaders beguiled by President Kennedy's engaging talk of a partnership with Japan. In fact, when the United States was willing to consult Japan, the Japanese were glad to comply. In August 1962, at a second meeting of the Security Consultative Committee, it was agreed that the two countries would keep each other more fully informed. More importantly, they agreed that the committee would meet thereafter at least twice a year.

In the matter of territorial return, Ikeda took a different approach from his predecessors. Instead of asking for the direct return of civil jurisdiction of the southern and southwestern islands, he pressed for greater participation in the welfare and development of the territories. Japan not only provided economic aid but also urged the United States to increase its economic assistance. The United States remained eager to keep control of these islands to insure the effectiveness of its military power in South Korea, Taiwan, and Southeast Asia as well as Japan itself, but the United States was willing to extend economic aid if doing

[41] *Asahi Shimbun*, 15 June 1969, p. 1.

so would placate Japan and the islanders, especially those on Okinawa.

Both Presidents Kennedy and Johnson in budget messages to the United States Congress stated the justification of American control of Okinawa: "To protect the security of the free world, the United States will continue responsibility for the administration of the Ryukyu Islands as long as conditions of threat and tension in the Far East require the maintenance of military bases in the islands."[42] Military leaders such as the commanding general of the Ryukus, who was also head of the civil adminstration took an even stronger position: "Loss of administrative rights would reduce or destroy the freedom of our military forces to act, and would seriously impair the usability of Okinawa as a base in defense of Free World interests."[43]

The Japanese leaders wanted to regain civilian control of their territories and also desired a larger say in the military use of the islands. The government consented to the continued use of the American bases (although the opposition parties wanted the bases dismantled) but wanted to be more actively involved in decisions about their use. Prime Minister Ikeda did not demand return of the islands; but he did insinuate himself indirectly into their civilian administration by increasing governmental grants to the inhabitants. President Kennedy reciprocated. Japan gave funds on an increasing scale and President Kennedy asked Congress to double the $12 million in economic aid to the islands.

After Attorney General Robert Kennedy's visit to Japan in 1962, President John F. Kennedy issued a statement to mollify Japanese and Okinawan sentiment by reaffirming that Okinawa, as part of the "Japanese homeland," would be returned as soon as international conditions permitted. In September 1962, the Japanese government took the initiative to suggest some form of joint consultation on Okinawa. The United States replied with a proposal for a consultative committee limited to economic cooperation matters to consist of the foreign minister and the American ambassador to Japan. Also proposed was a technical committee to be located in Okinawa which would consist of the high commissioner and representatives of Japan, Okinawa, and the United States. The high commissioner displayed some impatience at these moves and exercised fairly strict control over the local legislature and adminis-tration of travel to and from the islands.

Meanwhile, Russia and the United States were making significant progress on the Nuclear Test Ban Treaty. Russia's position as a major potential enemy of the United States was taken over by Japan's other

---

[42] Mikio Higa, "The Reversion Theme in Current Okinawan Politics," *Asian Survey*, Vol. VII, No. 3 (March 1967), p. 151. See also Mikio Higa, "Okinawa: Recent Political Developments," *Asian Survey*, Vol III, No. 9 (September 1963), p. 422.

[43] Higa, "Reversion Theme," p. 151.

near neighbor, Communist China. America was greatly concerned over the defense of Taiwan and South Korea, the two countries which buffered Japan from mainland China.

The annual joint ministerial meetings between Japan and the United States as well as the lower level Security Consultative Committee were forums for considering the strategic situation. The ministerial meeting was supposed to deal with economic affairs but the occasion of a top-level meeting was too valuable to forego consideration of defense interests. At the second ministerial meeting in Washington in December 1962, President Kennedy startled his Japanese cabinet guests at a luncheon by appealing for cooperation in stopping Communism: "I hope that in the months ahead thought can be given to what role we can play as partners . . . to attempt to prevent the domination of Asia by a communist movement which is in its essence today a belief not only in the class struggle but also in the international class struggle of a third world war."[44]

The Japanese ministers who were present, as well as the government in Tokyo, feared that this turgid prose was a summons to some kind of anti-Chinese crusade. As the Ikeda Cabinet had just approved an "unofficial" trade agreement arranged by members of the ruling party's dissident factions who had gone to Peking, they and businessmen in Japan wondered if their hopes for some small improvement in relations with China would be dashed. Officials of the United States tried to explain that the president's remarks were extemporaneous and not the beginning of a new policy and that they were asserted only to reflect alarm at the Cuban missile crisis of 1962. Unfortunately, President Kennedy's appeal foreshadowed the gradual drift into the disastrous war in Vietnam.

The third meeting of the Security Consultative Committee on 29 January 1963 dealt with the People's Republic and the current state of Japan's defense forces as well as the Cuban missile crisis and conditions in Southeast Asia. The fourth meeting on 10 October 1963 treated Japan's relations with both China and the Soviet Union as well as progress in the negotiations of the Test Ban Treaty.[45]

It was at the joint ministerial economic meeting after President Kennedy's assassination in 1963 that the question of French recognition of the Peking government as the Chinese government was discussed. France's step in formal recognition of the Peking government reflected its distance from the policy of the United States and its independent course. Prior to the next meeting on 26 January 1964, Foreign Minister

[44] *New York Times*, 6 December 1962, p. 11.
[45] Asahi, *Joyaku no Shoten*, p. 218.

Ohira met with Secretary of State Dean Rusk to discuss the situation. Ohira made it clear that Japan had no thought of exercising a similar independence in its foreign policy. At the committee meeting, Ohira discussed conditions in China and South Korea, while Secretary Rusk devoted himself to castigating the attitude of the Communist Chinese government. He pressed for greater Japanese assistance in dealing with the fearful spectre of Communist China. However, the Ikeda Cabinet failed to respond to American overtures to take a more active role in containment of Communist China. Ikeda's attitude had always favored peaceful economic means in domestic and foreign policy and did not move beyond old defense commitments despite the efforts of Kennedy and Rusk.

The result of the Ikeda leadership was to maintain security cooperation with the United States and slowly improve the quality of Japanese forces on a very modest scale. Initially, the trauma of the Security Treaty Crisis of 1960 reduced the willingness of Japan to permit any cooperation that might extend, even to a small degree, the use of more threatening equipment or forces either overseas or in Japan. However, earlier policies were continued. In particular, Ikeda never wavered on dependence on the American security guarantee of deterrence resting on the security treaty and American military bases in Japan. At the same time, Ikeda became as eager as his predecessors to maintain curbs to deal with American operations. Initial reluctance to take advantage of consultative participation was dropped after the dispatch of American forces to Thailand and this device was extended with respect to Okinawa. The attempts to curb or influence the deployment of American forces were less successful than hoped by the optimistic Kishi Cabinet.

Unlike other prime ministers, Ikeda did not attempt to win territorial retrocession but rather, in the case of Okinawa, he tried to win joint controls to initiate the process of territorial reversion. To this extent, he appealed to nationalist sentiment and the desire for greater independence in relations with the United States.

Despite some attempt to neutralize opposition criticism by calling for self-reliance in defense, Ikeda really yielded to pacifist and isolationist sentiment by keeping the defense forces to a modest size even in comparison with minor powers. The mission of these defense forces was also severely restricted by the refusal to even countenance any participation in direct military operations in the Far East outside Japan proper. The real underlying mission of the Japanese forces was to enable Japan to induce the United States to guarantee its defense, and its efforts were even more modest than was usually admitted.

In order to reduce international tension in the Far East and thus enhance its own security in a positive way, Japan refused to join any anti-Communist crusade against Communist China. The refusal to resolve the outstanding issues with South Korea also contributed to reduced cooperation of the American Allies in the area.

Without reversing security policy in any significant respect, the Ikeda government applied it in a more negative way than its predecessors. It lacked decisiveness and had far less appeal to nationalistic or independent sentiment in what was a fundamentally dependent relationship, though exercised in such a way as to give as little offense as possible to Japan's neighbors.

The security bargain Japan made to rearm gradually and to take over its own defense in exchange for temporary American protection was never fully carried out even during the Kishi or later Ikeda Cabinets when Japan had recovered economically and was able to increase its military effort. Leaders in the United States were disappointed at this failure but they did not impose any sanction for nonfulfillment of the security bargain by its Allies and thus they accepted it, even while complaining. As long as the United States cast itself in the role of protector of the non-Communist world against the Communist states, it feared to withdraw its protection. This, in effect, became a reinforcement of the American guarantees, and American forces provided a more credible deterrent, along with Japanese forces, while they remained in Japanese bases.

Japanese leaders' initiative was blunted by only a moderate need for their forces, the uncertainty of their role, and the pressure of continued pacifism at home. Their size and makeup, of course, would have depended on their mission and likely enemy which changed as East Asian relations changed. At the end of the Ikeda Cabinet, the Russian threat declined greatly and the focus of military attention shifted away from East Asia to Southeast Asia and particularly to Vietnam where the new rules of international conflict were to preclude an American military victory.

The Ikeda Cabinet concentrated its attention on Japan's economic problems. It strove to gain full entre to the councils of the industrialized states, especially in the international forums such as the Organization of Economic Cooperation and Development (OECD) and the General Agreement on Trade and Tariffs (GATT), and it concentrated on foreign trade in American and European markets. These policies were to produce the remarkable economic prowess that was so prominent under Prime Minister Sato.

The rather negative security policies based on a minimum defense, far from weakening Japan, may actually have strengthened it for the new era in which economic power was to count for much more than ever before.

4

Economic Partnership

THE IMPORTANT CONCERN that occupied Ikeda's attention as well as that of Japan's foreign officials and businessmen was the commercial relationship with the United States. Especially in trade and aid, Japan was dependent for its recovery and development upon the United States. This reliance was even acknowledged in the security treaty of 1960, and the words "mutual cooperation" were included in the name of the treaty to refer not only to defense but also to economic cooperation. The preamble to the treaty contained the phrase: "Desiring further to encourage closer economic cooperation between them and to promote conditions of economic collaboration between them." But the 1960s were a time of economic competition which subjected this ideal of collaboration to considerable strain.

Perhaps significantly the security treaty did not give any concrete details about how economic collaboration was to be increased. The United States had already aided Japan substantially ever since it tried to make it an ally as a consequence of the cold war. Even before that time it had aided Japan's recovery from the Second World War by helping to make its economy self-reliant. It had also sponsored Japan in various international agencies in which Japan was to play an increasingly important role as its trade increased and it once again became a major power in the economic affairs of the world.

President Kennedy's aim of increasing Japan's support for security reasons led him to seek to satisfy Japan's economic aims in creating what he called "a partnership." This provided the opportunity for Ikeda to meet his need for international economic support to supplement his emphasis at home on domestic economic growth and international trade. Both of these were likely to be popular and consolidate his political support. Concrete means of giving expression to the vague economic aims of the treaty were soon to be supplied.

Ikeda-Kennedy Alliance

The year 1961 opened with a new administration in Washington under President John Kennedy—one with which Ikeda was anxious to establish good relations. The rising tensions of the renewed cold war also made Kennedy anxious to gain increased Japanese support in order to strengthen the American position in Asia.

Early in 1961, Prime Minister Ikeda began to consider a trip to the United States. Earlier, when Prime Minister Yoshida and Prime Minister Kishi, visited Washington the trips had been opportunities to reveal dramatic plans or concessions with which to strengthen the Japanese political leader's position at home. However, these visits also usually involved concessions on the part of the Japanese for greater cooperation with the United States. When Ikeda broached the idea of a visit to America, his personal advisers were distinctly not enthusiastic. Kiichi Miyazawa, who had accompanied Ikeda on his two previous visits to Washington, immediately raised the question of China's reaction. What would be the impact on leaders in Peking, with whom the new Ikeda Cabinet was trying to improve relations in an unofficial way through the resumption of trade? It was suggested strongly that such a visit at this time would antagonize China, which would interpret any concessions made by Japan as a design to preserve American influence in Asia.

Another consideration was the clash of priorities of the two countries. The United States was chiefly concerned with military cooperation in its global struggle with the Communist states. However, the Japanese were anxious to distract attention from these matters and to concentrate on economic cooperation.

In spite of the feeling by some of his closest advisers that he should not make this visit to the United States, Ikeda began elaborate steps to prepare for the visit which was planned for June. He took care to familiarize himself thoroughly with foreign policy questions. Not only was Ikeda personally anxious to make the trip, but also certain party officials were eager for him to do so, and the chairman of the Liberal Democratic party's special investigation committee on economic cooperation thoroughly briefed the prime minister.[1] He urged that a concrete way be found to give some substance to the economic cooperation specified in article II of the new security treaty of 1960 in order to convince the interested public that it was not purely a military agreement.

[1] Morinosuke Kajima, *Nihon no Gaiko Seisaku* (Tokyo: Kajima Kenkyujo Shuppan Kai, 1966), p. 204.

He strongly urged as goals for the Japanese government the increase of trade with the Western bloc and a policy of loans to developing countries in the Asian area. He urged a joint Asian development fund and a liaison organ to coordinate aid to regional states. These were to become the basis of Japan's Asian policy.

The Chief Cabinet Secretary, Masayoshi Ohira, made the startling suggestion that the prime minister, foreign minister, and Miyazawa should all take their wives along on the trip to the United States, which would be the first time this had been done by Japanese officials. President Kennedy made a special effort to entertain suitably both the Japanese leaders and their wives in a successful series of social and political occasions well-calculated to appeal to the Japanese sensitivity to ceremony and prestige.

The meeting on 20 June between Kennedy and Ikeda was devoted to a number of areas which were particularly relevant to Japan, such as Kennedy's recent meeting in Vienna with the Russian Prime Minister Khrushchev, American relations with China, and the security and development of South Korea.

The belligerent attitude of Khrushchev, to which Kennedy, like Eisenhower, had been exposed, foreshadowed the confrontation of the Cuban missile crisis that was to come in the following year. Kennedy already had good reason to express cordiality to his Japanese visitors during their visit as he sought Japan as an ally in the troubles he expected in the future. Despite its truculence, Russia had agreed to reconvene the Geneva Conference to take up the Laotian crisis just before the Ikeda visit. However, the Chinese leaders in Peking were more disagreeable than the Russians, and they sharply criticized Kennedy's whole Asian policy.

There were also signs of renewed tension in the Taiwan Straits over the desire of China to reincorporate the island province into China which was prevented by American protection of Taiwan and its non-Communist regime.[2] Committed to military cooperation with the United States but faced with a potentially popular neutralist and pro-Communist China lobby among his opposition, Ikeda was in a similar position to Kennedy, who was committed to military cooperation with Taiwan but was faced with a potentially popular nationalist and anti-Communist China lobby among his opposition.

It was natural that with trouble in Laos and Taiwan Kennedy was anxious to see improvement in the relations between South Korea and Japan. These two non-Communist states were potential friends who could

---

[2] Roger Hilsman, *To Move A Nation: The Politics of Foreign Policy in the Administration of John F. Kennedy* (New York: Dell Publishing., 1967), pp. 302-20.

help each other greatly, and Kennedy urged Ikeda to settle his country's differences with South Korea. It was hoped that this would reduce tension in the region, enhance the chances for military coordination of the countries, and help the economic development of South Korea. Ikeda accepted this suggestion and promised to renew negotiations with South Korea.

Economic relations between the United States and Japan were discussed by Prime Minister Ikeda and Secretary of State Rusk. They covered a wide range of subjects including adverse American balance of payments, Japanese trade barriers, restrictions on Japanese cotton textile exports to the United States, and the threat of the European Common Market.

To give more concrete and regular high-level attention to the economic relations between the two countries, Rusk and the Japanese Foreign Minister Kosaka signed documents providing for an annual meeting of a Joint Trade and Economic Affairs Committee alternating between the two countries. When the president and the prime minister met aboard Kennedy's yacht on the Potomac on 21 June, they ratified the agreement reached by Rusk and Kosaka. The members of the committee from the United States were to be the secretaries of state, the treasury, the interior, agriculture, commerce, and labor; from Japan they were to be the ministers of foreign affairs, finance, agriculture, trade, labor, and the director general of the economic planning agency. The assignment of top level officials to such regular meeting in each other's country was just beginning to be instituted and gave some official recognition to the importance of their economic relations.

Such a cabinet-level committee had already been set up between Canada and the United States, and before Ikeda returned to Japan he stopped in Ottawa where he made a similar arrangement with Prime Minister John Diefenbaker. The purpose of these meetings was not to make formal agreements but to permit the respective senior officials to get acquainted and discuss informally their mutual problems in an effort to understand better the attitudes and problems involved on each side. The chief merit of the arrangement seemed to be the opportunity it offered to lobby the principal officials just below the head of government.

Kennedy and Ikeda also set up a committee for cooperation in cultural and educational matters and another committee for scientific interchange. These, however, were committees of lower-level experts which made them of less importance. Unlike his predecessor and successor, Ikeda did not press for the return of American-occupied Japanese territory in the Ryukyu Islands or the Ogasawara Islands.

This was not put among foreign policy objectives in public statements at the time, although the Ryukyu Islands were discussed by Kennedy and Ikeda, and both leaders pledged to make greater efforts to help the inhabitants of these territories. This was to give rise to American moves toward greater self-government of the islands and economic aid as well as Japanese economic assistance. Thus began the greater Japanese involvement in the islands which later led to the promise of their return to Japan by the end of the decade. The president's subsequent request for economic aid to the Ryukyu islands was severely cut by Congress but the United States did begin to increase its aid to the development of the islands.

The Japanese leader urged the desirability of greater economic aid to the developing countries of Southeast Asia and he proposed joint Japanese-American action. Japan felt it could not take on the major part of the burden of outside assistance alone and felt that the developing countries also needed substantial aid from the advanced Western countries, particularly the United States. The president was noncommital on this matter and would agree only to joint consultation on the economic aid to the Southeast Asia goal.

The final communique after the Washington meeting served Japanese objectives of emphasizing economic and non-military cooperation:

> The President and Prime Minister expressed satisfaction with the firm foundation on which the United States-Japanese partnership is established. To strengthen the partnership between the two countries, they agreed to establish a Joint United States-Japan Committee on Trade and Economic Affairs at the Cabinet level, noting that this would assist in achieving the objectives of Article II of the Treaty of Mutual Cooperation and Security.[3]

The Ikeda mission to the United States was a success both in affirming the policy of close cooperation with the United States in economic matters and in strengthening the Japanese leader's position in domestic politics. The fear of ill-feeling resulting from the earlier inability to welcome Eisenhower was dispelled and relations between the countries were judged to be on a more cordial level. In addition, the agreement to establish a Joint Trade and Economic Committee was considered a concession to Japan and even an acknowledgment of a higher status for it. To send almost the entire American cabinet half-way round the globe for a week in Japan was an indication of its greater importance such as was seldom evidenced by the United States to its other allies. The promise of increased economic aid to Okinawa was a further, although limited, concession from the United States.

[3]U.S., Department of State, *Department of State Bulletin*, Vol. XLV, No. 1150, 10 July 1961, pp. 57–58.

Economic Partnership

The trade between Japan and the United States, which the Japanese leaders rightly regarded as the most important relationship, began to receive more attention with the first meeting of the Joint Committee for Trade and Economic Affairs in Hakone, Japan, in early 1961. As American Secretary of State Dean Rusk explained, the importance of the meeting: "Not too many years ago the possibility of such a committee meeting would have seemed remote. Today it is a reality, and it is a reality because our partnership is solid, enduring, and expanding."[4] The visit to Hakone by five American cabinet secretaries at one time was quite a novelty and it attracted the attention of the press and officialdom in Japan.

In the year 1961, the economic slowdown had reduced the world demand for certain products, such as textiles. In consequence, there was a demand from American business and labor for relief through trade restrictions or tariffs to protect their home market in the United States against foreign imports. Japanese businessmen, however, were more anxious than ever to hold or to increase their share of foreign sales. The Japanese ministers at Hakone naturally pressed for greater trading opportunities for Japanese products. They argued at the meeting that Japan had purchased nearly a billion dollars more in 1960 from the United States than the United States had purchased from Japan. It was only fair, therefore, that the Americans help to balance this trade by buying more from Japan. In the meantime, Japan's heavy purchases of American products aided the American dollar and eased the drain of gold from the United States which suffered from continuing deficits in its overall payments abroad. Besides this, Japan had long suffered from an excess of purchases which was an undue strain on its economy. The United States could relieve this situation by taking more exports from Japan.

The Americans countered this argument by saying that the United States spent enormous sums on supplies for its military bases within Japan. Further, the American military personnel spent a great deal on recreation in Japan which earned foreign exchange for Japan. In giving aid to Asian countries, the United States made further purchases on foreign account within Japan. All these needed to be considered in a proper accounting. When these were included there was no imbalance of international payments between Japan and the United States.

Despite trade barriers in the United States, American restrictions were much less onerous than Japanese impediments to foreign trade in Japan. American automobiles and capital investments were excluded or kept

[4] *New York Times*, 1 November 1961, p. 4.

at a token amount by the Japanese government. It was true that Japan was asked to restrict the amount of its cotton exports under a voluntary arrangement, but it was still able to export to the world a large amount of textiles and at an increasing rate even to the United States. The American cabinet secretaries urged the Japanese to concentrate on the export of high quality goods and generally to work for expansion of world trade by joining the United States in its foreign aid program for developing countries.[5]

Japan and the United States had a common interest in maintaining access to the European market but this was threatened by the possibility of Britain joining the common market which was expected to erect high tariffs against Japanese and American exports. In the United States, the Democratic party had long favored low tariffs which would aid world trade, but the Reciprocal Trade Agreements Act, which permitted the American president to lower tariffs, was due to expire in 1962. Therefore, a new effort was needed to renew it and reaffirm a low tariff policy in the United States just when the feeling of protectionism was growing stronger in that country. To support their effort toward freer trade, the Kennedy team at the meeting urged the Japanese to lower their barriers to trade and foreign capital and consequently to increase trade, particularly vis-à-vis the United States. This was to be a long-continued plea which was to wait nearly a decade to see adequate response being taken by Japan in the face of sharp antagonism.

The Japanese responded, however, that they had been carrying out a reduction in quotas on many imports, which was a policy Ikeda strongly favored before efforts in this direction were almost halted by unfavorable economic trends and Japanese protectionist policy. Some of the lack of Japanese response to liberalized trade and investment was because of its long-held preference for preserving native ownership of Japan's industry and heavy reliance on home savings for investment. Japanese officials were reluctant to surrender any financial controls by which they might be able to protect Japan's previously weak position from foreign economic impact. The changing position of the United States in the direction of international financial weakness and the relatively greater strength of Japan and Europe were never given sufficient weight by the Japanese. It was assumed wrongly that the United States could make economic sacrifices indefinitely as the leader of the Western bloc. Unfortunately, many American officials also thought so in the early 1960s.

It was difficult as usual to restrict an economic conference to only economic matters. An American motive in agreeing to the committee

[5] Ibid., 5 November 1961, pt. 4, p. 5.

and its meetings was to strengthen the tie of Japan, as the strongest industrial power in Asia, to the Western bloc. The current phase of cold war supplied the impetus.

After Ikeda addressed the Hakone meeting of the economic affairs committee in November 1961, Secretary Rusk used the opportunity to urge Japan to go ahead with diplomatic negotiations with South Korea with a view to eventual economic cooperation between Japan and South Korea. When Rusk left the Hakone meeting to fly to South Korea, he was accompanied by a Japanese representative who went to discuss the revival of Japan-South Korean talks. Later General Chung-hi Pak, chairman of the Supreme State Reconstruction Council (as the ruling body in South Korea was called) then went to Japan to meet Ikeda at which time he agreed to further talks.[6] Japanese policy eschewed any active defense measures outside its own borders but in considering economic cooperation or aid to South Korea Japan was indirectly contributing to its own defense.

At a press conference on 9 November, President Kennedy used the occasion of the Hakone meeting to invite support for freer trade policies in preparation for the coming battle in the United States Congress over the Reciprocal Trade Act.[7] He said, "It [the Hakone meeting] succeeded in extending the concept of American-Japanese partnership to the economic and trade field and, I think, was a most important step forward in the relations between both of our countries . . . In addition, Japan also plays a key role in the economy of Asia and Free World economic objectives depend in a very important extent on her cooperation." The president echoed Japanese arguments on buying more from Japan to balance trade. "We cannot just sell and never buy," he averred. He also urged those who recognized the benefit of the large Japanese purchases from the United States to speak up "as loudly as those who are hurt."

Almost simultaneous with the Hakone meeting was a businessmen's conference in Tokyo which was attended by an eight-man delegation from the United States under A. N. Booth, president of the United States Chamber of Commerce. The thirty Japanese participants at the conference were headed by Taizo Ishizaka, president of the Federation of Economic Organizations. At this meeting, Booth said his mission came to Japan because the United States recognized that Japan was a leader in the free world and a country with whose fate the United States was closely linked.[8] He stated that although the United States was suffering from underemployment, which was caused by a recession,

[6] Ibid., 2 November 1961, p. 36.
[7] *Asahi Nenkan, 1962*, p. 284.
[8] *New York Times*, 7 November 1961, p. 14.

adverse effects from foreign trade were felt in only a few sectors of the economy. He added that the chamber of commerce opposed purely sectoral or regional approaches in favor of an overall national approach to clashes of economic interests. It was no good to complain of low wages in Japan: the United States must buy and sell competitively abroad where wages were a condition of the market. The point of view which he represented was economically liberal on trade, and the chamber backed President Kennedy on extension of the Reciprocal Trade Act, which was then before Congress.

Both the American and Japanese businessmen at the meeting feared the possibility of isolation from Europe with greater integration of the common market and British entry. As an alternative for Japan and the United States, the Japanese businessmen urged the creation of a Pacific Economic Community with Japan, the United States, Canada, and Australia as its nucleus. Later in the month, an American congressional sub-committee also urged that, in the event of the raising of European trade barriers, a Pacific Common Market be formed of those states plus New Zealand and other Pacific countries.[9]

Thus private business effort paralleled or led that of the governments in economic cooperation, although both government and industry had common interest in keeping open links with Europe as well as with each other. Japan was particularly anxious to gain freer entry into markets of the advanced European states, which were the major trading nations, both to insure its trade growth as well as to lessen its dependence on the American market. The American officials at Hakone promised to use their influence to support Japan's efforts to reduce discrimination against it by European governments. They also promised to discourage the practice of invoking article XXXV of the General Agreement on Trade and Tariffs (GATT), which permitted harsh measures against Japanese trade when disruption of American market from Japanese exports was feared.

Both Japan and the United States believed in the doctrine of freer trade, particularly as it applied to others. However, they were in less agreement about the urgency of sacrifice on the part of their own people or industries. Both Japanese and American officials were subject to political pressure for economic protection from supporting interests to which they were sensitive. As a champion of economic liberalism, the American leaders continued to favor freer trade, and a report was issued, the Herter-Clayton report, calling for wider presidential power to make general tariff reductions instead of being compelled to trade item for item.[10] Despite this, Kennedy was to consider some restrictions in favor

[9] *Asahi Nenkan, 1962,* p. 363.
[10] *New York Times,* 2 November 1961, p. 36.

of domestic textile interests in order to weaken protectionist opposition and, thus, permit the more important liberalizing measures to pass through the Congress.

The Problem of Textiles

The perennial economic debate between Japan and the United States centered on textiles. American manufacturers felt Japanese exports to the United States cut into the domestic producers' markets. This problem was handled by persuading the Japanese government and industry to restrict exports rather than by protective legislation on the part of the United States or European countries. This policy was supported by a growing resistance to the Japanese products within the United States by various labor groups.

On 16 February 1961, the Amalgamated Clothing Workers of America general executive board instructed its 385,000 members to refuse to cut any Japanese cloth imported after 1 May of that year. The boycott was claimed to be a measure of self-defense against the refusal of Japanese clothing manufacturers to set voluntary quotas on shipments of men's and boys' suits to the United States, and it was intended to curb low-wage imports from the Far East. The failure of a Japanese plan to set a ceiling on exports at 60,000 suits triggered the action. Since Japan had sold only 40,000 suits the previous year, compared to 20 million produced in the United States, the threat of Japanese competition did not appear very great to the Japanese. However, it was claimed that compared to an average hourly union wage of two dollars in the United States workers on the imported garments were paid only fourteen cents an hour in Japan. The executive council of the Textile Workers Union claimed that wool fabrics from Japan, Italy, and other countries displaced the equivalent of 16 percent of domestic output.

The boycott attempted against Japan would have supported protective measures by American authorities. However, because President Kennedy was anxious to cooperate with Japan and wished to lower trade barriers through a reciprocal tariff procedure, he requested a withdrawal of the boycott. He was successful in this despite the pressure from labor and management in the textile and clothing industries for protection against foreign competition.

In the spring 1961, negotiations began between the two countries to see if Japanese cotton textile makers and exporters would accept voluntary restrictions on their trade. The Japanese proposed that they would not exceed a 30 percent increase over their 1960 exports and finally after consideration the United States responded with a proposal that Japan should not exceed the previous year's exports by more than 5 percent. However, the Japanese manufacturers were dissatisfied with this counter-proposal of limitations and the discussions between the countries were halted.

One of the difficulties experienced by the Japanese textile manufacturers in 1961 was the general drop in world prices for their product. They naturally were anxious to increase their export sales to compensate in part for the losses threatened by the decrease in prices. The economic slump also had an adverse effect on Ikeda's campaign for liberalization of Japan's barriers to trade by reducing or removing fixed quotas on imports and thus opening its own market further to foreign traders and eventually to investors desiring to do business directly or in partnership in Japan.

In April 1961, the Japanese government freed imports of raw cotton and wool from the limited quotas, which had the effect of permitting the small- and intermediate-sized firms to manufacture larger quantities of textiles and thereby increase domestic competition just when there was a drop in world prices. Except for a brief improvement in May, the slump continued in both the domestic and export demand for textile products. Japanese industry was further adversely affected by the settlement of a strike by the Japanese Textile Workers' Conference in August with a large wage increase to be met by dwindling revenues. By October 1961, sales promotion organizations were trying to hold up prices by large-scale buying of textiles to stabilize the market but unfortunately the effort was fruitless.

Japan liberalized its trading restrictions just when demand was falling and costs were rising, but it was unable to offset the decline of export sales. Business leaders had feared just such destabilizing consequences for liberalization. Their criticism and the need for temporary restrictions on imports to ease the adverse balance of payments dealt Ikeda's liberalization program a severe blow from which it never fully recovered. The few initiatives toward reducing quotas did not go very far and when pressure from the United States increased later in the decade for more progress in Japanese trade and capital liberalization Japan had still not taken major steps to reduce its own protectionism while objecting to it in others.

President Kennedy proposed an international textile conference which finally met in Geneva under the sponsorship of the countries that had signed the General Agreement on Trade and Tariffs (GATT). The short-term remedy agreed upon at the conference was that those countries not presently limiting imports of textiles could ask exporting countries to limit themselves to the previous year's levels. Those presently limiting imports would prepare draft agreements providing for increases of imports starting in 1962.

Japan had begun the bilateral negotiations with the United States under the interim plan on cotton exports for 1962. An agreement was finally reached with the United States providing for only an 11.2 percent increase in cotton exports over 1960 under the so-called voluntary quotas. The United States, however, reduced the number of restricted items from sixty-four to twenty-seven so that there was some concession to Japanese demands. Japan also proceeded with its liberalization schedule to abolish restrictions on imports of rayon, mixed fiber, silk goods, wool and synthetic fabrics. In October, Japan reluctantly signed the interim agreement of the GATT countries but complained that the results were too favorable to the interests of the United States. When meetings were reopened later that month to consider long-term measures Japan submitted its proposals for preventing undue restrictions on textiles but substantive discussions were not scheduled until December.

Not long after the Hakone conference, Japan was shocked to learn that President Kennedy might be inclined toward some substantial restrictions. On 20 November, he asked the tariff commission if an import fee equal to the 8.5 percent cotton export subsidy should be imposed on cotton content of imported textiles.[11] The Japanese ambassador to the United States, Koichiro Asakai, protested to the state department that it would be difficult to explain to the Japanese people that the United States followed a liberal trade policy if it took such a protectionist step. The Japanese government similarly found this proposal difficult to understand.

In December, Vice-Foreign Minister Ryuji Takeuchi protested to Ambassador Reischauer in Tokyo that the effect of this import fee would be equivalent to a 10 percent tariff increase except that in the case of carpets it would amount to an increase of 30 percent. He also pointed out that Japanese textiles had a 40 to 50 percent American cotton content. It should be noted that what the president had proposed was, in effect, that the American textile importer should pay the equivalent of the cotton subsidy so that the imported textile goods would bear a cost proportionate to that of the American cotton textile industry.

The damage to Japanese-American relations threatened by these restrictions was highlighted by the testimony of Professor Hunsberger of Johns Hopkins University before the Congressional Joint Sub-Committee on Foreign Economic Policy. He urged that the government consider doubling the trade with Japan by the end of the decade and thereby increase it from $1.5 billion to $3 billion.[12] If this were done the United States should not consider any restrictions on trade. The small disadvantage to some sectors of American industry could easily

[11] Ibid., 1 December 1961, p. 10.
[12] Ibid., 26 November 1961, p. 1. There was no inkling at this time that the Japanese-American trade would increase nearly fourfold in the decade, let alone double.

be compensated for and factors of production could be transferred to give relief to any injured groups. Hunsberger also appealed to government defense objectives, by saying that Japan was important as an ally in Asia and that as a trading partner it was second only to Canada. Therefore, the United States should follow liberal trade policies and give friendly treatment to Japan and urge it on the other advanced countries to maintain their military cooperation. National needs and those of the free world would thus be served and they should take precedence over any minor injury to the domestic economy. Japan was cooperating with the United States on major international questions as well as in defense and if Japan were to shift to a neutralist policy it would have adverse consequences for the American defense position.

The Hunsberger argument was influential and was a factor in the passage of the Reciprocal Trade Act. The confrontation between protectionists and free traders in the United States was extended from January 1961 until October 1962 when Congress enacted the new Reciprocal Trade Act giving the president considerable freedom to reduce tariffs. The tariff commission gave support to freer trade by reporting to the president that the cotton import fee that had been discussed was unnecessary. However, it did not oppose completely any protective measures.

To avoid the pressure in the United States for further protection, voluntary limits on Japanese exports were nevertheless accepted by Japan. These were contained in temporary agreements such as the bilateral annual cotton agreements, and a long-term agreement on an international multilateral basis was reached on 9 February 1962 by the Cotton Goods Committee of GATT. Under this agreement, the nineteen cotton goods importing countries agreed that when an importing country's market was disturbed, the standard of the previous year, up to three months of the alleged crisis, should be applied to the following year; from the second year, a 5 percent increase; and from the third year another 5 percent increase over the previous year should be allowed. The restricting country should indicate at least some degree of liberalization in an agreed period and participants should not practise other limitations during the period. The agreed period was to be for the following five years. The Japanese exporters complained that by accepting the voluntary quotas agreed upon with the United States, the amount of the American market they lost would go to European exporters who did not have the same restrictions. The Japanese government, however, accepted the international decision and it went into effect on 1 October.[13]

The year 1962 proved to be an extremely poor one for Japanese textile

[13] *Asahi Nenkan 1963*, p. 399.

manufacturers. Despite a record volume of exports, continually falling prices in cotton and wool goods, of as much as 20 to 50 percent, produced shrinking returns. The Japanese government resorted to stringent measures to force its producers to curtail production except in special export categories. The generally unfavorable situation was a part of the adverse balance of payments which finally forced the Ikeda Cabinet to modify its policy of growth and liberalization by May 1962 with a policy of "a balanced economy," which imposed credit restrictions to check excess importations but which required a business slowdown.

After the inauguration of the special partnership by Kennedy and Ikeda in 1961, Japan had achieved considerable attention from American leaders, who strove through cabinet-level conferences and liberal trade measures to insure Japan's support for their policy aims. Despite the cordiality and goodwill displayed by the high-level officials and a generally favorable trend on specific issues such as textiles, the American leaders still acted to mollify domestic protectionists in the United States. They also collaborated more closely with their European allies.

Seeking Further International Support

Japan desired to enter the exclusive European sector of the advanced nations to gain fuller recognition and to gain remission of special economic discrimination against it in the form of high duties or quotas. Japan had already become a participating member of the Development Aid Committee (DAC) of the Organization for Economic Cooperation and Development (OECD), which was a multilateral group consisting of Japan, Canada, the United States, and several Western European states formed for the purpose of aiding developing countries. Japan participated in the consortium, which it sponsored, for loans to India and Pakistan. Japan thus not only participated as an advanced, or semi-advanced, country in aid-giving but did so as a member of an international group of advanced Western states. Because of the extensive Japanese restrictions on its currency and imports, Japan could not become a full member of OECD and GATT. However, under the Ikeda Cabinet efforts were begun to remove some restrictions on imports.

The discrimination against Japan was due to the fear of excessive exports of low-priced Japanese manufactured goods with which European industry could not compete. Even before the Second World War, Britain's textile and ship-building industries were hard pressed by Japanese competition which resulted in attempts to restrict Japanese exports in the peace negotiations after the war. This economic conflict of interest was sufficient to result in somewhat more stringent quotas or tariffs being applied to Japanese goods, especially where the European industry had not modernized itself sufficiently to compete with Japanese manufacturers or in areas in which wages were too high.

The Ikeda government took as a chief objective in 1962 the elimination of economic discrimination in the form of unusually high tariffs and low quotas against Japan, especially from Western Europe. This relief was sought through improved commercial agreements as well as by means of the prime minister's goodwill visit to Europe in November. However, he was not very successful in his efforts to improve relations except in Britain, where his persuasion resulted in a return visit by Prime Minister Harold Wilson to Japan. Between these two countries, a treaty of commerce and navigation was negotiated granting most-favored-nation treatment to Japan, with the proviso that it would be limited by Britain's entry into the European Common Market, if Britain gained entry into that organization. Particularly important to Japan was the agreement to limit Britain's privilege of restricting Japanese imports when any market disruption was feared by Britain. Japan also agreed that, on products requiring careful treatment, in emergency situations, it would accept restrictions on such goods going to Britain. Japan, thus, was pledged anew to the hated voluntary quotas, but its commerce was put on a firm footing for the first time since before the Second World War.

Although the reception and relationship with the major Western European states was not like that accorded to Ikeda in the United States, the prime minister called for similar intimacy to be developed with Western European countries and the reduction of trade barriers in his policy speech of 10 December 1962.[14] At the same time, he reaffirmed the special importance of American trade to Japanese prosperity. As the American cabinet secretaries pointed out at the second economic committee meeting that year, even the $300 million spent annually by the American military authorities alone in Japan was more than all the Western European countries together purchased from Japan.

In December 1962, the second Japan-United States Economic Affairs Committee meeting was held in Washington and the Japanese strongly urged modifications of the protective "buy American" policy adopted by the Kennedy Administration to ease the drain on United States gold. The United States maintained that if such a policy were not followed it would have to adopt even more stringent restrictions on Japanese trade. It also argued that the agreed voluntary quotas on textiles were necessary to enable the liberal American trade policy to continue. During the previous year, American-Japanese trade had been almost in balance despite the buy American policy. The American officials expressed the view that Japan exaggerated the economic discrimination against it and was unduly pessimistic about Western Europe's attitude towards it. Finally, the United States evidenced its economic support of Japan by

[14] Tsuji Kiyoaki, ed., *Shiryo Sengo Nijunen-shi,* Vol. I: *Seiji* (Tokyo: Nihon Hyoran-Sha, 1966), pp. 641–2: Ikeda policy speech to 42nd Diet.

its willingness to support Japan's entry to OECD.[15]

Some of the clash of interests grew less sharp as economic conditions improved in 1962. In Japan, the adverse balance of payments halted and the cabinet was able to ease some of its restrictive financial measures. The prices of textiles also began to recover, and the improved trend abroad relaxed some of the pressure from American industry and labor for restrictions on Japanese imports. The generally unfavorable American balance of payments, which was to be a permanent feature of the decade of the 1960s, was due to its ambitions overseas military and aid commitments and unbalanced budget at home which countered its favorable foreign trade earnings where exports continued to exceed imports in value throughout the 1960s, until 1970. To meet the unchanging drain of gold and dollars President Kennedy asked the Congress on 18 July 1963 to pass an interest equalization tax on foreign securities purchased by Americans.

Canada was excepted from this tax because of the adverse impact on its development which was mainly financed by American imvestment. On 31 July, Japan's Foreign Minister Ohira, one of Ikeda's most intimate advisers and leading lieutenants of his party faction, went to the United States to see Kennedy, Rusk, and Treasury Secretary Douglas Dillon to see if Japan could receive some special consideration as well. It was hoped that some exemption could be made on new stock issues as Japan depended heavily upon the issues it floated in the American market for current financing of its major industries. Despite the fact that Japan was a major trading partner with the United States, which bought more from the United States than it sold, Japan was to be treated the same as those countries that were a destabilizing factor. The only concession was an agreement to an ad hoc consultative committee to consider the situation. A vague promise was given to take some unspecified steps in case Japan was found to be seriously hurt.

The United States approached Japan to cooperate at the Geneva tariff meeting, which was to be held in May 1963, now that the president had obtained further power to make tariff concessions under the new Reciprocal Trade Act. In March 1963, the Assistant Secretary of Commerce, James Roosevelt, went to Tokyo to open the American Trade Center. While there he seized the opportunity to press the Japanese Minister for Trade, Takeo Fukuda, to support the American moves for new tariff cuts at the Geneva meeting. Fukuda objected that Japan's trade was still subject to special discrimination in Western Europe as well as to voluntary quotas for the United States. Christian Herter, who had been the previous secretary of state for the United States

[15] *New York Times*, 7 December 1962, p. 59.

and who was now the new special ambassador for the Geneva tariff conference, went to Tokyo in April. He talked to Ikeda and Foreign Minister Ohira as well as to political and business leaders to get support from Japan for this policy of tariff cuts. While the Japanese promised to cooperate as a matter of principle, they were not prepared to make any sudden dramatic tariff cuts at this time. As the two countries were in the process of negotiating the contentious three-year cotton agreement, it was not a propitious time to ask for concessions from Japan, which already felt pressed too far on voluntary quotas for the United States and Britain.

Whether correct or not, the Japanese image of itself continued to be one which exaggerated its weaknesses before the imagined strength of the American economy. Both sides were more conscious of their own domestic political pressures than the compulsion of arguments relying upon philosophical principles that were good in the long run but not quite so effective in solving immediate issues. Both governments were responsive to domestic businesses and to their economic bureaucracies and therefore should have had a better appreciation of their mutual problems. At the GATT meeting in May 1963, Japan did support initiatives for tariff reductions of American representatives, but the negotiations were to continue until 1967 before substantial tariff reductions were finally agreed upon.

The third economic committee meeting was scheduled to be held in Japan in November but the American delegation turned back at Hawaii because of the assassination of President Kennedy. When both Ikeda and Ohira went to the United States for the president's funeral on 24 November 1963, they had a chance to talk to Lyndon Johnson, the new president, and they agreed to a meeting of the committee at the earliest opportunity.

The committee finally met at the end of January 1964 in Tokyo. In the final communique of the meeting the American delegation agreed that the United States would strive to solve its general balance of payments problem and that, if Japan's balance of payments with the United States became very unfavorable, appropriate steps would be taken with regard to the issue of new securities as promised earlier. The usual statement about cooperation in expanding trade was repeated and both parties agreed to keep in touch on GATT tariff discussions. They also agreed to support the Geneva Conference on Trade and Development by finding ways to increase imports from developing countries.

On 28 April 1964, the achievement of advanced status was conferred by full membership in the Organization for Economic Cooperation and Development. Japan had freed its trade and currency to the degree that it was able to meet the requirements of the chief organization of the advanced industrial states. Its acceptance in what was mainly an organization of Western European and North American states for aid to the developing countries was also a symbol of fuller acceptance by Western Europe which Japan hoped would now extend to trade as well. Since Japan was also interested in influencing the Asian region, it could hope for more support there from the advanced states through greater cooperation in aid.

Despite the claims of the Ikeda Cabinet that Japan had moved a long way in liberalizing trade by the removal of quotas or quantitative restrictions on many products, the apparent liberalization was more truly a mark of the extraordinarily large number of products that had been restricted earlier. Japan was certainly the slowest among the advanced industrialized states to remove wartime and postwar restrictions. Those products that remained restricted or were closely controlled were ones which foreign traders especially wished to sell to Japan, such as passenger cars, computers, large electric generators, and dairy products. As a member of GATT, Japan was permitted to continue to exclude only a limited number of products for security reasons or for a few other agreed purposes. However, Japan continued to limit more products than most of the other major non-communist states—products not permitted to be excluded by GATT rules. Although some relaxing of restrictions on passenger car imports were considered under Ikeda, it was to be nearly a decade later, under Sato, before substantial moves were finally undertaken on this sensitive item.

The practice of "voluntary restraints" by Japan was required in areas other than textiles or competitive manufactured products. It was also relied upon with respect to fishing even on the high seas in the Pacific Ocean—to protect depletion of resources by excessive catches. At the time of the peace treaty in 1951, the fishing industries in the United States and Canada wished to eliminate entirely Japanese fishing in the eastern Pacific. For the sake of getting the peace treaty signed, the question of fishing rights was put aside and handled by a separate treaty. This treaty was to continue until June 1963 and thereafter unless a party gave notice of withdrawal.

The signatories met as the North Pacific Fisheries Commission to consider changes but did not reach an agreement. The Japanese were intent on extracting an admission of the principle of equality of use of resources but the United States and Canada were not prepared to concede this principle. The Americans and Canadians wanted a continuation of restraints which in fact would be a prohibition on Japanese fishing for salmon and trout in the northeast Pacific and for halibut in the Gulf of Alaska. At a meeting in Tokyo, the United States and Canada dropped the explicit acknowledgment of the voluntary restriction principle but still wished to retain the substance by any other wording.

The various economic clashes which accompanied Japan's growing strength were resolved fairly amicably by Ikeda and Kennedy, particularly in contrast to the Sato-Nixon clashes that were to come later when Japan was relatively much stronger and the United States much weaker. The Ikeda and Kennedy Administrations began their terms with considerable enthusiasm and goodwill toward each other. They strove to adjust their relations to accord a higher status to Japan in the light of Japan's growing strength and importance. This partnership policy was under considerable pressure within Japan from opposition parties and groups which demanded a more neutral, less pro-American, and hence more independent policy. The policy was also under pressure in the United States from particular industries, both labor and management, to make no major concessions to Japan beyond a token share of the market or resource involved.

Despite these pressures, which grew more severe in times of international tension, the two leaders persisted in a liberal policy which checked attempts to impose greater barriers and permitted the total volume of trade and financial transactions to grow to a considerable level for Japan. From this point of view the liberal and cooperative policy in economic matters must be judged a success.

In the sense that many important barriers and threats of more severe restrictions remained, the principles of economic liberalism were never carried far enough. Nor could economic groups and political leaders in Japan feel they were treated as "equal partners" even though they did appreciate the economic benefits received from the good economic and political relations at the official level. Not only the Western European countries but also the United States insisted on conditions which, in the case of fishing, were based on the guardian or paternalistic roles of the occupation and the 1951 peace settlement.

It seems fair to say, therefore, that the economic relationship during the first part of the 1960s was something less than a partnership and that on specific issues in conflict there was little disposition to depart in any substantial way from the application of restrictions and essentially unequal relations. The acceptance of the restrictions was a sacrifice to the wider area of concord and mutual benefit.

5

Return To Asia

ALTHOUGH THE SAN FRANCISCO PEACE TREATY was signed by Japan and most of its Asian neighbors, it did not fully settle the differences between them and Japan. Japan realized that it would have to take positive action to restore friendly relations. It was chiefly through reparations, economic aid, and trade that Japan gradually gained entry to the markets and access to the raw materials of its Asian neighbors, both of which it badly needed. In doing so, it eventually restored diplomatic relations with most of its neighbors. However, the region never regained its prewar importance for Japan, which was increasingly integrated much more closely with the advanced economies of North America, Australia, and Western Europe.

Japan, however, has been anxious to retain the markets for its manufacturers as well as its access to raw materials in Asia not only because they are valuable for Japan's own economic development but also because friendly trade relations reduce tensions and may contribute to a greater and more satisfying role in East Asia. It is in this region that it emphasized policies contributing to its three major goals of prosperity, security, and recognition as a leading world power.

The important initial purpose of the war reparations was to effect a reconciliation with those non-Communist neighboring states most inimical to Japan. Japan's reparations and aid policies resemble somewhat the American Marshall Plan of economic aid to Western Europe or American economic assistance to West Germany. The relatively underdeveloped Asian neighbors, however, were not able to utilize this aid as quickly and effectively as Japan had been able to do through its highly trained population and effectively organized political and economic system. Still, the provision of grants, loans, and investments greatly facilitated the trade which immediately benefited Japan's own economy and helped the economic development of its neighbors. It also had the effect of making Japanese trade and investment more welcome and reducing hostility to it.

Japan also cooperated with the United States in signing a peace treaty with Taiwan. Although Taiwan did not demand reparations from Japan, it did receive valuable military and economic support from both the United States and Japan. Japan established a large trade and made large industrial investments in Taiwan, but these steps aroused the hostility of Peking and this antagonism was to constitute one of Japan's most serious foreign policy problems right into the 1970s.

Japan also joined the United States in giving economic aid to other Asian countries. This was added to the reparations of the particular countries, but the amount did not increase under Ikeda because of the economic recession during his tenure of office. Like trade, the economic aid contributed to Japan's own economic development and it gave Japan better access to its neighbors' markets and resources. However, in the case of trade with Peking Ikeda would have pursued a more aggressive role if he had not been checked by pressure from Taiwan and the pro-Taiwan leaders in his own party.

Avoiding direct military commitments in the Asian region in accord with Japan's conception of its limited defense policy was valuable in reducing, if not entirely avoiding, antagonism from both the Southeast Asian countries and the communist states in East Asia. It was indirect commitment to the United States in its use of Japanese bases and facilities in Japan that prompted the communist fear of "Japanese militarism."

Japanese Reparations

Japanese reparations generally have taken the form of the transfer of goods and services. These goods and services were usually provided by direct Japanese government grants which were used to purchase Japanese products or to pay for Japanese technical services in the recipient country. Reparations and reparations-like payments were made to former occupied countries or to those injured by Japan before and during the Second World War. The countries receiving these reparations included the Philippines, Burma, Indonesia, Vietnam, Laos, Cambodia, Thailand, and South Korea. Despite the misuse or neglect of some goods provided for by reparations, chiefly in the Philippines, these transfers have been unusually successful as they were easy to carry out and were, or could be, used to supply capital goods badly needed by the recipients to rehabilitate their economies or to undertake productive enterprises.

The ostensible purpose of reparations and the chief impetus for them was to obtain redress for injury arising out of aggression. Where the

Japanese government did not recognize an obligation arising from aggression, such as in the cases of Laos and Cambodia, Japan nevertheless agreed to payments and loans for the sake of reconciliation of the differences with the respective countries.

Because these reparations payments have been used for economic assistance, they have been listed by Japan as part of its aid to developing countries. They constituted a very large amount of economic aid and were almost the only direct grants given by Japan. They were intended to pay for items selected by the recipients without limitations placed upon their selection except that the goods and services must be from Japan. These stipulations corresponded very closely to the type of aid advocated in the West and have been accepted as part of Japan's aid effort by other members of the Development Aid Committee of the OECD. In addition, the Japanese government agreed to sponsor private loans in the reparation agreements.

At the time of the negotiations for the peace treaty in 1951, the United States had signed a defense treaty with the Philippines to obtain its adherence to the Japanese peace treaty, thus providing protection against any renewed Japanese aggression. The adherence of countries such as the Philippines was considered essential to concluding a general Japanese peace treaty. However, even this proved to be insufficient to insure Philippine ratification and therefore provision for reparations were inserted into the peace treaty.[1] On the basis of this article, Japan began to negotiate a reparations agreement with the Philippines, but it was not until 1954 that the Philippines felt sufficiently satisfied with the arrangements to ratify the peace treaty even though it had been signed at San Francisco in 1951. Because of the initial demands for billions of dollars in reparations, the negotiation of reparations agreement had made little progress until the Philippines was prepared to reduce its claims in 1954.[2] In May 1955, an agreement was reached between the countries on $550 million to be provided in goods and services over the next twenty years from an outright reparations grant, and the Japanese government was to sponsor an additional $250 million in private loans. The agreement was finally signed on 9 May 1956 but did not go into effect until 23 July.

Diplomatic and trading relations flourished thereafter, but Japan was still disliked and regarded with suspicion in the Philippines. To obtain some of the same privileges in doing business and traveling in the

[1] U.S., Department of State, *United States Treaties and Other International Agreements*, Vol. III, pt. 3, "Treaty of Peace with Japan," TIAS 2490, 8 September 1951, Art. XIV, pp. 3180-81.

[2] J. L. Vellut, "Japanese Reparations to the Philippines," *Asian Survey* III (October 1963), 497-500.

Philippines as were enjoyed by other countries, a treaty of amity, commerce, and navigation was finally negotiated and signed in 1960, but not without great political opposition and criticism.[3] However, even this agreement did not allow permanent residence to Japanese, as the people of the Philippines feared Japanese economic control. The result was that the commercial treaty between the countries has not been ratified to this day.

Despite the corruption that attended the handling and awarding of goods resulting from reparations and the failure of the Philippines government to utilize the opportunity to undertake an effective development program based on them, the reparations have, nevertheless, provided some productive goods and beneficial services to the Philippines. The Japanese businessmen and the officials who were most concerned simply accepted the reparations as necessary to encourage trade on a substantial scale. The chief motive of trade in economic cooperation (or aid) policy was thus fully served both before and during the term of the Ikeda government. The motive of assistance to a developing country for its economic growth, even if intended largely to build Japanese markets and to supply resources, was probably not as effectively achieved. However, if the Japanese reparations are compared with the vast sums of money given to the Philippines after the war by the United States, the Japanese effort is no worse—and perhaps even better—in productive outcome than that of the United States. Relatively less Japanese aid has been dissipated in immediate consumption or extravagant expenditure than was true of America's aid.

The amount of reparations grants to the Philippines was more than half the total that Japan supplied to all countries. The relatively large amount reflects the extent of damage and hostility aroused in the islands as well as the importance the United States placed on patronizing its former colony. Placating the Philippines and the United States for the sake of a peace treaty was thus a major step in Japan's progress in strengthening its position in the region and internationally.

Although the Philippines was one of the most important Japanese neighbors and the most difficult one with which to reach reconciliation through reparations grants and loans, Burma and Indonesia were also important in settling reparations claims. As soon as these two countries achieved their political independence after the Second World War, they had joined the ranks of the allied powers occupying Japan. As they had been occupied and controlled by Japan during the war, they had to be appeased by reparations.

[3]Lawrence Olson, "The Politics of Flower Arrangement, Aspects of Japanese-Philippine Relations," *American Universities Field Staff Reports Service*, East Asia Series, Vol. IX, No 13 (Japan), (26 December 1961), pp. 4–7.

Burma refused even to go to San Francisco Peace Conference but, in fact, did reach agreement with Japan prior to that reached with the Philippines. In 1954, an agreement with Burma was concluded for reparations of $200 million in goods and services over a ten-year period and a peace treaty was signed on 5 November 1954 between the two countries.[4] Besides the reparations grants, Japan also agreed to sponsor private loans in that country to the amount of $50 million. There was little action on the private loans, not through lack of interest, but because one impractical project after another was rejected by the Japanese.[5]

Burma pressed for additional amounts of reparations starting in 1959. Article V of the peace treaty between Japan and Burma, provided for reconsideration if any other country received an unequal amount of reparations, and as the Philippines obtained $550 million, Burma claimed it should be treated equally. It asked for another $200 million in grants and an equal amount in private financing of capital goods and technical assistance. The Burmese foreign investment law was modified to permit foreign ownership of joint enterprises up to 50 percent although the lack of Burmese investment was a serious problem.

It was not until March 1963 that an agreement for economic and technical cooperation finally was signed for a grant of a further $140 million.[6] The government funds were to be used over the next twelve years, and, in addition, it was agreed that yen credits to the amount of $30 million would also be provided over the next six years. These negotiations, however, concluded the reparations—it was agreed that no further demands would be made. The new agreement was ratified in October 1963 and went into effect the next month.

In 1952, Indonesia signed, but did not ratify, the San Francisco peace treaty pending a settlement of reparations claims. Like the Philippines, Indonesia began by demanding an enormous amount in reparations—$17.2 billion. As no payment had been received by 1957, Indonesia felt it necessary to do something drastic about the adverse balance of payments with Japan and to obtain some capital resources for economic development. Negotiations began with a reparations figure of the modest proportions of $250 million, significantly lower than the original demand. These discussions were interrupted by a change in cabinet in Indonesia after which the new prime minister, Kartawidjaja Djuanda, proposed negotiations on the basis of $400 million in reparations and $400 million

[4] Lawrence Olson, "Japanese Activities in Burma, Comments on Japan-Burma Economic Relations," *American Universities Field Staff Reports Services*, East Asia Series, Vol. IX, No. 12 (Japan), (30 November 1961), pp. 3-10.

[5] Ibid., pp. 7-8.

[6] Japan, Tsusho Sangyo Sho, Boeki Shinko Kyoku, *Keizai Kyoryoku no Genjo to Mondai Ten 1968* (Tokyo: Tsusho Sangyo Chosa Kai, 1968), pp. 172-73.

in economic aid. To the accompaniment of worsening internal disorder in Indonesia and a visit of Prime Minister Kishi to talk with President Sukarno, a final settlement was reached by the end of 1957. Reparations were fixed at $225,444,000 in the form of Japanese goods and services over an eleven-year period, and all uncollectable foreign trade debts to the amount of $174,556,000 were cancelled. For "economic coopera-tion" over the next twenty years, Japanese private companies would extend loans and investments to the amount of $400 million. After normal relations were fully established, the two governments were to take steps to strengthen economic relations in trade to effect the elimination of discriminatory treatment.

The internal disorder in Indonesia in 1957 led not only to the demise of the party regime and civil war but also to the seizure of Dutch businesses which was followed by nationalization of industry. Japanese firms were asked to take over the Dutch oil installations. As a result, Japanese business had an opportunity to replace Dutch interests. One of the areas affected by this opportunity was the economic cooperation agreement reached in 1960 to assist Indonesia's oil organization, Permina, to restore and expand production of oil wells in the Atjeh region of North Sumatra. Japan supplied equipment and technicians for surveys and drilling, and in return received 40 percent of any increase in oil production. To cooperate, the Japanese created the North Sumatra Oil Development Company with majority control in the government but with a third of the shares held by private Japanese firms.

When it is remembered that the Pacific War was precipitated by Japan in 1941 at least partly through the desire to gain access to Indonesian oil, the interest of Japan in Indonesia today can be easily understood. Japanese government and private participation in Indonesian development and especially in the supply to Japan of its key export commodity of oil has become a major achievement of its economic cooperation policy. Indonesian friendship is important. When Sukarno became increasingly less aligned with the West and more cooperative with the Communist bloc leaders, Japan, not surprisingly, was reluctant to join the United States or Britain in trying to enact sanctions against him.

The three formerly French-controlled Indochinese states of South Vietnam, Laos, and Cambodia also signed the San Francisco peace treaty as each was anxious to claim reparations from Japan. In 1956, the Republic of Vietnam asked to discuss reparations but it was a few months before the Japanese ambassador in Saigon did propose $8 million as reparations and $12 million in loans as economic cooperation. The South Vietnamese, however, wanted $250 million, and only later indicated they would reduce this demand to $200 million. Despite the enormous discrepancy between this amount and the amount the Japanese were willing to consider, the leading vice-president of the Federation of Economic Organizations, Uemura Kogoro, was sent to Vietnam by the foreign minister of Japan in 1957 to negotiate an agreement. He offered $25 million but had to cancel the negotiations when the Vietnamese proved adamant in their demands for more. Shortly after, Prime Minister Kishi went to see President Ngo Dinh Diem. They agreed only that a solution should be reached soon. Because of the success of the Indonesian negotiations, the Japanese leaders were anxious to resolve the Vietnam problem, and Uemura returned to Vietnam once more. This time Japan proposed $26.5 million in reparations and Vietnam demanded $63.6 million; on cooperation loans Japan offered $11.5 million and Vietnam asked for $60 million. With such a discrepancy, progress was impossible. It was not until January 1960 that the problem was finally settled through the efforts of Foreign Minister Fujiyama with reparations grants of $39 million in total to be paid in installments over a five-year period. Most of this was to be used to build a power plant at Danim, and, in addition, a loan of $7.5 million was made for operating expenses of the power complex and another of $9.1 million for fertilizer plants. In this case, the settlement was closer to what Japan thought to be reasonable and the amount was considerably smaller than had been made with other countries. Japanese interest in Vietnam was not as great as in other places and consequently the Vietnamese bargaining position was considerably weaker. In fact, Vietnam was lucky to get what it did. As it was, there was severe criticism from the opposition parties and groups in Japan which denounced the American policy of supporting South Vietnam. The criticism was directed at the settlement with the South Vietnamese regime, a settlement which would only benefit the business organizations in Japan.

Laos and Cambodia also asked for reparations but Japan was reluctant to provide any further concessions. Without admitting to compensation for aggression, Japan did agree to moderate payments for the sake of postwar reconciliation with these countries. An agreement was made with Laos for $2.8 million over a six-year period from 1959 and one was made with Cambodia for $4.2 million over a five-year period from 1960.

A special yen agreement was made with Thailand to provide it with $26.8 million in Japanese goods and services over an eight-year period from 1962.

While these economic arrangements with Laos, Cambodia and Thailand were not reparation payments, they did serve the purpose of reparations by smoothing trade relations and reducing war-induced antagonisms.

TABLE 5.1
REPARATIONS AND SIMILAR GRANTS

Country	Time Period	Amount of Payment (in millions of dollars)		
		Reparations	Non-Repayable Economic and Technical Cooperation	Special Yen Payments
Burma	10 yrs. from 1955	200.00		
Philippines	20 yrs. from 1956	550.00		
Indonesia	12 yrs. from 1958	223.00		
South Vietnam	5 yrs. from 1960	39.00		
Laos	6 yrs. from 1959		3.00	
Cambodia	7 yrs. from 1959		4.00	
Burma	12 yrs. from 1965		140.00	
South Korea	10 yrs. from 1965		300.00	
Malaysia	3 yrs. from 1968		8.17	
Singapore	3 yrs. from 1968		8.17	
Thailand	8 yrs. from 1962			28.00

SOURCE: Japan, Tsusho Sangyo Sho, Boeki Shinko Kyoku, *Keizai Kyoryoku no Genjo to Mondai Ten 1968* (Tokyo: Tsusho Sangyo Chosa Kai, 1968), table 2.8, p. 170.

The Japanese preferred to call the grants economic aid and stressed the fact by referring to the arrangements as economic and technical cooperation agreements.

South Korea was the final area involving reconciliation and large-scale grants and credits. South Korea was in a different category from the Southeast Asian countries, and it took twenty years to reconcile differences with Japan. South Korea had suffered incorporation into Japan in 1910 as a dominion, or colony. Ikeda responded to American pressure to improve relations with South Korea. The change of regimes in South Korea in 1960 and 1961 brought a greater inclination of the new South Korean leaders to settle outstanding differences over compensation for the period of Japanese rule and for fishing rights and territorial claims. Some trade already existed between the countries, but there were no regular diplomatic relations. Under the military rule of General Pak in 1962, a provisional economic cooperation agreement was concluded for $300 million in grants for Japanese goods and services and $200 million in long-term credits. The Japanese Overseas Economic Cooperation Fund, which was established in 1961, provided funds for twenty years at 3.5 percent, an unusually low interest rate for Japanese aid credit. The fund was intended for use in the South Korean settlement.

The steps to finally establish relations with South Korea were slowed in 1962 and then postponed until after Ikeda was replaced in power. All moves toward normalization between the countries were strongly resisted by the opposition parties in both Japan and South Korea. Ikeda apparently was not willing to risk the confrontation planned by the left-wing parties and groups which aimed at creating as big a commotion as they had done in 1960 over the security treaty. As the final settlement was resolved only in 1965 under Prime Minister Sato, the cooperation fund hardly was used at first and no extra capital was provided for the fund in the budgets of 1963 and 1964.[7] Even the initial capital for the fund was quite insufficient for the contemplated South Korean credits.

The hesitation to move forward in South Korea was an exception to other Asian moves when Japanese businessmen were eager and trade prospects were good. While the South Korean economy had not entered an advanced stage, trade and joint enterprises were almost certain to prosper once normalization was achieved. Reparations and commercial settlements in Southeast Asia had been fairly easily approved in Japan, but those cases tended to be the province of officials, politicians, and businessmen and were relatively isolated from the general public which was uninformed and uninterested. South Korea was a different matter. It was a country with which Japan had a long intimate relationship and about which most Japanese had definite opinions. South Korean questions were important in Japanese politics, both as they affected major policies of the government and opposition parties and as they affected the handling of the South Korean minority in Japan—the only large ethnic minority group. The commercial objectives, therefore, took second place to the political considerations.

Government Loans and Credits

In addition to grants for reparations, loans and credits to foreign governments have been an important form of aid from Japan. Loans were made between governments but they were closely tied to the provision of Japanese capital goods and services. Lines of credit provided advance supplier's credit up to an agreed amount on behalf of a foreign government. Since the Japanese government preferred to refer to these by region or yearly totals, it is often difficult to calculate the exact amount of individual agreements and amounts going to a particular country. The largest government loans and credits went to India and Pakistan in cooperation with consortia established to assist the development plans of those two countries as part of an international effort. Before and during the Ikeda Cabinet these amounts were exceeded only by the reparations paid to the Philippines and Indonesia. In addition to promoting commercial relations, the loans represented Japanese aims to maintain good relations with important neighbors and also to obtain

[7] John White, *Japanese Aid*, (London: Overseas Development Institute, 1964), pp. 38–40.

TABLE 5.2
JAPANESE GOVERNMENT LOANS BEFORE AND DURING THE IKEDA CABINET
(IN MILLIONS OF DOLLARS)

Date of Loan	Receiver Country	Amount
February 1958	India (1st)	50.0
July 1959	Paraguay	3.8
November 1960	South Vietnam	7.5
August 1961	India (2nd)	80.0
November 1961	Pakistan (1st)	20.0
January 1962	Brazil	17.5
January 1963	Pakistan (2nd)	25.0
May 1963	India Supplement (2nd)	15.0
September 1963	Pakistan (3rd)	30.0
October 1963	India (3rd)	65.0
September 1964	India (4th)	60.0
October 1964	Pakistan (4th)	30.0
February 1965	Brazil (Refinancing)	7.7
March 1965	Brazil (Refinancing)	24.9

SOURCE: Japan, Tsusho Sangyo Sho, Boeki Shinko Kyoku, *Keizai Kyoryoku no Genjo to Mondai Ten,* 1968 (Tokyo: Tsusho Sangyo Chosa Kai, 1968), pp. 144–46.

acceptance among the developed nations as a leading participant in granting aid.

As well as government loans and government lines of credit, credits were also given to private Japanese suppliers to enable them to finance export sales on a deferred-payment basis to buyers of plants, capital equipment, and ships on a favorable long-term basis. These were called "export credits" and usually were financed through the Export-Import Bank which also handled most of the government-to-government arrangements. Both the export credits and the government credits and loans were partially financed by the commercial banks which usually took up to 20 percent of the amount.[8]

Private investment took place in two main areas. First, Japanese capital was used to finance a wholly owned Japanese firm doing business in a foreign country. Second, Japanese entrepreneurs often formed a consortium with foreign investors to underwrite ventures in another country. This private investment was included in Japan's aid or economic cooperation to developing countries because it undoubtedly contributed to the purpose of development and because it also received protection from the government. The Japanese government made some funds available at advantageous terms through the Export-Import Bank and the Overseas Technical Cooperation Agency for lending to the private firms concerned. It also provided insurance for investment principal

[8]Kiyoshi Kojima, "Japan's Foreign Aid Policy," in *Papers on Modern Japan 1965,* ed. D. C. S. Sissons (Canberra; Australian National University, 1965), p. 131. See also, White, *Japanese Aid,* pp. 54–58.

and investment profits thereby creating a stable climate for investment by the private sector.

Japanese private investors were restricted severely in the Philippines and in Indonesia, despite the so-called normalization of diplomatic relations. Indonesia did not permit the formation of any joint companies and the Philippines forbade Japanese participation in local firms pending a trade treaty. For example, up to September 1963 total private investment in Southeast Asia, including South and East Asia, was only $85.2 million compared to Latin America which was $148.6 million, the Middle East which was $137.4 million, and other areas which was $5.6 million.[9] The private investment pattern contrasts with the government loans and credits. The greatest amount of government aid went to Southeast Asia, which received $315.1 million compared to Latin America, which received $285.5 million, the Middle East, which received $48.7 million, and other countries, which received a total of $17.8 million.[10]

Japanese technical assistance was an early and important form of aid which, like direct grants, was financed wholly by the Japanese government. This assistance had never amounted to a great deal in terms of dollars compared with financial and capital aid, nor did it compare in size with the advanced countries as a percentage of total aid. Nonetheless, it enabled Japanese techniques, which were appropriate for developing Asian countries, to be transmitted. Technical assistance took the form of receiving trainees in Japan in connection with the Colombo Plan and technical cooperation schemes of a regional or multilateral character. Another form of this assistance was the dispatch of Japanese technicians to Asian countries to teach and to demonstrate Japanese techniques. Also, Overseas Technical Training Centres were established to carry out demonstrations of improved techniques. Finally, pre-investment surveys for development plans and programs proved increasingly beneficial and sought after by the developing countries.

Japanese contributions to multilateral agencies were relatively small but the contributions enabled Japan to participate as a donor to the World Bank and agencies such as the International Development Agency, the International Finance Corporation, the United Nations Special Fund, and others.

However, it was only in 1961 that Japan succeeded in coming close to the amount of aid recommended by international agencies, which was 1 percent of its national income. Thereafter, it became increasingly difficult to approach that amount as Japan's national income increased rapidly. In 1962 and 1963, it was not economically feasible to increase aid at the same rate as the national income.

[9] Kojima, "Japan's Foreign Aid Policy," appendix II, p. 148.
[10] Ibid., appendix I.

TABLE 5.3
JAPANESE AID DURING THE IKEDA CABINET, 1961–64
(IN MILLIONS OF DOLLARS)

Official Funds	1961	1962	1963	1964
Bilateral grants				
Reparations	65.1	66.8	62.1	57.8
Technical assistance	2.4	3.6	4.5	5.8
Other grants	0.3	4.2	10.1	5.1
Government long-term capital				
Direct loans	26.8	12.5	60.3	49.1
Other	0.9	−7.5	−8.8	−11.6
Grants to multilateral agencies	2.0	2.2	2.9	3.2
Capital subscriptions to multilateral agencies	9.4	5.0	9.2	6.5
Subtotal	106.9	86.8	140.3	115.9
Private funds				
Direct investment	98.4	68.4	76.7	39.3
Export credits	180.7	130.3	50.6	135.7
Multilateral portfolio investment	−4.6	0.7	—	0.3
Subtotal	274.5	199.4	127.3	175.3
Total	381.4	286.2	267.6	291.2
National income (in billions of dollars)	41.32	46.68	52.93	60.08
Percentage of national income	0.92	0.61	0.51	0.48

SOURCE: Japan, Ministry of Foreign Affairs, Public Information Bureau, *Japan's Foreign Aid*, Japan Reference Series, No. 2-67, p. 12.

As seen in table 5.3, Japanese aid as a percentage of its national income actually declined continuously throughout the Ikeda regime from 1961 to 1964. This was not due to any desire to decrease aid as a policy objective, but, as already noted, it was due to the rapid increase of national income in spite of foreign exchange problems and setbacks in the world market for products such as textiles. Nevertheless, it certainly seems to be true that allied with this there was no concerted effort during the Ikeda Cabinet to increase aid substantially. The situation reflected the relative quiet on the international scene and Japan's increased concentration on internal affairs in an effort to avoid disturbances to the internal political equilibrium. The falling percentage of Japanese aid became the object of external criticism as Japan became a full-scale member of the international organizations concerned with trade, aid, and international finance.

International Economic Cooperation

Economic aid or "cooperation" is handled either by multilateral international organizations containing a large number of members or by direct bilateral arrangements between the donor country and the recipient. Sometimes both methods are combined, as in the Colombo Plan for assistance to British Commonwealth countries which Japan joined as a donor in 1954. In the Colombo Plan, the full membership meets regularly to discuss general policy and to make recommendations. A donor country, such as Japan, then makes direct bilateral arrangements with a recipient country to send and receive trainees or technicians or to take other assistance measures. In 1956, when Japan became a member of the United Nations, it also became a contributor to the Special Fund, the International Bank for Reconstruction and Development, the International Finance Corporation, and the International Development Association. It has been also a member of the consortia for India, Pakistan, Nigeria, and Colombia.

Most countries participating in the international agencies preferred to make their donations bilaterally. Such an arrangement allowed them to control the terms of the agreement and to insure that their own trade and industry received some benefit from the donated funds. In Japan's case more than 90 percent of its aid was bilateral and its participation through the international agencies during the Ikeda Cabinet was modest. However, during the Ikeda Cabinet, as with the previous cabinet, Japan exerted itself to be accepted into the councils of the major advanced states in order to strengthen its international status. It wished to insure more attention to its own demands for freedom to enter world markets and eliminate discrimination against it. Participation in aid-giving and in multilateral discussions about it had the advantages of giving Japan a foothold in the group of the more powerful states and greater influence in both world and regional affairs where it had both commercial and political interests.

Japan joined the Development Assistance Group, which was composed of the principal donor countries and whose main concern was the principles of the aid programs. Almost the only requirement of Japan was that it submit reports of its aid activities. However, the group did apply some pressure on Japan to conform more to the aid practices of the advanced states and to report on these practices in more detail. It also

TABLE 5.4
COMPARISON OF JAPAN AND SOME MAJOR WESTERN DONORS, 1961-62
(IN MILLIONS OF DOLLARS)

Country Giving Official and Private Aid	1961	1962
United States	4531.0	4520.0
Britain	863.8	836.7
West Germany	800.4	681.4
Japan	371.1	281.9

NOTE: The Japanese figures here appear to be based on those of earlier Ministry of Foreign Affairs publications such as used by Kojima, "Japan's Foreign Aid Policy," p. 130. The sums in table 5.3 are from later ministry compilations and are slightly larger for Japan.

SOURCE: John White, *Japanese Aid* (London: Overseas Development Institute, 1964), table 2, pp. 46-47.

provided another forum by which Japan could associate closely on a more equal basis with the major states. Later the Development Assistance Group became a committee of OECD.

The OECD, which was a successor to the agency which coordinated postwar European recovery with American aid, undertook to guide greater efforts of the advanced states to help the developing countries. When OECD itself discussed aid conditions and measures to increase joint aid efforts on 17 November 1961, Japan was invited to attend the ministerial council in Paris and was represented by the Economic Planning Agency Director General, Aiichiro Fujiyama.

In November 1962 Japan applied for full membership in OECD and an invitation for it to join was issued the following July. The Diet failed to ratify the invitation and Japan's formal admission to OECD was delayed until 27 April 1964.

Although Ikeda had strongly supported the gradual elimination of various restrictions on imports, control over foreign exchange and currency was strictly maintained as had been the case for nearly thirty years. Japanese officials were surprised when Western Europe freed its currency, and Japan became the only major non-Communist country to continue to control all private foreign exchange transactions. Among the eighty-two members of the International Monetary Fund (IMF), Japan was classed under article XIV of its charter as a country that could place restrictions on the movement of capital or ordinary exchange transactions due to its postwar financial difficulties. Each year the chief of the Exchange Restrictions Bureau of the IMF came to Japan to confer on its status. In 1961, the Development Assistance Committee recommended that Japan change to an article VIII country, which permitted a country to free exchange transactions, provided liberalization of trade proceeded to the 90 percent level by October 1962. The 1962 OECD annual report stated that exchange stability was the first principle upon which Japan's growth policy rested but that there was no international instability warranting continued trade and currency restrictions. Japan had come to the position where it should have begun to change over to article VIII status.

The United States had been undergoing considerable difficulty due to a shortage of foreign exchange to carry on its defense and aid programs abroad. In March 1963, the Clay report to President Kennedy was made public; it proposed that Japan give aid loans on more flexible and favorable terms, increase the loans, and permit the United States to reduce its assistance. This recommendation was criticized in Japan on the basis that it might weaken other countries if the United States strengthened its exchange position at the expense of countries such as Japan. [11] In effect, the Japanese felt that if the Western nations wanted Japan to give more aid they should help it by opening their doors wider to Japanese exports.

Perhaps this international urging together with the pressure from the United States and International Monetary Fund prevailed upon Japan to take the plunge and free its currency. Japanese officials indicated that Japan was prepared to switch to article VIII status by the beginning of the new fiscal year in April 1964. In early 1964, the necessary arrangements were made when Japan became the twenty-fifth country to make the change among the IMF members. Thus the yen began to regain its convertibility after three decades of tight control.

Japanese Regional Trade

Although advanced countries have acknowledged the need to increase trade with the developing countries, they have, in fact, increased trade among themselves even more, because the developing economies simply cannot grow fast enough to take full advantage of the growth of world trade. Other serious problems limit the growth of the developing and would-be developing countries, as many advanced countries can often produce cheaper and better quality agricultural products and manufactured goods than the developing countries. The less-developed countries, such as India whose population has grown more rapidly than its food output, have often been forced to rely upon imported food from the advanced countries. Before the Second World War, the less-developed areas were a chief source of food and agricultural products for the world, but now they are often unable to compete even in these items with countries such as Canada and Australia. The internal unrest, political upheavals, and radical political experiments that have taken place since the war have had further disastrous consequences for their trade.

Japan's trade with advanced countries, such as the United States, increased in volume so rapidly after the war, that the portion going to East Asia declined. This was a contrast to the prewar period when most of Japan's trade was in Asia, particularly with Korea, Manchuria, China, and Taiwan. Thus Prime Minister Ikeda's attempt at a partnership with the United States and Western Europe followed the course of its enormous trade expansion with advanced countries. It is probably not surprising that aid policy and relations with Asia received relatively less attention during the Ikeda Cabinet while relations with the Western states received the greatest attention.

As seen in table 5.5, the share of Japan's trade with Asia dropped during the 1950s. It tended to hold its own during the Ikeda Cabinet.

[11] White, *Japanese Aid*, p. 16.

TABLE 5.5
SOUTHEAST ASIAN SHARE OF JAPAN'S TRADE

Year	Percentage of Total Imports	Percentage of Total Exports
1951	26.6	40.0
1956	22.7	34.7
1961	16.8	32.6
1964	16.3	26.7

NOTE: "Southeast Asia" follows Japanese usage here, including the area from Korea to Afghanistan but excluding the communist states.

SOURCE: Saburo Okita, "Japan in South and Southeast Asia; Trade and Aid," in *India, Japan and Australia: Partners in Asia?*, ed. J. D. B. Miller (Canberra: Australian National University, 1968), p. 131.

Exports considerably exceeded imports which shows the effect of economic aid, particularly reparations, which enabled Japan to continue to send substantial amounts of capital goods to this major developing area despite the whole range of obstacles in importing from countries such as Indonesia and India. However, Japan showed an interest in these countries through its aid policy. Whatever the effects on the recipient states, there is no doubt that the aid policy greatly benefited Japan's own industry and trade, and it helped to consolidate Japan's indispensability to the developing states, some of which were major non-communist countries of the region. The fact that the program was fairly modest but closely linked to Japan's own development plans increased the likelihood of continued mutual benefit. The commercial character of Japan's program was probably its chief strength, as it limited the dubious projects which were showy and unproductive and aimed instead at long-term development, which was desirable for both parties. This is something that cannot be said as easily of the American, British, and Soviet aid to some countries, such as Indonesia.

The great emphasis of Japanese policy upon trade and trade-promoting aid may also have had an important economic consequence. As in the slogan "trade, not aid" which many developing countries voiced in their frustration at the obstacles to their development and the lack of assistance they received, trade was regarded as much more beneficial than aid. Aid through loans had the obvious disadvantage of requiring debt repayment, a burden which was less involved in ordinary trade transactions. The process of renegotiation and settlement was not likely to insure cordial relations between the two parties. Even when aid was in the form of a one-way transfer of funds or of goods and services, it was apt to be fortuitous and not easily controlled by the receiver country. It was generally felt that such aid projects were likely to be poorly conceived and relatively unproductive in contrast to ordinary commercial transactions. Increased trade may directly result in growth of domestic production and employment of a permanent and cumulative nature. The advanced states were reluctant to increase trade with the developing countries on terms disadvantageous to themselves. Where the donor country, such as Japan, looked to the developing country as a source of essential raw materials—as in the case of Indonesian oil—the aid was a much firmer basis for both parties, provided the receiver country considered it beneficial. Japan was also influenced by its special position of extreme dependence on foreign trade and its fear of the vagaries of international politics which could easily threaten its commerce with the distant Western states.

Even though Japan's trade with Asia was shrinking in relative amount compared to its total trade, this trade still increased considerably. As total Japanese exports increased almost fourfold from $2.5 billion to $9.8 billion from 1957 to 1967, its Asian trade increased more than threefold from $868 million to $2630 million. At the same time that the Asian region's exports rose by 23 percent between 1960 and 1965, its exports to Japan rose by 83 percent. Second only to the United States, Japan received more of Asia's exports than any other country.

Despite Japan's steady internal progress and continued trade expansion, the prevailing Japanese attitude to economic aid remained ambivalent. Perhaps because its own recovery was so recent it was hard to turn from the previous attitude of concentrating on rehabilitation during the rule of the Ikeda Cabinet. As one of Japan's leading economists has written:

> Prevailing feeling in the government and among people in general was that the rehabilitation of the war-devastated economy should receive highest priority, and there was little room left for assisting other nations in view of the low standard of living of the people of Japan.
>
> In addition, there has been a general feeling that in pre-war years Japan was unnecessarily involved in the affairs of other Asian countries and this involvement had eventually brought catastrophe to the Japanese people.
>
> There has also been a feeling that in view of persisting memory of Japanese military occupation of other Asian countries, it was considered more desirable not to touch upon problems of those countries. In short, the general attitude in Japan was "let us not be involved in others' affairs and let us concentrate our efforts on rehabilitation of our own economy." [12]

---

[12] Saburo Okita, "Japan in South and Southeast Asia: Trade and Aid," in *India, Japan, and Australia: Partners in Asia?*, ed. J. D. B. Miller (Canberra: Australian National University, 1968), p. 137.

However, Japan was being prodded from abroad to change its attitude. We have already noted the positive steps the Japanese government took to gain entry to the meetings of the major powers in organizations such as the Organization for Economic Cooperation and Development, as well as participation in that of the General Agreement of Trade and Tariffs and the International Monetary Fund. In Paris in December 1964 at the first meeting after it joined OECD, the Japanese Minister of Trade, Yoshio Sakurauchi, immediately pressed for elimination of discriminatory treatment toward Japanese trade by the organization members. This represented the old absorption in Japan's own immediate material objectives. Nevertheless, here as in its ministerial meetings with the United States Japan was also pressed to take a broader viewpoint and reconsider its own barriers to foreign commerce with Japan. Also, Japan's greater involvement in international councils was emphasized when specialized agencies connected with the United Nations, such as the International Monetary Fund, the International Bank for Reconstruction and Development, the International Development Association, and the International Finance Corporation, held their joint annual general meeting in Tokyo in September 1964.

Particularly interesting is the Japanese experience at the first meeting of the United Nations Trade and Development Conference. The economic cabinet ministers had met to consider Japan's position at the meeting and had decided to avoid any commitments and took a protective attitude toward their own trade. Kiichi Miyazawa, the director general of the planning agency, did urge expanded trade with the developing countries but he also said it should benefit the advanced nations and that developing countries needed to make more effort to help themselves. The negative Japanese attitude was very unfavorably remarked upon at the various committees at the trade conference so that the foreign ministry adviser Asakai hurried back to Japan to see if a change could be made on their decision to avoid any commitments. A meeting of the economic ministers was called and Prime Minister Ikeda brushed aside the cautious warnings of the ministers of trade, agriculture, and finance. It was decided that Japan would take a flexible position to increase the importation of primary products from the developing countries, to give them tariff relief on special manufactures, and that Japan would aim at bringing its aid up to 1 percent of its national income. The Japanese representatives at the trade conference then volunteered to aim for the 1 percent level. Thus it seems to have been the developing countries that changed the Japanese attitude, and it was Ikeda who helped enunciate a new and more positive aid policy which was to animate the next cabinet.

Although Japan's trade was world-wide and most of it was with the advanced countries outside the Asian region, the importance of the Asian

TABLE 5.6
MAJOR TRADING NATIONS' SHARE OF FAR EASTERN TRADE, 1960–64
(PERCENTAGE OF TOTAL REGIONAL TRADE)

Country	1960	1961	1962	1963	1964
Japan	10.9	12.5	13.3	14.3	19.3
United States	11.9	13.6	14.4	14.8	16.7
Britain	8.1	8.3	8.5	8.2	7.5
West Germany	4.3	4.3	4.0	3.8	4.6
Australia	2.0	3.1	2.7	3.4	3.9
Holland	1.7	1.7	1.8	1.8	2.7
China	2.4	2.1	2.3	2.7	3.3
France	2.9	2.2	2.0	1.9	2.0
New Zealand	0.2	0.3	0.2	0.3	0.4

NOTE: The "Far East" here includes Burma, Thailand, Cambodia, Laos, North Vietnam, Brunei, West Irian, Macao, the Ryukyus, North Korea, South Vietnam, Malaya, Singapore, Sarawak, Sabah, Indonesia, the Philippines, Taiwan, Hong Kong, South Korea, Communist China, and Japan. This differs considerably from "Southeast Asia" as used in table 5.5. For Japan and China, only their trade with the region is included.

SOURCE: Donald C. Hellman, *Japan in the Postwar East Asian International System* (McLean, Va.: Research Analysis Corporation, 1969), p. 24, table 3.

trade was relatively great. In 1964 it surpassed American trade with the region as a whole, and became first or second in importance in the trade of nearly every single country in the region.

As table 5.6 shows, Japan and the United States, among the principal trading nations in Asia, carry on two or three times the trade of their nearest competitor among the other seven countries listed. The United States and Japan are economically very important to each country in the region, but the trade of any one country in the region is comparatively unimportant in terms of the United States' and Japan's overall trade. This would seem to justify some indifference by the two leading powers to the countries in the region. But the expected indifference is contradicted by the constant embroilment of the United States in the wars and the politics of the region and Japan's own prewar expansion and present economic activity there. Perhaps the relative lack of economic dependence from the Japanese side gives Japan strength in dealing with Asian countries since they cannot injure Japan's economy seriously by withholding support or obstructing its trade and investment.

The most likely source of military threat to Japan was from its neighbors in the region. An even more likely occurrence, however, was the disturbing impact on Japan of wars or insurrections in neighboring areas such as Korea, the Taiwan Straits, or Southeast Asia, which might threaten the free passage of Japan's commerce including the essential oil from the Middle East. Japan therefore developed financial ties which were also intended to strengthen friendly local incumbent governments thus reducing those threats.

In addition, Japan's status as an important Asian state was enhanced by its improving economic relations with its neighbors. Also, during this period the Asian area stopped declining as a trading area for Japan in comparison with the rest of the world. Japan's trade with Asia stabilized and began to increase at about the same rate as the rest of Japan's trade. Thus, at the same time that trade with Asia retained considerable importance to Japan, Japan continued to grow in importance as a partner of every Asian country by virtue of its expanding and modernizing economy.

The China Problem

Perhaps nowhere was Japan's diplomacy called upon to serve its goals in more challenging circumstances than with its Chinese neighbors on the mainland and on the island of Taiwan. Because both regimes considered themselves to be one state and Japan had been compelled by the United States to recognize and sign a peace treaty with the government on Taiwan, its principal link with the mainland was through trade. Thus the private unofficial negotiations over trade became the means not only of carrying on commercial relations but also of considering questions of defense. By implication, questions of status and influence of the two Chinese governments were also discussed.

This situation resulted from the Chinese Civil War, which in 1949 produced the government of the People's Republic of China under the Chinese Communists on the mainland and the Republic of China under the Chinese Nationalists on the island of Taiwan. At the time of the San Francisco peace conference in 1951, Britain recognized the People's Republic of China as the government of China while the United States recognized the Chinese Nationalists. However, both countries agreed that Japan could decide itself with which one to make peace. Neither Chinese government was invited to the San Francisco conference. However, when the Japanese peace treaty was due to be ratified by the American senate, John Foster Dulles, who had been the chief architect of that treaty, visited Japan, and explained that a majority of senators threatened not to ratify the treaty unless Japan chose to make peace with the Chinese Nationalist government on Taiwan.

Prime Minister Yoshida would have preferred more time to consider recognition of Taiwan as the legitimate government of China when even Britain refused to do so.[13] Fearing to jeopardize the opportunity to obtain Japan's political and economic independence under the San Francisco treaty, he submitted to American pressure. On 18 April 1952, Japan signed a separate peace treaty with Taiwan. Ironically, this was

---

[13] Shigeru Yoshida, *Kaiso Junen* (Tokyo: Sincho Sha, 1957), Vol. III, pp. 71-74.

the same day the the San Francisco treaty went into effect and gave Japan its independence. However, the Japan-Taiwan treaty applied only to territories under the control of the Chinese Nationalist Government.[14]

The mainland Chinese denounced the treaty.[15] From the time the People's Republic was formed in 1949, it had feared the American forces and the revival of Japanese military power. Even before Japan was linked to Taiwan in a peace treaty and before the outbreak of the Korean War, China concluded the Treaty of Friendship, Alliance, and Mutual assistance with the Soviet Union on 14 February 1950 to protect it from Japan and the United States. Article I of that treaty stated that in the event of China or the Soviet Union, "being attacked by Japan or any state allied with her and thus being involved in a state of war, the other Contracting Party shall immediately render military and other assistance by all means at its disposal."[16]

This Sino-Soviet alliance failed to deter Japan and the United States from later concluding a security treaty simultaneous with the San Francisco peace treaty, which linked Japan militarily with the United States and therefore indirectly with Taiwan. In the meantime, China and the United States had become principal antagonists in the Korean War although each took care to prevent the Sino-Soviet treaty from being activated and respectively claimed that their forces were volunteers or engaged in a United Nations peace-keeping task. Although Japan was not directly involved in the war, it did provide bases, supplies, and repairs for American forces engaged in defending South Korea and Taiwan. Japan, at American request, began to expand its own military forces.

The Japan-Taiwan treaty gave Japan a stake in the preservation of the Taiwan regime which was a challenge to the status of the mainland government. Japan was also responsible for defense of the Nationalists through its willingness to allow use of its bases by American forces for this purpose. The Chinese government's chief policy goals toward Japan became the elimination of the Japan-Taiwan treaty, the removal

[14] United Nations, Treaty Series, *Treaties and International Agreements Registered or Filed and Reported with the Secretariat of the United Nations*, Vol. CXXXVIII (1952) No. 1858, "Treaty of Peace Between the Republic of China and Japan, Exchange of Notes, I," 28 April 1952, p. 48.

[15] China, Chinese People's Institute of Foreign Affairs, *Oppose the Revival of Japanese Militarism*, "Foreign Minister Chou En-lai's Statement on the Announcement by the United States of America of the Coming into Effect of the Illegal Separate Peace Treaty with Japan," 5 May 1952, pp. 18, 22-25.

[16] China, Chinese People's Institute of Foreign Affairs, *Oppose the Revival of Japanese Militarism*, "Treaty of Friendship, Alliance and Mutual Assistance Between the People's Republic of China and the Union of Soviet Socialist Republics," 14 February 1950, pp. 1-4.

can military bases in Japan, and the prevention of the revival
:se military power. The chief means available to influence Japan
relations, and China pressed for its status and defense objectives
with Japan in return for cooperation in trade matters. For its part, Japan
utilized trade negotiations to reduce China's fear and hostility toward
Japan. The trade negotiations were kept at a strictly unofficial level
by conducting them through the auspices of members of the Japanese
Diet and businessmen while Japan itself continued to cooperate with
the United States and Taiwan at the official level.

Japan's attitude toward China was essentially a "two-Chinas" policy.
The conduct of affairs at the official level with Taiwan and indirectly
through trade relations with Peking was referred to as the "separation
of politics and economics" *(seikei bunri)* and it was anathema to the
mainland government which wished official relations to be confined to
it. The separation of politics and economics had the advantage of enabling
Japan to cooperate with the pro-Taiwan policy of the United States
while carrying on increasingly intimate relations at every level except
the official one with China. Despite China's seeming isolation Japan
was gradually to develop more extensive commercial and cultural relations
with China than it had with any other country.

However, trade between Japan and mainland China was inhibited by
embargoes. At the height of the cold war in 1950, the North Atlantic
allies instituted an embargo on strategic goods to the Communist-bloc
countries. Later, additional goods were placed on embargo for China
in an effort to isolate it. Upon gaining its independence, Japan was
induced to join in prohibiting a particularly wide range of goods to
China. Even the modest revival of traditional trade in raw materials
from China, such as soy beans, coal, and salt, was cut back with the
consequence that Japan came to rely upon the United States for these
products.

China attempted a counter-embargo by which it insisted it would only
trade certain goods desired by Japan if Japan permitted export of some
items on the Western allies prohibited list. Despite these obstacles, trade
agreements were made between the countries and trade gradually increased. The prohibited items were also gradually reduced in number
and embargo terms modified.

Beginning in 1952, private trade missions consisting of members of
the Diet and businessmen were dispatched from Japan to make periodic
agreements with the International Trade Promotion Council in Peking.
The Diet members came at first from all the political parties and formed
their own league to promote trade with China. They consulted with
the prime minister and had his approval for the trade with China. Firms

interested in the trade formed their own export-import association. Unofficial Chinese trade missions were also welcomed in Japan to display their products and acted for the Peking government in this exchange.

Resident missions were proposed as early as the second trade agreement of 1953 but were not started until more than ten years later. In 1958, the Japanese negotiators in China agreed to seek semi-official privileges such as the right to fly the national flag by visiting missions. In reprisal, the Taiwan government began to instigate anti-Japanese boycotts and to restrict Japanese trade transactions in an attempt to halt what appeared to be *de facto* recognition of China by Japan. American officials also objected sharply to improved trade arrangements between Japan and China. Prime Minister Kishi yielded to this pressure by denying the Chinese the right to fly their flag on their visits to Japan. China reacted angrily by delaying execution of the new fourth trade agreement and a large-scale contract to buy Japanese steel. When two Japanese young people tore up a Chinese flag on display at a special Chinese stamp exhibit in a Nagasaki department store without being charged by police, Chinese authorities considered this an additional insult. They broke off trade relations and cancelled the steel contract.

In the Japanese prime minister's visit to Taiwan, he indicated sympathy for Chiang Kai-shek's hope of reconquering the mainland which did not endear him on the mainland. As almost all trade was cut off for nearly two years, Japanese businessmen involved in the trade were greatly dismayed and relations with China were severely strained.

Despite the Chinese discouragement with its failure to normalize relations through trade, its irritation at the Kishi Cabinet, and the extremism to which the regime had been prone ever since 1958, Peking did not give up its contacts with Japan and it did not give up its ambitions to influence Japanese foreign policy. In March 1959, a Japanese Socialist party delegation led by the secretary general, Asanuma, went to Peking where he joined the Chinese leaders in denouncing United States imperialism as the common enemy of the Japanese and the Chinese people.

On 7 August 1960, when Chinese Prime Minister Chou met Kazuo Suzuki, managing director of the China-Japan Trade Promotion Council in Peking, he made it clear that China regarded trade to be inseparable from politics. There was therefore an insistence by China that trade should be conditional on good political relations leading ultimately to full recognition by Japan. Prime Minister Chou stated the "three political principles" of Sino-Japanese trade which were that Japan should not adopt a hostile attitude towards the People's Republic, that it should not follow the American "conspiracy to create two Chinas," and that it should not obstruct the normalization of relations between the two governments.[17]

Tatsunosuke Takasaki, who had been president of the Manchurian Heavy Industry Company during the Second World War and an architect of the Japanese-Indian steel cooperation in 1953, had met Prime Minister Chou En-lai in Bandung and was a strong advocate among the Liberal Democrats of normalization of relations with China. He also believed in trade and joint investment, as in the steel industry, as a way to build Asian solidarity.[18] In October 1960, he was invited to Peking and at a dinner for him given by Prime Minister Chou, Japan was criticized by Chou not only for its failure to establish friendly relations with China but also for its support of aggression against China through the Japan-United States security treaty. Takasaki did his best to deny these allegations and to inform the Chinese of the pacific attitude of Japan. He also strongly urged the establishment of unofficial relations with regard to permitting air transport, postal service, cultural contacts, fishing rights, aid to ships, and radio broadcasting between the two countries.[19] Although Takasaki's visit was unofficial, it was considered by the Chinese to be approved by the new Ikeda Cabinet. In return, Liao Ch'eng-chih, who was chairman of the Asian-African Regional Committee and later a deputy chief of the ministry of foreign affairs in Peking, was invited by the Japan-China Trade Promotion Council to Japan on a private basis.

The Japanese government at the bidding of the new prime minister, Ikeda, set up a special foreign policy discussion group to advise him and the foreign minister on policy. This group met in December 1960 to consider the question of China. The Liberal Democratic party's foreign policy investigation committee also took up some of the issues at stake. As with each new prime minister, foreign policy change was considered.

To re-establish trade, China accepted recommendations of the Japan-China Trade Promotion Council in Japan which suggested that it accept "friendly" Japanese companies which pledged to respect the three political principles enunciated by Chou En-lai.[20] These companies tended to be small but they included some set up by big trading companies. They could be induced to undertake political agitation in Japan on China's

[17]Gene T. Hsiao, "Communist China's Trade Treaties and Agreements (1949-1964), "*Vanderbilt Law Review,* Vol. XXI, No. 5 (October 1968), p. 640. See also, Chae-Jin Lee, "The Politics of Sino-Japanese Trade Relations, 1963-68," *Pacific Affairs,* Vol. XLII, No. 2 (Summer 1969), p. 130.

[18]Donald C. Hellmann, "Japan's Relations with Communist China," *Asian Survey,* Vol. IV, No. 10 (October 1964), pp. 1088-89.

[19]Tatsunosuke Takasaki, "Shu On-rai to Kaidan Shite," *Chuo Koron,* February 1961, pp. 251-52.

[20]Lee, "The Politics of Sino-Japanese Trade Relations, 1963-68," p. 130.

behalf and worked together with various left wing groups and parties favoring China trade. This was the part of the trade called "friendly trade." In December 1962, it was given more formal status in a protocol between the Japanese and the Chinese.[21]

The friendly firms, however, did not have the credit sources, long-term credit, or stable supply of machinery and fertilizer desired by China as did the big Japanese trading and manufacturing concerns. As a result of talks between Prime Minister Chou and Japanese Diet member Kenzo Matsumura (who was to become the leading Liberal Democratic proponent of normalizing trade and political relations with China) trade restrictions were lessened.

As we have seen, Ikeda tried to appear more independent of the United States than his predecessors had been and he expressed an increased sense of confidence based upon Japan's resounding economic progress. In 1962 he reached toward Western Europe to balance American dependence by some favorable response in trade and economic affairs with others. With China, the growing trade provided the basis for extensive contacts despite the lack of formal diplomatic relations—relations which were to become unique as China's contacts deteriorated with nearly all the countries which had been friendly to it in the preceding decade. China became more isolated and came to value the relationships with Japan despite its annoyance with the dominant factions among the Japanese Liberal Democrats which persisted in participating in the global ostracism of China on—the official level, at least.

At the same time that Ikeda permitted relations with China to improve, which pleased the pro-China elements in his own party as well as the opposition, he was careful to continue his cooperation with President Kennedy, which required support for Taiwan in the United Nations. One issue in which Japan became involved created problems in its two-Chinas policy. The Taiwan leaders who controlled the China seat in the United Nations clung to China's old claims over Mongolia, which had become a Soviet satellite after the Russian revolution. Therefore, they were determined to veto the request for Mongolia's admission to the United Nations on the basis that it was still a part of China.

A veto of Mongolia's admission to the United Nations was sure to antagonize the Soviet Union and might lead to an increase in the United Nations members preferring the Peking government to the Taipei government. The Kennedy administration feared any such deterioration in Taiwan's position as the representative of China in the world organization. Japan had regularly voted to postpone the question of which Chinese

[21] Haruhiro Fukui, *Party in Power* (Berkeley and Los Angeles: University of California Press, 1970), p. 232.

government should have Chinese representation in the United Nations, which would include a permanent seat on the Security Council. The China question took the form of which government should be recognized as the legitimate occupant of China's place, as China had been a founding member of the organization. Over the years since 1949 as more governments recognized the Peking regime, especially among the newly-independent nations which established diplomatic relations with it, the number of votes in the United Nations in favor of replacing Taiwan with the Peking government grew larger. In the meantime, the Taipei government continued to represent China in the United Nations although the member nations supporting it shrank in number.

American government leaders tried to persuade the Taiwan politicians to permit Mongolia's admittance and not to cast a vetoing vote against it. The Americans feared such action on Taiwan's part would crystallize antagonism towards it and, possibly, cost the island its United Nations' seat. The Ikeda government, therefore, at the urging of the United States used its persuasion on Taiwan not to veto the admission of Mongolia. Japan was in a good position to do this as it had signed a peace treaty with Taiwan and had established cordial diplomatic ties with it. As a result of Japan's persuasion, the Taiwan government refrained from exercising its United Nations' veto of Mongolia. Ikeda's cooperation with the United States thus favored Taiwan by strengthening its position in the United Nations, but it antagonized China and the Soviet Union even though it allowed Mongolia to join the United Nations.

At this time, the United States leaders decided to change their tactic of proposing postponement of debate on the China question each year in the General Assembly of the United Nations. They began to fear defeat on such a proposal and so sponsored a resolution to make the seating of China in the United Nations a "substantive question," which would require a vote of two-thirds of the members of the General Assembly to decide which government should represent China. To the annoyance of not only China and the Japanese opposition parties but also those among the Liberal Democrats favoring better relations with China, Japan became a co-sponsor with the United States of the substantive question resolution. Outside the Liberal Democratic party, this decision of the Ikeda Cabinet was considered to be subservience to the United States.

Japan's ambassador to the United Nations, Katsuo Okazaki, in speaking to the General Assembly, explained that Japan's action was not hostile to Peking. But strong dissatisfaction remained even in conservative circles that Japan had taken an unfriendly stance against mainland China. During the remainder of Ikeda's term of office as prime minister Japan's government voted against the resolution presented annually in the General

Assembly to seat Peking in place of Taipei.

Ikeda, therefore, was prepared to maintain previous Japanese policy favoring Taiwan as far as formal relations were concerned, which pleased the United States. The United States was confronted by renewal of the cold war in Laos and shortly thereafter in both Cuba and India as well. President Kennedy was anxious for Japanese support although he was aware that military matters had to be treated with caution for the sake of Japanese domestic peace.

Relations between Japan and China improved considerably with the negotiation of a semi-official trade memorandum. Liao Ch'eng-chih and Tatsunosuke Takasaki both signed a memorandum on 9 December 1962 for a five-year period in which trade was expected to average about $100 million a year each way. This was to involve deferred payments and medium-term credit to purchase Japanese plants. It had a semi-official character since it was expected that it would be partially financed by the Japanese Export-Import Bank and was supported by leaders of the Liberal Democratic party.[22] In contrast to friendly trade, which was arranged directly by the companies concerned at the Canton trade fairs, the semi-governmental trade was sponsored by the Liberal Democratic party members of the Diet with the support of the prime minister and his cabinet. The detailed trade arrangements were negotiated by Japanese businessmen and Chinese officials in Peking.

As a result of the Liao-Takasaki memorandum, the export of a large vinylon plant by the Kurashiki Rayon Company was approved in July 1963. This involved deferred payments of $20 million for five years at 5.5 percent, part of which was financed through the Export-Import Bank. By 1964, other similar contracts were under consideration including another vinylon plant from Dai Nihon Boseki Company and a 12,500-ton freighter from the Hitachi Shipbuilding Company. Thus, large Japanese business organizations were beginning to show interest in the trade with China.

The Ikeda government also permitted the exchange of trade missions. A Chinese group under Sun Ping-hua arrived in Tokyo for discussions in August 1964, and later a Japanese group went to Peking under a minor official of the ministry of trade. The ministry had always been more responsive to those Japanese business interests pressing for trade with China than the foreign ministry, which generally reflected a pro-American, pro-Taiwan, and anti-China bias. Since the exchange of trade missions came so soon after French recognition of the Peking government, it was assumed that Japan was taking advantage of the opportunity to establish closer relations with China. The exchange of

[22] Lee, "The Politics of Sino-Japanese Trade Relations, 1963–68," pp. 130–31.

trade missions was provided by the Liao-Takasaki memorandum as was an exchange of newspaper correspondents. Liao was also made president of a new China-Japan Friendship Association in Peking, an honor which reflected China's esteem of Japan.

The rising tempo of trade relations did not go unnoticed by Taiwan whose leaders became increasingly perturbed. They were particularly disturbed by the vinylon contract which they thought to be tantamount to giving economic aid to China. In Taiwan, heads of government ministries made a strong protest, and the Nationalist Chinese ambassador in Tokyo, Chang Li-sheng, asked Japanese Foreign Minister Ohira to cancel the contract. However, the Japanese leader said that it was a private transaction on the same terms made to other countries and did not represent any favoritism to China.[23]

Ikeda seemed almost to court the disapproval of both Taiwan and the United States as he was quoted to have said that the Nationalist hope to conquer the mainland was probably a dream rather than a practical hope. He later qualified this statement to take the more formal official position that he opposed the use of force by either Chinese regime to change the status quo in China.

The tension with Taiwan over trade was further complicated by an incident involving Chou Hung-ch'ing, an interpreter from China with a trade group in Tokyo. He had fled from his hotel room and at one point indicated that he wanted to go to Taiwan. There was further confusion in the Japanese justice ministry, which handles all foreign entrants to the country, and in the ministry of foreign affairs, which grants visas, as to the proper disposition of the case. In the interim, Chou reversed his decision and decided to return to China. The Japanese complied and issued a visa for him to return there. Taiwan suspected that this concession was made to appease China and they strongly protested to the Japanese. In Taipei, mobs attacked the Japan Air Lines office and the Japanese embassy and a trade boycott was begun against Japan.

To mollify Taiwan, Bamboko Ono, vice-president of the Liberal Democratic party, was sent to Taiwan. He was followed by former Prime Minister Yoshida. They sought to reassure Chiang Kai-shek that Japan preferred Taiwan over China. On his return, Yoshida signed a letter addressed to Chang Ch'un, secretary general of the president's office, in which Yoshida said the Japanese government would not approve the export of the Japan Spinning Company's vinylon plant to China through the Export-Import Bank during 1964 and would step up consider-

---

[23] Masayoshi Ohira, *Shumpu Shuu* (Tokyo: Kajima Kenkyujo Shupan Kai, 1965), p. 125. Chang resigned and returned home in protest.

ation of Taiwan's request to limit all plant exports to China to purely private credits.[24] However, no such Export-Import Bank credits were approved throughout the remainder of the decade.

Foreign Minister Ohira confirmed the initial pledge to stop Export-Import Bank credits to Peking. These assurances were sufficient to restore good relations with Taiwan. The Japanese government policy thus failed to conform to that advice put forward by the foreign ministry officials as early as May 1963 when it was stated that terms for trade to China should be equivalent to those given by Western European countries; Export-Import Bank credits for aid to underdeveloped countries should go to the free world and be withheld as much as possible from China; the reactions of the United States and Taiwan to deferred payment transactions with China should be fully taken into account.[25] Insofar as the reactions of Taiwan were taken into account and credits withheld from China, the principle of equivalent treatment of China could not be adhered to.

In 1964, the trade with China reached $310.4 million surpassing trade with Taiwan, which was only $278.7 million. In 1965, China trade reached $469.7 million, again well ahead of the increased Taiwan trade of that year, which was $375.2 million. In that year, it was three times the pre-Ikeda peak of 1956 and China became Japan's fourth largest trading partner after the United States, Australia, and Canada.[26] At the same time, China's trade with the Communist bloc and especially the Soviet Union continued to diminish, which probably explains Chinese willingness to ignore the failure of their Japanese policy.

Japan's trade with China thus began to assume quite significant proportions despite the pessimistic and contrary expectations of the United States. It represented a victory for the Japanese plan of asserting its own independence of both the United States and Taiwan by continuing and increasing the trade. Perhaps this fact also helped encourage China to swallow the Japanese persistence in favoring the United States and

[24] Partial text of letter in Nitchu Boeki Sokushin Giin Remmai, *Nitchu Kankei Shiryo Shu, 1945-1966,* (Tokyo: Nitchu Boeki Sokushin Giin Remmai, 1967), pp. 477-78; *Mainichi Shimbun,* 5 August 1965. Commentary in "Hamon Nageta Yoshida Shokan no Kaishaku, Nitchu Kankei wa Kewashiku Naru," *Asahi Janaru,* Vol. VII (21 February 1965), p. 7. Chang Ch'un came to Japan in August 1964 to ask that the credit denial be continued. Both Foreign Minister Ohira and Director General of the Planning Agency Miyazawa claim that Ikeda did not agree to this but Chang received the impression that Ikeda agreed to continue to restrict government credits to China. In the outcome, the Yoshida pledge has been continued and adhered to.

[25] Haruhiro Fukui, "The Japanese Liberal Democratic Party and Policy-Making," (Ph.D. thesis, Australian National University, 1967), p. 317. The material referred to here does not appear in the published version of the thesis, *Party in Power.*

[26] Lee, "The Politics of Sino-Japanese Trade Relations, 1963-68," p. 131. See especially table I.

Taiwan in political matters and to tolerate its success in separating economics and politics by ignoring its political demands.

The Japanese use of policies of trade promotion, reparations, grants, loans, credits, and investment can only be viewed as a great success. However, even after Japan had recovered from the Pacific War and was well on the way to new rapid growth, it still tended, under Prime Minister Ikeda, to regard most of its policies as contributing to trade promotion in the pursuit of its prosperity goal. Despite a rather ambitious enunciation of regional and global status objectives, the Ikeda Cabinet did not really try to make its economic foreign policies the basis of a more vigorous Asian policy as the next cabinet did.

Even in Japan's awkward position with respect to the two Chinas, it managed to use trade as a means to bring these regimes into profitable and peaceful relations with it. Because of its profitable trade with the Western world Japan was eventually able to face Asia with more and more confidence. China's more dramatic and forceful foreign policy did not prevail over Japan's modest economic initiatives. It was Japan that accomplished its aims, not China.

Behind American military protection and the buffer states of South Korea and Taiwan, Japan maintained its cooperation with its great power ally but used its economic capabilities to aid and mollify its communist and non-communist neighbors and at the same time, to promote its own prosperity and reduce hostility toward it. Japan also laid the basis of economic and political leadership in the region, which was developed further under Prime Minister Sato. Domestic liberalization measures as well as aid activities enhanced Japan's global status and its activity in the Asian region as it became a full member of the most prestigious international organizations.

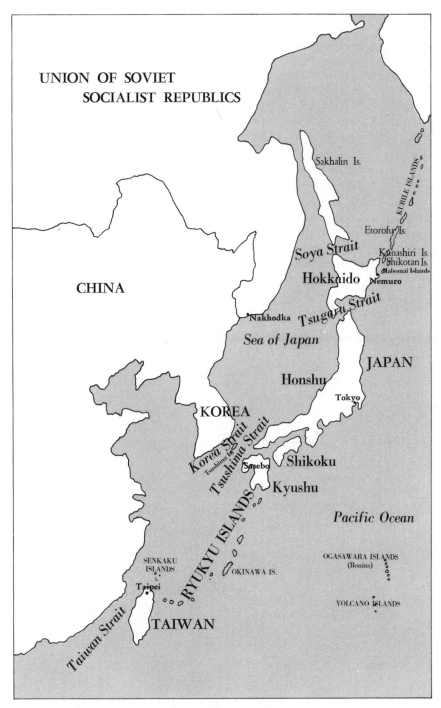

Fig. 2 Japan and Security Treaty Area.

6

Self-Reliant Defense

ALTHOUGH THE BASIC DEFENSE POLICIES of Japan changed very little under
Prime Minister Sato, they were challenged by the large-scale entry of
the United States into the Vietnam War and the subsequent withdrawal
policy which resembled earlier attempts by Presidents Truman and
Eisenhower to disengage the United States from direct intervention in
East Asia. Despite the great unpopularity of the Vietnam War within
Japan and among American allies, Prime Minister Sato gave diplomatic
support of a verbal nature to the United States as its great power ally
in its East Asian policy.

There was no disposition of Japanese leaders to arouse fear or hostility
toward Japan by any direct military intervention outside Japan, not even
to sell military equipment of any importance. In addition to the limited
mission of Japan's forces to defense of its own territory, Japan had
only slowly built up its conventional forces to a position in which it
would have a minimum impact on the strategic balance in the region
and avoid arousing fears in its Communist neighbors. In its security
policies, therefore, it continued to aim at reducing hostility towards
it from any major power as well as its weaker neighbors.

The slogan "self-reliant defense" continued to be used to appeal to
nationalist sentiment in an effort to gain support of the electorate for
the government's defense policy. Because its own forces were limited
and it was dependent upon American protection, the Japanese government
sought expression of the desire for greater independence and higher
status in territorial recovery. This was implemented by negotiating for
the return of both the Ogasawara and Ryukyu Islands from the United
States.

As the opposition parties mounted a new campaign directed at discontinuing Japan's security cooperation with the United States at the termination of the fixed term of the revised security treaty in 1970, the Japanese government sought to counter the opposition's appeal to greater national independence through ending military cooperation with the United States. It advocated the return of the remaining American-occupied islands, but qualified this by cooperating with the United States to the extent of continuing the American use of the bases in the territories to be returned but insisting that the bases were to be denuclearized and subject to consultation and Japanese agreement on their combat use. The prime minister, after first insisting on free use by Americans of the bases in Okinawa, agreed with the opposition on requiring a non-nuclear use of the bases but did not go as far as the opposition in demanding the removal of all bases. However, some leaders of the government indicated that the security treaty would probably be reconsidered by about 1975 and possibly replaced then by other arrangements. The Japanese government was able to join with the opposition in demanding the unqualified return of the northern islands from the Soviet Union, which was an issue that had prevented a final peace treaty between the countries. However, the opposition Socialists went further than the government and demanded return of all the Kurile Islands and Sakhalin Island, not just the southern Kuriles.

Security policies were tied together by the desire for greater independence and international status under conditions in which the restrictions of older policies of great power cooperation and dependence were increasingly irksome when challenged by the shift in relations among them and by increasing domestic economic strength.

Even though Japan was careful to avoid any direct participation in the Vietnam War, the American decision to intervene on a large scale affected the foreign policy of Japan under the Sato prime ministership. Another important influence on foreign policy was the change in economic relations between the two countries, signaled by the change from a constant deficit in Japan's international payments vis-à-vis the United States to a very large and growing surplus. This latter fact indicated a relative weakening of American economic strength and a great increase in that of Japan.

Prime Minister Sato, as the leader of the dominant faction within the ruling Liberal Democratic party, was inclined to take no more new initiatives in policy than his predecessor Ikeda. He clung stubbornly to the previous policy of close collaboration with the United States even in the face of the momentous change in American policy to disengage from East Asia by reducing its involvement in the Vietnam War. Previously, American policy had been dominated by a rigid anti-Communist attitude from the time of the Berlin confrontation and formation of NATO with the attendant manning of overseas bases and large overseas garrison forces.

The United States took over the historic Japanese defense policy to maintain control over Taiwan and at least part of Korea. Despite the development of detente in Europe with the death of Stalin and the consequent weakening of the Western alliance against the Soviet Union, the flare-up of the cold war under Khrushchev reconfirmed for the Kennedy and Johnson administrations the continued validity of their cold war strategy.

In Europe, however, the cold war continued to abate with the successful conclusion of the Nuclear Test Ban Treaty and the Western European allies' refusal to participate in the Vietnam War in which the United States had only the aid of its East Asian Allies, South Korea, Thailand, and the Philippines as well as its South Pacific Allies, Australia and New Zealand. The Cultural Revolution gave some semblance of militancy to the Chinese regime which nevertheless carefully refrained from any direct participation in Vietnam hostilities. The Johnson administration scrupulously refrained from any encouragement of the Nationalists for a return from Taiwan to the mainland.

Once the decision was made to reduce the attempts to stamp out Communism in Asia with American military power, the new Nixon adminstration of 1969 revived the old doctrine of giving the major responsibility for self-defense to its Asian allies with only financial and technical assistance from the United States. This policy was referred to as the Nixon Doctrine although it was similar to earlier policies such as the policy of the Truman administration in 1949 and of the Eisenhower administration after the Korean truce of 1953 when it pressed Japan to take over most of its own defense.

In its protected position behind Taiwan and South Korea, Japan could afford to let the United States bear the costs of its regional and global ambitions. Once the United States ceases to define its national interest in acting as the policeman of Asia, Japan might be faced with the need for some form of greater self-reliance in defense in accord with the clear intent of the Nixon Doctrine of allied self-reliance.

Agreement with South Korea

The Sato government showed considerable initiative in normalizing relations with South Korea. At the beginning of his incumbency, a new prime minister usually has a free hand in charting his policy approach. He may also be able to solve some of the issues that have come up in the course of the inner-party campaign for president of the ruling political party, an office which is the essential qualification for the position of prime minister. This is especially true if there is a realignment of party factions behind the new president and prime minister.

Sato was the chief rival and leader of the dissident coalition which ranged against Ikeda. When Sato became prime minister, he was supported by a more conservative and anti-Communist coalition than Ikeda had experienced. The dominant coalition was led by quite a few who had been prominent in lobbying for a solution to the Korean problem in order to increase trade and aid to South Korea to the mutual economic benefit of the two countries and the strengthening of the anti-communist regimes. The selection of Sato as prime minister to replace the ailing Ikeda encouraged inner-party agreement and action on normalizing relations with the Republic of Korea.

The populations of South Korea and Japan harbored quite antagonistic feelings towards each other which made it impossible for the respective governments to safely ignore public attitudes. However, the extremely anti-Japanese regime of Syngman Rhee was eventually succeeded by the more pragmatic government of General Pak, which was willing to resolve the outstanding issues on a basis agreeable to Japan. Within a year of Sato taking office, a treaty and associated agreements were signed by the two governments resolving the outstanding issues except for the dispute (which still continues) over the ownership of some tiny islands lying between Japan and South Korea. Two particularly important aspects of the agreements were the apparent Japanese recognition that the Republic of Korea was the only "lawful government in Korea" and the willingness of Japan to give extensive grants and loans for South Korean economic development.

In both countries, the process of ratification by the parliamentary bodies was difficult and was only accomplished by pressure and sharp maneuvering by government leaders.[1] This reflected the attempt of the opposition parties to arouse strong popular feelings as well as a more radical and intractable Socialist party leadership in Japan. The Japanese Socialists hoped to arouse the same opposition to the Japan-South Korean treaty as they had done in the 1960 security treaty struggle against the government. But in the case of the Korean agreements they were frustrated because there were not the same enormous public interest and demonstrations that there had been in 1960.

The Sato leadership managed to reach the essential stage of House of Representatives' approval before the opposition parties could disrupt ratification.[2] This was not accompanied by the same disorder in the

---

[1] Mark J. Mobius, "The Japan-Korea Normalization Process and Korean Anti-Americanism," *Asian Survey*, Vol. VI, No. 4 (April 1966), pp. 241–48.

[2] Hans H. Baerwald, "Nikkan Kokkai: The Japan-Korea Treaty Diet," in *Cases in Comparative Politics, Asia*, ed. Lucian W. Pye (Boston: Little, Brown, 1970), pp. 19–57; includes texts of treaty, agreements and protocols of 22 June 1965.

Diet or campaign of condemnation by the newspapers which disrupted the Kishi Cabinet in 1960, nor, of course did the treaty have the same importance as the security treaty. As Japanese businessmen and politicians expected, agreement with South Korea and the Japanese trade and aid which followed greatly facilitated the economic recovery and development of South Korea with the consequent strengthening of the Pak regime. However, it was precisely the Japanese responsibility for supporting the Republic of Korea that bothered Japanese opposition party leaders and even some in the ruling Liberal Democratic party.

Even though the United Nations had some formal responsibility for the Republic of Korea as the legitimate government of the peninsula, there was a competing Communist government in the north. By significantly supporting the south, Japan was contributing to deepening the division of the two halves of the country even if it could do nothing to solve the problem of reuniting them. The opposition Socialists in Japan not only deplored creating further obstacles to Korean unity but also claimed to fear that a kind of Northeast Asian Treaty Organization (NEATO) was being created analogous to NATO. Prime Minister Yoshida had rejected the Dulles proposal of a NATO-type alliance but Japan, like South Korea, Taiwan, and the Philippines, already had bilateral alliances with the United States.[3] Japan was thus indirectly linked with a series of anti-Communist defense treaties. Although American leaders had pressed Japan for years to settle its dispute with South Korea, the two countries had failed to come to an agreement until 1965.

The settlement with South Korea made no provision for any military cooperation with Japan. The Sato Cabinet never departed from its limited defense conception which prevented any direct military support for South Korea.

The policy of economic aid and cooperation pursued by the Sato government was similar for South Korea and Taiwan. By strengthening these countries and supporting their governments, Japan helped them indirectly to defend themselves. The Japanese policy of stabilizing the East Asian region by economic support of non-Communist governments was thus extended from Southeast Asia to Northeast Asia through the settlement of the South Korean problem.

Doubly protected by the American defense of South Korea and Taiwan as well as of Japan itself, the Sato government had little incentive to create a self-reliant defense system. It also did not have to worry about defending more-distant Vietnam as long as the United States was doing so and did not press Japan to participate. Even though it lay beyond

---

[3] South Korea and the Philippines also had token forces, which were paid for by the United States, fighting in Vietnam with the United States against communist forces.

the Far East, as defined in the security treaty, there did remain the fear that, if American involvement led to considerable use of Okinawan bases by the United States, an attack might be invited there which would be close to Japan—especially if China were to become a participant.

Okinawa's Military Significance

The fear of indirect involvement in Vietnam was raised in 1965 when the American embassy in Japan reported that American B-52 bombers from Guam would land in Japan at Itazuki Air Base to avoid a typhoon. The Japanese government accepted the report, which did not involve any consultations and consequent Japanese approval, because the movement was temporary and did not involve any change of forces in Japan. The Socialist party, nevertheless, denounced the use of Japan by the planes which were being used to bomb North Vietnam and the party asserted that the planes would indirectly involve Japan. As a consequence, they demanded a rejection of the report.

Fortunately the weather improved and permitted the bombers to be routed to Okinawa from which they departed on 29 July for their mission over Vietnam. Foreign Minister Shiina told reporters on 30 July that the dispatch of the planes to Okinawa was fully within American rights but the use of the planes to bomb Vietnam caused misgivings among the Japanese people nonetheless.

On 2 August, during an exchange in the House of Representatives, Sato told Kozo Sasaki, chairman of the Socialist party, that the dispatch of the B-52 bombers was disturbing. The use of Okinawan bases as departure places for the bombing of Vietnam was arousing the Japanese public, he said. The prime minister thought the matter could be resolved by expressing the government's and public's concern to the American authorities. However, the three opposition parties protested directly to the American embassy and staged demonstrations there. The Okinawan Legislature itself passed a non-partisan resolution of protest. It was announced in Washington that there was no plan to use Okinawa regularly as a place from which to bomb Vietnam. The American Ambassador, Reischauer, in a speech in Boston on 3 August, stated that the United States had lost the respect of the Japanese people by intervening in Vietnam and indicated that the moving of planes of the Strategic Air Command to Okinawa had caused grave misgivings in Japan. To Japanese reporters in Tokyo, the ambassador said he had only been reporting Japanese sentiment and indicated some sympathy with American government motives by pleading for Japanese understanding of the need to meet defense responsibilties.

Concern over Vietnam and Okinawa continued. In March 1966, Prime Minister Sato told the House of Councillors budget committee:

If Okinawa is attacked from abroad, the United States, which has administrative control, will undertake its defense. But we cannot sit idly by while our countrymen of Okinawa are killed. Japan will consult with the United States and take responsibility for defense. The United States will agree to our demands, and I intend to see that it does.[4]

To objections by the Socialists that this statement did not accord with the position taken by Prime Minister Kishi in 1960, Sato said the next day, "It is unnecessary for me to change my opinion."[5] He had come close to saying that Japanese forces would be dispatched to Okinawa in case of attack, but, on 16 March in response to discussions between Liberal Democrats and Democratic Socialists, he took a less forthright stand. He told the upper house budget committee, "I spoke frankly from keen nationalistic feeling. To the extent that the United States had administrative rights, naturally the Self-Defense Forces cannot be mobilized and dispatched under Constitutional doctrine, the Treaty conception, or the Self-Defense Forces Law."[6]

Japanese public antagonism to the Vietnam War was led by the opposition parties which naturally focused on the need for the return of Okinawa to enable Japan to exert more control over American forces and curb its use for military purposes. Unlike Ikeda, Sato was willing to press for the return of the lost territories. He was the first postwar prime minister to visit Okinawa where he had said: "I know very well that the postwar era has not ended as long as Okinawa is not restored to the fatherland."[7] Spurred by popular fear of war and the desire for return of the occupied territories, Sato embarked on a diplomatic campaign for restoration of the islands to Japan.

In July 1967, he attended the inauguration of General Pak as president of South Korea where he had the opportunity to meet and talk with Vice-President Hubert Humphrey of the United States and the Chinese Nationalist Vice-President Yen Chiu-kan. Humphrey proposed that Sato should bring up the return of the Ogasawara and Ryukyu Islands when he met President Johnson in the fall. In September, Sato made a trip to Taiwan, Burma, Malaysia, Singapore, Thailand, and Laos. In Thailand he indicated support of the American conduct of the Vietnam War by stating that he did not think peace would be attained by halting the bombing of North Vietnam. While this statement may have pleased his hosts and may have been intended to win American accommodation

---

[4] *Asahi Shimbun*, 11 March 1966, p. 1.
[5] Ibid., 12 March 1966, p. 1.
[6] Ibid., 16 March 1966, evening edition, p. 1.
[7] *Asahi Nenkan 1966*, p. 314.

to Japanese wishes, it was counter to the widespread opposition to American intervention in Vietnam even among some of the Liberal Democrats in Japan. Despite this verbal encouragement, the Japanese prime minister was careful to avoid any direct participation by Japan in Southeast Asian defense, nor did he promise any military aid or even permit weapons to be sold to belligerents. Sato only offered economic assistance.

On 8 October 1967, the prime minister left on another trip, this time to Indonesia, Australia, New Zealand, the Philippines, and South Vietnam. More than two thousand radical university students clashed with the police in Japan and one person was killed in an unsuccessful attempt to halt Sato's departure. Although his visit to Saigon lasted only three hours because of his decision to return suddenly to Tokyo on hearing of the death of former Prime Minister Yoshida, Sato did manage to talk to both Chairman Nguyen Van Thieu and Prime Minister Nguyen Cao Ky. His very presence in such places as Taiwan and Vietnam implied approval of the American policy toward China and Vietnam which would impress Washington but at the cost of sharp opposition in Japan. American policy was anathema to the opposition parties and radical students.

Because of its proximity to Japan, South Korea continued to play an important role in the relationship of Japan and Okinawa. The economic progress of South Korea caused the Communist leaders of North Korea to become more hostile and belligerent. When the American intelligence ship, the *Pueblo*, was captured by North Korea in Janaury 1968, fear of a renewal of the Korean War was revived. The United States deployed B-52 bombers from Okinawa and moved the aircraft carrier *Enterprise*, into the Sea of Japan in an effort to deter the North Koreans from any further action.

When the nuclear-powered *Enterprise* stopped briefly in Sasebo, Japan, it was greeted by hostile demonstrations in which all the opposition parties, including even the Buddhist Komei party, took part. The Soviet government delivered a note of protest to the Japanese ambassador in Moscow objecting to Japan's military cooperation with the United States which was engaged in the war in Vietnam. It charged that Japan was involved in American aggression by permitting nuclear and non-nuclear ships of the American Seventh Fleet to stop in Japanese ports and then proceed to military operations off Vietnam.[8]

The Japanese government replied that calls of warships were an authorized obligation under the security treaty and this included nuclear-powered warships which had been calling on Japanese ports for some time. The Japanese Socialists charged that the *Enterprise* was deployed

[8] *New York Times*, 31 January 1968, p. 8.

for war duty from a Japanese port without prior consent as required by the treaty with the United States. Saburo Eda, vice-chairman of the Socialist party, said the treaty was dragging Japan into American quarrels through the *Pueblo* affair and the movements of the *Enterprise.* In the Diet, the prime minister rejected the charge that the call of the *Enterprise* constituted the introduction of nuclear weapons into Japan. Sato also denied that the treaty in any way involved Japan in American quarrels.

Despite the disclaimers, American bases in Okinawa and Japan and the right for warships to call at Japanese ports were vital to the effective defense of South Korea in 1968 as they had been during the Korean War. Japan was required by the treaty to permit these actions. The threat of hostilities in the immediate vicinity of Japan only made the quickening opposition to the American military bases and operations in Japan and Okinawa sharper and more vocal.

The B-52 bombers remained in Okinawa in considerable numbers. Foreign Minister Takeo Miki, a leading rival of the prime minister within his own party, expressed strong dissatisfaction over their presence as a factor contributing to the tension in the Far East.[9] The prime minister himself, however, refrained from any criticism of American policy, although the Okinawan Legislature passed resolutions asking that the bombers be removed. When Miki met with American Ambassador Alexis Johnson on 27 May 1968 to consult on Okinawa, he pressed for the return of administrative rights to Okinawa as soon as possible with the bases under the same restrictions as those in Japan proper as, he asserted, was overwhelmingly desired by the Japanese people. Ambassador Johnson defended the American position by pointing out the vital role played by Okinawa (under American administration) as an advance defense post, a supply base, a communications center, and a deterrent to attack (with nuclear missiles deployed there and free of Japanese curbs).

The prime minister and American authorities were challenged by several incidents in May. On 2 May 1968, the Maritime Safety Agency detected high radiation levels during the visit of the American submarine, *Swordfish,* to Sasebo. Although the high reading was detected only briefly and no discernible cause was located after careful investigation, the incident was given much publicity and was seized upon by opponents of the bases and the treaty. In consequence, the Japanese government felt compelled to ask for suspension of visits of nuclear submarines until better detection and safety measures were taken. The visits were

[9] Frank Langdon, "Strains in Current Japanese-American Defense Cooperation," *Asian Survey,* Vol. IX, No. 9 (September 1969), p. 708.

cancelled for six months and Japanese requests were complied with in an effort to allay public fears.

Almost simultaneous with the radiation scare was the crash of an American airforce jet which struck a building at Kyushu University during a night flight from Itazuke airbase. This provided further cause for agitation against the American bases and the treaty although the Johnson adminstration was already embarked on a policy of reducing bases and personnel to lessen the defense costs. It was decided to put Itazuke airbase on standby status and plans were pushed forward to close some American military facilities in Japan, to transfer some to the Japanese Self-Defense Forces, and to convert others to joint use. All night training flights were immediately cancelled at Itazuke airbase and the American authorities even agreed to move the base if the Japanese could find a suitable alternative site. Local authorities proved unanimously opposed to the location of any new base in their jurisdictions.

Thus, events conspired in 1968 to highlight Japan's indirect responsibility for American policy of defending anti-Communist regimes in Vietnam and Korea. The objectives of return of occupied Okinawa and limitations on American use of bases there appealed to the desire for greater independence on the part of Japan but did not go so far as to meet the demands of the opposition in Japan for completely eliminating the bases and ending the security treaty. Another means to greater independence was the buildup of Japan's own forces and the sharing or takeover of some of the bases. Sato directed his government's policy towards this end also.

Defense Buildup Plans

The Second Defense Buildup Plan overlapped the Ikeda and Sato prime ministerships from fiscal years 1962 to 1966, a period ending on 31 March 1967. Although the plan had modest goals for defense forces and a modest aim of withstanding an external attack until American forces could arrive, it achieved an enormous improvement in the quality of the defense forces by eliminating obsolete American equipment and modernizing the anti-aircraft defense. Tactical deployment of seven squadrons of F-104-J fighter planes as well as Nike Ajax high-altitude, anti-aircraft missiles provided an up-to-date type of air defense. By the end of the period of the plan the airforce comprised twenty-three of the twenty-four squadrons of planes that had been projected. The BADGE system of radar and fighter-director centers, which permitted interception by air of enemy aircraft, was not completed in time because of the stoppage of American military aid when the United States Congress judged Japan able to finance fully its own defense equipment. However, in 1968 this system was operational.

The Maritime Self-Defense Force surpassed slightly the projected amount of 140,000 tons. This represented the early stage of the concept of Munenori Akagi, who had been director general of defense in 1959, and it put special emphasis on anti-submarine defense to protect Japanese shipping, which was the country's lifeline in the sense of supply of essential fuel for the economy. The projected helicopter carriers and thirty-nine anti-submarine escort vessels were eventually to encompass 470,000 tons of shipping.

For the defense of island territory, it was natural to rely on air and naval defense as long as no overseas land fighting was envisaged. However, attention was also given to the ground force. Japan's Ground Self-Defense Force had the mission of defending its shores in the event of external attack. The long-planned goal, set as early as the beginning of the 1950s, of about 180,000 men was not reached even by 1966. Only 171,500 men were included in the ground force, which was caused in part by the difficulty in recruiting an all-volunteer force in a period of prosperity and pacifism. However, the ground force was organized and deployed in greater accord with Japan's own priorities. Initially, joint Japanese and American plans were made on the assumption of the need to prepare for a Soviet invasion from the north. There originally had been six area corps with an authorized strength of 12,700 men each and four composite divisions of 6,000 men each. Contrary to American practice, these were reorganized into smaller units, but with the necessary structure and equipment for expansion in case of need. They could also be deployed more widely. It was now possible to strengthen the eastern and central sections of Japan near its large cities on whose protection the American plans did not put a high priority. The defense against a northern attack was modified to permit a more even coverage of the entire country as far as Japanese forces were concerned. This also had the benefit of more convenient deployment in the event of any internal uprising.

Active consideration of a Third Defense Buildup Plan began in 1965 when there was pressure from within the defense agency for a more ambitious defense plan. Director General Junya Koizumi indicated to the foreign affairs committee of the House of Representatives that no important increases were to be requested: "I am not contemplating any big defense force increases in land, sea, or air arms. Rather, I would like to have the main emphasis put on qualitative improvement and modernization of the existing forces."[10] The mission of the Japanese forces thus remained substantially the same as before for the period

[10]Tomohisa Sakanaka, "Boei Ryoku Seibi no Hoko to Mondaiten," *Asahi Shimbun Anzen Hosho Mondai Chosa Kai, Nihon no Jiei Ryoku,* Vol. VIII of *Nihon no Anzen Hosho* (Tokyo: Asahi Shimbun Sha, 1967), p. 94.

TABLE 6.1
JAPAN'S MILITARY EXPENDITURES, 1958-72

Defense Buildup Plan	Year	Amount of Expenditures (in billions of dollars)	Percentage of Budget	Percentage of GNP
First Defense Buildup Plan	1958	0.4	10.9	1.25
	1959	0.4	9.0	1.00
	1960	0.4	9.0	1.00
	1961	0.5	9.0	0.95
Second Defense Buildup Plan	1962	0.6	8.50	1.01
	1963	0.7	8.05	1.00
	1964	0.8	8.49	0.98
	1965	0.8	8.24	0.97
	1966	1.0	7.74	0.94
Third Defense Buildup Plan	1967	1.1	7.47	0.90
	1968	1.2	7.28	0.83
	1969	1.3	7.22	0.84
	1970	1.6	7.16	0.78
	1971	1.9	7.23	0.72
Fourth Defense Buildup Plan	1972	2.67[a]	7.00	—

NOTE: [a]Yen converted at 300 to the United States dollar instead of 360 which was used for previous years.

SOURCE: James William Morley, ed., *Forecast for Japan: Security in the 1970s* (Princeton: Princeton University Press, 1972), table 1, p. 11, with additions.

of the new plan which ran from 1967 to 1971: to meet an attack in a local conventional war while relying upon American forces with the assumption that the security treaty would continue in effect.

The Third Defense Buildup Plan fixed upon a sum of 2,365,000 million yen, or about $6.5 billion, over the five-year period as the result of hard bargaining between the defense agency and other agencies such as the finance ministry, ministry of trade, foreign ministry, and the Economic Planning Agency. As usual, the defense agency hoped for 2 percent of the national income, but after the final decision was made by the prime minister the figure was set at 1.16 percent, or about 0.92 percent of the gross national product. In absolute terms, the overall amount was double that of the previous five-year plan.

The revised defense plan was intended to insure a greater capability in the seas adjacent to Japan, to strengthen the air defense system for major points, to enhance air and land mobility, to improve the quality of men and equipment, to raise the overall capability through education and training, to increase the research and development capacity, and to modernize the equipment. It was intended to increase the number of ground force personnel from 171,500 to 179,000. Most of the additional funds would go to replace equipment. On-going expenses would consume nearly 70 percent of total defense funds. About one-half of the remaining amount was for replacing obsolete weapons. An important feature of the new plan was that much more weaponry and equipment would be obtained from the domestic defense industry, and Japan would be less dependent upon American imports. The third plan concentrated on improved anti-aircraft and anti-submarine capability of the Maritime Self-Defense Force.

Although the Third Defense Buildup Plan provided for a considerable improvement in the Japanese Self-Defense Forces, two aspects are especially noteworthy. The amounts devoted to defense were a declining proportion of the government's budget and of the gross national product, even though the actual amount spent was doubled. That is to say, that though the amount spent increased, it was a smaller burden on the budget and on the economy of Japan than previous plans had been. Another aspect of note was the comparison with other major countries— and even with more minor ones. What Japan spent on defense was comparatively small, both in absolute amounts and in proportion to its total budget.

The expenditures for defense purposes by the Japanese government in 1969 were 483,810 million yen, or about $1,344 million. Very clearly, Japan, which had an economy comparable to Britain, France, or West Germany, was making a very small effort towards its own defense. In 1966, because Japan was spending 1 percent of what the United States spent on defense, Senator Frank Church persuaded Congress

TABLE 6.2
ECONOMIC BURDEN FROM MILITARY EXPENDITURES IN 1970

Country	Percentage of GNP
Israel	26.5
United Arab Republic	19.6
Soviet Union	11.0
China	9.5
United States	7.8
Poland	5.2
Britain	4.9
West Germany	4.9
France	4.0
South Korea	4.0
Switzerland	2.1
Japan	0.8

SOURCE: Percentage GNP as estimated in the Institute for Strategic Studies, *The Military Balance 1971-1972* (London: Institute for Strategic Studies, 1971), table 3, "Defence Expenditures and National Economies," pp. 60–61; for China see p. 41.

to stop any military aid funds to Japan. At that time, these grants amounted to 18.5 percent of the Japanese defense budget.[11]

The Growing Need for Self-Reliant Defense

The decision of the Johnson administration in 1968 to halt the bombing of North Vietnam and to begin the Paris peace talks marked what seemed to be a new era in East Asian defense. The Nixon adminstration's gradual but continued withdrawal from Vietnam and its bid for detente with the Chinese government led to some response from China with the conclusion of the Cultural Revolution and a return to more conventional diplomacy in that country. The call from the United States for increased self-reliance upon the part of its Asian allies and lesser American involvement in combat operations in the area signaled a return once more to a policy of disengagement.

Although the United States indicated that it would stand by its defense commitments in the region, the extent to which this would be carried out was not clear until later challenge and response would indicate in what America would involve herself. The possibility was growing that the United States might become less willing to protect Japan and Japanese interests to the same extent as before as its stake in the region began to erode or its position in the region began to change its character. Should this be the case, Japan might need to develop its conventional armament to the level of a state such as West Germany if it hoped to pursue a strong policy to protect its non-Communist neighbors or even its own territory and shipping.

Prime Minister Sato, like Prime Minister Ikeda before him, talked about "self-reliant defense" in order to appeal to Japanese nationalist feeling which was impatient and fearful of American military bases. The phrase had popular appeal and had the merit of attracting some support for Japan's defense forces and government policy. It also relied upon national resentment of American forces and enforced involvement in American Asian strategy.

The period of 1968 to 1969 proved to be a time of intense political competition in Japan in which the major issues were the American bases and the security treaty. The reason was that the year 1970 would end the ten-year term of the security treaty and Japan could then unilaterally abrogate the treaty on one year's notice, which the opposition parties said they would do if they were to win a majority in the Diet. The appeal for self-reliant defense was one way to try to outbid the opposition in appealing to nationalist feeling. However, it remained to be seen whether Sato, in fact, would support more than the token defense

[11] Ibid., pp. 102–103

expenditures and work for a quantitative improvement when it came time to discuss the Fourth Defense Buildup Plan.

Associated with Japan's self-reliant defense was the changing character of the war in Vietnam. The pressure on the United States to end the inconclusive war was a result not only of the failure of the United States to defeat North Vietnam but also of the steady inflation in the United States through a failure to control prices at home and the continued export of inflation abroad through such media as Euro-dollars with the weakening of American competition in foreign trade. Internal problems such as racial strife, war protests, student radicalism, and pollution added incentive for America to pursue a more modest foreign policy.

The Nixon administration soon acted to reduce the American military role in Asia through troop withdrawals from Vietnam. The president also announced new guidelines for his Asian foreign policy.[12] When he was traveling to Southeast Asia in July 1969, Nixon indicated at a press conference in Guam that the United States would insist that both internal and external aggression be dealt with increasingly by the Asians themselves except when they were threatened by a nuclear power such as Communist China. The president repeated an earlier statement on the matter: "The role of the United States in Vietnam or the Philippines or Thailand or any of these other countries which have internal subversion is to help them fight the war but not to fight the war for them." This constituted a renewed call for self-reliance on the part of the allies of the United States so often demanded by American policy-makers since the Second World War but with such meager results in the case of Japan. Once more commitment of United States troops was to be reduced and some type of economic measures were to be considered in their place.

President Nixon also said the United States would stand by its current alliance treaties because to withdraw would pave the way for other wars. Greater self-reliance of its allies backed by materiel, air, and naval support became the essence of what was to be called the "Nixon Doctrine." As the United States was still a Pacific power, it had a stake in Asian stability. In Bangkok during his trip, Nixon said, "Our determination to honor our commitments is fully consistent with our conviction that the [Asian] nation can and must increasingly shoulder the responsibility for achieving peace and prosperity in the area."[13]

The logical inconsistency, of course, was the possibility that fully carrying out its commitments (defense guarantees) might require more,

---

[12] *New York Times*, 26 July 1969, p. 1, "Nixon Plans Cut in Military Role for U.S. in Asia."

[13] U.S., Department of State, *Department of State Bulletin*, "President Nixon's Round-the-World Trip," Vol. LXI, No. 1547 (25 August 1969), p. 154.

not less, use of American intervention. The continued withdrawal of ground forces from Vietnam, however, indicated that American participation in Asian hostilities was being definitely reduced and gave increasing force to the Nixon Doctrine. The 1970 incursion of American forces from Vietnam into Cambodia seemed to have been in the nature of a rearguard action and not a cancellation of the Nixon Doctrine. The state department was left with the job of giving a more precise meaning to the doctrine.

Undersecretary of State, Elliot L. Richardson, explained the doctrine in his speech to the American Political Science Association in New York on 5 September 1969:

> The nature of our assistance to nations threatened by internal subversion will hereafter depend on the realities of each separate situation. In some cases, assistance in economic and political development may be enough. In other cases, aid in the form of training and equipment may be necessary. But, the job of counter-insurgency in the field is one which must be conducted by the government concerned, making use of popular support, its resources, and its men. Large-scale intervention from abroad is, of course something else again and must be considered against the backdrop of the total obligations and interests of the American people. [14]

The implication for Japan can be deduced from this statement even though the main thrust of the new Nixon policy was directed toward Vietnam and Southeast Asia. If the United States took a more passive role toward the relatively small weak states, it would probably expect considerably more from the healthy and more capable ones in Northeast Asia, such as Japan. Before taking office the president had called on Japan to take on some of the American role in regional defense. [15] However, after assuming his new responsibilities and being fully briefed by officials, he realized that Japan was unwilling to consider such a burden under its current and past policies. If Japan was unwilling to accept responsibility for aid in the defense of other Asian countries, it was still better able to undertake more of the burden of its own defense which it had promised to do long before and about which its leaders constantly talked under the guise of "self-reliant defense." It only remained to be seen if this would enable anything more than the modest token forces created under the first three defense plans. If

---

[14] U.S., Department of State, *Department of State Bulletin*, Vol. LXI, No. 1578 (22 September 1969), p. 258, "The message the President carried to the nations of Asia."

[15] Richard M. Nixon, "Asia after Vietnam," *Foreign Affairs*, Vol. XLVI, No. 1 (October 1967), pp. 111-25.

withdrawal from Vietnam lessened tension in the region or encouraged detente between the United States and China, it might reduce the need or desire for American intervention in Asian affairs. Japan might be forced to increase its defense effort if it wished to maintain a strong non-Communist influence in the region. Or, in the case of an attack upon it, Japan might be forced to acquiesce from a weak military position, which it had come to accept under the United States.

Discussion of a Fourth Defense Buildup Plan began nearly three years in advance of the implementation of the plan, which was to run from 1972 through 1976. The reasons for the advanced discussions were that the campaign against the security treaty was at its height, new directions for American policy were evident in the Nixon Doctrine, and negotiations over the return of Okinawa had already begun. The American decision to return civil jurisdiction of Okinawa to Japan in 1972 resulted in the need for Japan to increase its defense effort to permit cooperation in the defense of Okinawa. Nuclear weapons were to be withdrawn and the American military bases there were to be put under the same restrictions as those in Japan proper. Agreement was also reached that Japan would build its own Phantom jets under the new plan. Defense bills were passed providing for increasing reserves to 70,000 men and the recruiting of a new maritime reserve. In 1969, considerable interest was shown in protecting Japanese shipping which brought the vital fuel oil supplies from the Middle East. Even under the projected plans, Japan's forces would be insufficient for this operation. [16]

Within the defense agency, planning projections for as long as ten years ahead were produced in 1969. In its Plan for Future Buildup of Self-Reliant Defense Forces, the agency was reported to have concluded that there were possibilities of direct and indirect aggression from the Soviet Union but that China did not pose a threat as long as the United States defended South Korea and Taiwan. The agency believed that North Korea lacked the ability to undertake direct aggression but it might help support an indirect aggression. [17] This belief led to contingency planning of what was possible rather than what was probable—it was precisely this type of approach that contributed to the escalation of the arms race between the United States and the Soviet Union. However, the government in Japan was careful never to name openly any country

[16] U.S., Department of State, American Embassy, Tokyo, *Summaries of Selected Japanese Magazines, 6-20 October 1969*, pp. 17-20; from *Toyo Keizai*, "Strategic Concept of Autonomous Defense," 6 September 1969.

[17] U.S., Department of State, American Embassy, Tokyo, *Daily Summary of the Japanese Press*, 15 August 1969, pp. 7-8; from *Tokyo Shimbun*, 11 August 1969, "*JDA Having Difficulty in Expression of Threat in Preparing Defense White Paper.*" Yoshinobu Kawamoto, "Kokubo Shiso no Shin Dankai," *Sekai*, November 1969, pp. 157-58.

as even a hypothetical enemy and was reluctant to encourage even clear statements of military objectives. Once the outlines of settlement of the Okinawa question were agreed upon, systematic consideration of long-range strategic plans began between diplomats and military experts of both the United States and Japan.

When the Japanese prime minister received President Nixon's formal agreement for the return of Okinawa, he immediately called a general election because he thought he was in the advantageous position of obtaining a promise with great nationalist appeal. During the election campaign, some Liberal Democrats, such as Yasuhiro Nakasone, who was to become the new director general of the defense agency, tried to match the opposition in nationalist appeal by suggesting that in the mid-1970s the security treaty might be replaced by a looser arrangement with the United States whereby Japan would be more responsible for its own defense, and, hence, more independent of the United States.

The election was a resounding victory for the Liberal Democrats who won more seats than before and who even added additional members when conservative independents joined the Liberal Democrats after the election. The election was a disastrous defeat for the Socialists who lost nearly one-third of their seats in the House of Representatives. In general, the election results seemed to reflect the Japanese public's acceptance of Sato's defense policy and a rejection of the Socialists' demand for treaty abrogation. The Liberal Democrats approved the leadership policy of continuing the security treaty indefinitely when its fixed term expired in June 1970. This did not require any new negotiations or government legislation so the expected 1970 crisis over Okinawa and the security treaty failed to materialize.

Upon assuming the director generalship of the defense agency, Nakasone said little about his campaign proposals for reviewing and replacing the security treaty. It was generally expected by the Liberal Democrats that if defense conditions changed radically the situation could be reviewed and new and more suitable arrangements made. If conditions of threat declined, the treaty might be replaced with a looser kind of friendship treaty. If not, and if the United States wished to continue to defend Japan, the treaty might be extended for another fixed term.

The new defense agency director general did not completely abandon the attempt to give some content to a more self-reliant defense effort. In a budget committee debate on 18 March 1970, he said that under the Fourth Defense Buildup Plan an attempt would be made to secure command of the sea and air in the vicinity of Japan through patrols of fighter planes and bombers against ships bent on attack or invasion of Japan. He said that it was not proper to possess offensive aircraft carriers, but it was possible to maintain aircraft carriers for anti-submarine operations. In his estimates of developments for the decade beginning in 1972, Nakasone assumed a high degree of continuity of conditions in the Far East and cooperation with the United States. Most important, he assumed that constitutional limitations dealing with offensive war potential and economic checks would continue to operate. The three non-nuclear principles (not to make, not to store, and not to let others introduce nuclear weapons) would be observed, civil control over military policy would continue, and foreign policy would be based on peaceful measures. Defense force units would be small, highly mechanized, and armed with the most modern weapons and equipment. Defense would be carried out as far as possible with Japan's own forces to reduce reliance on the United States. Invasion was to be intercepted offshore. Fighter patrols, bomb- and torpedo-carrying planes were to be used as well as ground support and ground attack aircraft.

The concept of primary reliance on Japanese forces for conventional air and sea protection and the plan to supplement it by American cooperation seemed to incorporate the essential principle of self-reliance of the Nixon Doctrine. It did not involve any responsibility for neighboring countries except additional provision for Okinawa after 1972 when it would be returned to Japan. The Liberal Democratic party hoped the situation of the 1960s would be changed so that the American security arrangements would become supplementary to Japanese self-defense efforts. [18]

In 1969, the discussion concerning the protection of Japanese tankers in the Indian Ocean or Straits of Malacca was premature despite the improvements planned and the hopes for an independent and effective defense. Business and defense experts doubted whether either a Fourth or Fifth Defense Buildup Plan would provide sufficient maritime strength for such a task. [19] In October 1970, this seemed to be confirmed when the defense agency director general indicated the Fourth Defense Buildup Plan was expected to cost $14.4 billion. This would double the cost of the previous plan but still would not constitute forces sufficient to guard distant shipping.

The first Defense White Paper, which was issued in October 1970, was intended to emphasize the inoffensive nature of Japan's military effort. [20] However, China did not accept this interpretation and waged a vigorous propaganda campaign charging Japan with militarism and

[18] Hajime Ikeda, "Security Research Council, LDP Maps Basic Defense Policies," *Japan Times Weekly*, International Edition, Vol. X, No. 24 (13 June 1970), p. 3.

[19] Tetsuya Senga, *Waga Kuni no Anzen Hosho, Getsuyo Kai Report*, Security Series No. 2, 10 March 1969 (Tokyo: Kokumin Seiji Kenkyu Kai, 1969), pp. 42-48. Udai Fujishima, "Jishu Boei o Meguru Sei-Zaikai no Omowaku," *Bessatsu Chuo Koron: Keiei Mondai*, Autumn 1969, pp. 92-93.

[20] Japan, Boei Cho, *Nihon no Boei, Boei Hakusho* (Tokyo: Okura Sho Insatusu Kyoku, November 1970).

pointing with alarm to the defense plans. The White Paper repeated all the customary denials against nuclear arms, strategic bombers, and assault aircraft carriers and asserted Japan's limited aim of repelling direct aggression against Japan through local control of the seas and air. Apparently, the Chinese cries of alarm were aimed at deterring Japanese leaders from developing any more significant military force.

Return of the Southern and Southwestern Territories

On a visit to the United States, Prime Minister Sato pressed for the return of the American-occupied islands. In January 1965, a joint communique issued by Sato and President Johnson stated:

> The President and the Prime Minister recognized the importance of United States military installations in the Ryukyu and Bonin Islands for the security of the Far East. The Prime Minister expressed the desire that, as soon as feasible, the administrative control over these islands will be restored to Japan and also showed a deep interest in the expansion of the autonomy of the inhabitants of the Ryukyus and in further promoting their welfare. Appreciating the desire of the Government and people of Japan for the restoration of administration to Japan, the President stated that he looks forward to the day when the security interests of the free world in the Far East will permit the realization of this desire.[21]

Among the opposition parties, the Japan Socialists wanted the occupied islands returned at once and all the American military bases removed. The other parties also favored return of the islands and limits placed on the use of the bases by the United States with the aim of their gradual removal. Sato too appealed to Japanese nationalism by asking for return of the administration of the civilian population on the islands, but he did not demand any specific restrictions on the military use of the bases which were to be left under American control.

During the early Sato prime ministership, reversion of the islands on a step-by-step approach was considered. One method was to begin with the gradual integration of the educational system with that of Japan. The leading advocate of this approach was Kiyoshi Mori, director general of the prime minister's office and the official in the cabinet responsible for Okinawan affairs, who went to Okinawa in August 1966 to investigate the feasibility of this step. The negative attitude of U. Alexis Johnson, the new American ambassador, discouraged this approach and after consideration Prime Minister Sato put an end to it. Instead, the prime

---

[21] U.S., Department of State, *Department of State Bulletin*, Vol. LII, No. 1336 (1 February 1965), p. 135.

minister began his campaign to win complete reversion of the islands by verbal support of American policy in the Vietnam War.

After feverish personal diplomacy throughout East Asia and the South Pacific in the summer and fall of 1967, Prime Minister Sato departed for Washington in November to visit President Johnson. He had demonstrated Japan's verbal support of American policy in Vietnam in a Kennedy-like display of public relations but he did not commit Japan to any active support of American policy. He succeeded in extorting from the United States the promise of return of the least important American-occupied territories of the southern islands, such as the Bonins and Volcano Islands or Ogasawaras. It was agreed that the civilian control of the islands would be returned to Japan although the United States would retain bases there. At the same time Japan was to gradually assume much of the responsibility for defense of the area.

In the joint communique with President Johnson in which the return of the Ogasawaras was promised, Prime Minister Sato also asked for the return of the Ryukyus centering on Okinawa. The president said agreement was likely to be reached in a few years on a date for reversion of these islands but that military bases played too vital a role in the security of Japan and other countries of the Far East to permit an immediate decision. Seizing upon the only time mentioned, which was "a few years" but translated in Japanese as "two or three years," the prime minister told a news conference: "The period for return appears to be two or three years. There is no need to change our policy of a non-nuclear return. If the Japanese people firmly believe in maintaining their security, Okinawa will be returned quicker without waiting even three years." [22] On 5 December 1967, in his policy speech to the Fifty-Seventh Extraordinary Diet, the prime minister said:

> Under present unstable Asian conditions we, of course, cannot overlook the role Okinawa is playing for the defense of the Far East including Japan. . . . If our people are united and have the spirit to defend themselves by their own hand and consider a realistic policy, they will contribute to the stability of Asia. The future return of Okinawa to the fatherland is dependent on this. [23]

The prime minister apparently tried to reassure the United States that Okinawa, in Japanese hands, would still be available for use in the defense of South Korea and Taiwan by American forces and that when it was returned Japan would participate in its defense. He was

[22] *Asahi Nenkan 1968*, p. 281.

[23] Japan, Gaimu Sho, "Sato Naikaku Sori Daijin Shoshin Hyomei Enzetsu," *Waga Gaiki no Kinkyo*, No. 12, Shiryo, pp. 3-4.

also appealing to Japanese nationalism in the desire for return of Okinawa by urging the Japanese to support the government's defense policy in order to accomplish its aim. The Japanese leader thus used the issue of Okinawa in such a way to help obtain his "self-reliant defense" and to try to outbid the opposition parties, which were continuing their efforts to create a crisis in 1970 when the Security Treaty's fixed term expired. It is doubtful if Sato intended to suggest that the government would undertake a type of defense effort requiring a significant increase in expenditures or responsibilities beyond any territory under its own jurisdiction. The phrase "self-reliant defense" thus had virtually no new meaning as far as the government's intentions were concerned.

In 1968, the pressure of the opposition in Okinawa became so severe that it raised doubts in the minds of American officials about retaining administrative control and unfettered use of the bases there. In October 1968, the first popularly elected chief executive in Okinawa, Chobyo Yara, was the candidate of the opposition parties and he advocated the immediate return of the islands and the removal of the bases.

Foreign Minister Miki decided to run for president of the Liberal Democratic party against Sato and resigned his position, thereby removing a spokesman for the critical elements within the ruling party. He was replaced as foreign minister by Kiichi Aichi, who was a personal follower of the prime minister. When Aichi began negotiations with the Nixon administration on the return of Okinawa, the prime minister reversed himself somewhat and insisted that the question of nuclear weapons on Okinawa should be kept open. He may genuinely have believed the United States might not negotiate if Japan started with a demand of a non-nuclear return. Or he may merely have tried to create a position from which to retreat in order to make some concession to the opposition within his own party which was determined to put its own candidate in as party president and prime minister.[24] After numerous visits of Foreign Minister Aichi to Washington the main points of agreement on the return of Okinawa were reached and the text of the joint communique to be issued when Sato went to Washington was agreed upon.[25]

On 20 May 1969, the prime minister graciously yielded to pressure within the Liberal Democratic party and instructed the foreign minister to press for the return of Okinawa without nuclear arms and asked that the bases on Okinawa be subject to the same restrictions as those in Japan proper.[26] Although the American defense secretary, Melvin

[24] Frank Langdon, "Strains in Current Japanese-American Defense Cooperation," *Asian Survey*, Vol. IX, No. 9 (September 1969), p. 719.
[25] *Asahi Evening News*, 11 October 1969, p. 1.
[26] *Asahi Shimbun*, 20 May 1969, p. 1.

Laird, told the House of Representatives appropriations committee that Okinawa's chief value was as a support of conventional combat operations in the Western Pacific in the region of China, Korea, Japan, Taiwan, and the Philippines American officials were reluctant to concede a completely non-nuclear return of Okinawa if the Vietnam War was still in progress in 1972, the year agreed upon for the return of the islands. They considered unrestricted American use of the bases essential to maintain the Vietnam War.[27]

When the prime minister went to Washington in November, he and President Nixon formally issued a joint communique. The provision for return of Okinawa was as follows:

> The President and the Prime Minister also recognized the vital role played by United States forces in Okinawa in the present situation in the Far East. As a result of their discussion, it was agreed that the mutual security interests of the United States and Japan could be accomodated within arrangements for the return of the administrative rights over Okinawa to Japan. They therefore agreed that the two Governments would immediately enter into consultations regarding specific arrangements for the accomplishing of the early reversion of Okinawa without detriment to the security of the Far East, including Japan. They further agreed to expedite the consultations with a view to accomplishing the reversion during 1972, subject to the conclusion of these specific arrangements with the necessary legislative support. In this connection, the Prime Minister made clear the intention of his Government, following reversion, to assume gradually the responsibility for the immediate defense of Okinawa as part of Japan's defense efforts for her own territories.[28]

Thus, Japan succeeded in obtaining a definite time for the return of Okinawa. Yielding to domestic critics, the prime minister said he would submit the final agreement to the Diet and the president of the United States would submit it to the American senate. After lengthy negotiations, it was made ready for submission to the respective legislative bodies in 1971 with final return of the islands planned for 15 May 1972.

Japan appeared to have obtained all that it had asked. The communique not only indicated a willingness to return and set a definite date for

[27] T. B. Millar, *The Indian and Pacific Oceans: Some Strategic Considerations*, Adelphi Papers, No. 57 (London: Institute for Strategic Studies, May 1969), p. 9. See also Michio Royama, *The Asian Balance of Power*, Adelphi Papers, No. 42 (London: Institute for Strategic Studies, November 1967), pp. 8-9.

[28] *New York Times*, 22 November 1969, p. 14.

it but applied the same limitations to the bases on Okinawa as to the American bases in Japan proper:

> The President and Prime Minister agreed that, upon return of the administrative rights, the Treaty of Mutual Cooperation and Security and its related arrangements would apply to Okinawa without modification thereof. . . . The Prime Minister was of the view that, in the light of such recognition on the part of the Japanese Government, the return of the administrative rights over Okinawa in the manner agreed above should not hinder the effective discharge of the international obligations assumed by the United States for the defense of countries in the Far East, including Japan.[29]

Although purposely vague, this provision was intended to insure that any changes in equipment or the dispatch of American forces abroad for combat operations would be subject to consultation and Japanese approval as applied to the American bases in Japan proper.

American officials were anxious to insure that the Japanese leaders acknowledge their obligation to permit dispatch of material and forces where and when required, while Japanese officials were anxious to insure that they could exercise their own judgment in deciding if such steps were necessary or desirable. The phrase "should not hinder . . . including Japan" implied that Japan ought not hinder military action which was designed to defend Taiwan and South Korea whenever the United States deemed it necessary. The Japanese text simply said that there would be no hindrance to effective discharge of international obligations assumed by the United States to these other countries.[30] This implied that Japan should not hinder American actions designed to defend Taiwan and South Korea. However, the Japanese version could be interpreted to mean that, even if it disagreed with the United States, Japan would not hinder the United States from defending those countries. Critics of the Japanese government leaders leaped upon this interpretation to insist that Japan would docilely accept the American lead as it had done so often in the past.

The provision for a non-nuclear return of Okinawa in the agreement was extremely vague:

> The Prime Minister described in detail the particular sentiment of the Japanese people against nuclear weapons and the policy of the Japanese Government reflecting such sentiment. The President expressed his deep understanding and assured the Prime

---

[29] Ibid.

[30] The Japanese text reads: "Beikoku ga otte iru kokusai gimu no koka-teki suiko no samatage to naru yo na mono de wa nai." *Asahi Nenkan 1970*, p. 245.

Minister that, without prejudice to the position of the United States Government with respect to the prior consultation system under the Treaty of Mutual Cooperation and Security, the reversion of Okinawa would be carried out in a manner consistent with the policy of the Japanese Government as described by the Prime Minister.[31]

Critics of the government in Japan condemned the failure of the communique to commit both parties not to bring nuclear weapons into Japan and thus foreclose the nuclear option. The government leaders were loath to spell out their policy, which was not to possess, make, or let others bring nuclear devices into Japan, but they also refrained from committing themselves to follow such a policy in the indefinite future.

Their opponents feared that this provision might have the opposite effect after reversion, of permitting the United States to bring nuclear weapons into Okinawa or even its bases in Japan proper. They even thought the phrase "without prejudice to the position of the United States Government . . . Security" might have the effect of insuring that the Japanese leaders would agree to the desire of the United States to bring in nuclear weapons if the Americans deemed it necessary. The effect of such an interpretation would be to increase the possiblity of nuclearization of Japan in the future. The vague wording did seem to be broad enough to encompass such a change in policy, which has been referred to by critics as "Okinawanization" of Japan. Insofar as Japanese government policy is concerned, it has always left open the possibility that it might someday want to have nuclear weapons brought in, and it seemed very doubtful that this provision widened the possibility of nuclearization of Japan more than before. It seemed more likely that the wording of the clause was intended to insure that the Japanese authorities had a veto in case the United States wanted to bring nuclear weapons into Okinawa.

On 1 December 1969, Prime Minister Sato provided his interpretation of the agreement in his speech to the Sixty-Second Extraordinary Diet, just before the general election, which he had called to take advantage of the American agreement to return Okinawa:

> The general principles of the return of administrative rights to Okinawa are a return in 1972, a return without nuclear weapons, and a return with restrictions that apply to bases in Japan proper. Our country has been able to realize Okinawa return with our basic position fully carried out . . . [The Nixon-Sato talks] have

---

[31] *New York Times*, 22 November 1969, p. 14.

mutually reaffirmed the maintenance of the Japan-United States Security Treaty after 1970.[32]

He also explained that the security of Japan's neighbors, South Korea and Taiwan, was a matter of grave concern to Japan from the point of view of Japan's security. If security of these countries was threatened, the United States would have to obtain Japan's agreement to dispatch combat forces.

This explanation by Sato was intended undoubtedly to indicate that Japan would have an open mind in case of future threats or hostilities and that it did not intend to prevent the United States from using Japanese bases to protect its neighbors. This was a necessary attitude to win American agreement to return Okinawa, but it merely reaffirmed the intent of the two security treaties and the defense policy of the previous twenty years or so. It was nevertheless provocative to Peking which seized upon the fears of Japanese critics. In a radio broadcast, the Chinese government stated, "The Nixon-Sato discussions put importance on strengthening the Japan-United States security system and much of them tried to change the treaty into a military alliance of wider scope in order to plan aggressive policies against China and Asia."[33] These exaggerated charges were intended to excite fear within Japan of Japanese militarism, and to bring pressure from abroad on the Japanese leaders to deter them from such a course. Despite the Chinese campaign against the Liberal Democratic leaders, the government won the general election with a majority in the House of Representatives and their chief critics, the Japan Socialists, lost the election quite heavily. While these political results were not due solely to defense policy, the return of Okinawa was undoubtedly a popular move and the Chinese Communist leaders were unable to help the Socialist party with which they had established cordial relations.

Return of the Northern Territories

Japanese leaders also had the objective of regaining some of the northern territories it formerly owned but which, since the war, had been under Russian control. Previously in 1956, the Soviet Union promised to return a few of these islands but because Japan insisted on the return of more of the islands, none was returned. One major obstacle to solving this territorial question was the Russian objection to the American bases in Japan.

The Soviet Union had agreed during the 1956 negotiations that the island of Shikotan and the Habomais Islands would be returned upon

---

[32] *Asahi Nenkan 1970*, p. 262.
[33] Ibid.

the conclusion of a peace treaty with Japan but the Soviet Union was unwilling to concede the return of the southern Kurile Islands of Kunashiri and Etorofu, as demanded by Japan. Moscow contended that when Japan gave up claim to the Kurile Islands and the southern half of Sakhalin in the San Francisco peace treaty of 1951, it also gave up Kunashiri and Etorofu.[34] Japan argued that the two islands were historically and legally inherent parts of Japanese territory and not part of the surrendered Kuriles.[35] The Soviet Union insisted in return that their status had been settled. Although it had not been a party to the peace treaty, it refused to reconsider the issue.

Some in Japan, including the Japan Socialist party, claimed Japan's prewar boundaries to the north and wanted return of all of the Kuriles and southern Sakhalin Island. On the other hand, the Japanese government spokesmen, several times in the 1956 negotiations, had briefly been willing to concede even the southern Kuriles.[36] Different scholars have emphasized different reasons for the official government stand for the return of the two islands, Kunashiri and Etorofu.[37] These interpretations include pressure from the American government, public opinion in Japan, and conservative party faction disputes. Apparently, American officials feared Japanese-Soviet rapprochement when Japan was negotiating outstanding issues with Russia in 1956. John Foster Dulles, the American secretary of state, was reported to have said that if Japan bargained away all the Kurile Islands the United States should consider the annexation of Okinawa.

At the time of the 1960 treaty crisis, the Soviet Union had tried to make the withdrawal of all foreign troops from Japan a condition for the promised return of the island of Shikotan and the Habomais Islands, but Japan denounced this move as a unilateral attempt to amend the 1956 agreement. In preparation for a visit to Moscow, Foreign Minister Shiina of Japan met the Soviet Foreign Minister, Andrei Gromyko, in New York in November 1965. Gromyko agreed to consider the question of safety measures for northern waters off Shikotan and the Habomais but said the question of the territorial rights of Kunashiri and Etorofu

[34] U.S., Department of State, *United States Treaties and Other International Agreements*, Vol. III, pt. 3, "Treaty of Peace with Japan," TIAS 2490, 28 September 1951, pp. 3169-328. See Article II (C).

[35] Japan, Ministry of Foreign Affairs, Public Information Bureau, *The Northern Territorial Issue*, Japan Reference Series, No. 5-68, 1968. Japan, Ministry of Foreign Affairs, *The Northern Territorial Issue*, 1970.

[36] Donald C. Hellmann, *Japanese Foreign Policy and Domestic Politics* (Berkeley and Los Angeles: University of California Press, 1969), pp. 37, 59 and 146.

[37] Ibid., pp. 41-73, 149-58. James W. Morley, "The Soviet-Japanese Peace Declaration," *Political Science Quarterly*, Vol. LXXII, No. 3 (September 1957), pp. 370-79. Douglas H. Mendel, *The Japanese People and Foreign Policy* (Berkeley and Los Angeles: University of California Press, 1961), pp. 193-214.

was closed. In January 1966, when Shiina went to Moscow, he delivered a letter to Prime Minister Kosygin from Prime Minister Sato requesting the return of the northern islands. In his reply, Kosygin repeated the Soviet position previously stated by Gromyko that Russia would not negotiate the matter of Kunashiri and Etorofu, but if Japan wanted to sign a peace treaty, the island of Shikotan and the Habomais Islands would be returned. The prime minister indicated to the Fifty-First Diet on 28 January 1966 that Japan would not jeopardize its defense, which rested in the United States bases, against the Soviet Union just to get back a few tiny islands:

> . . . under postwar conditions one country cannot insure its security alone. The demand of some to unilaterally abrogate the United States-Japan Security Treaty and insure security by a declaration of neutrality is too illusory. I believe it is Japan's national interest to strive to guard itself with its own efforts in addition to continuing to maintain the United States-Japan Security system in order to insure its own peace and security. [38]

As with the United States and Canada, regular ministerial meetings were begun with the Soviet Union to increase friendly trade and economic intercourse. When the next Foreign Minister, Takeo Miki, went to Moscow for the first such meeting in July 1967, Prime Minister Kosygin proposed taking some interim steps toward the incomplete peace settlement between the two countries. Japan was still not prepared to bargain with respect to security questions and had nothing to give up except some territory over which it had no control. Therefore, no progress was made.

On 15 September 1967, Senator Mike Mansfield of the United States attracted a great deal of attention when he attended the Shimoda conference of Japanese and American scholars and politicians. At the conference, he proposed a great power meeting on Japanese security and territorial questions. [39] He thought both the United States and the Soviet Union could make mutual concessions with respect to the southern and northern occupied territories which they held in the process of a joint guarantee of Japan's security. He also thought it desirable that China be included in the joint guarantee.

This sensible proposal was too far in advance of the thinking that continued to dominate the four countries' leaders although it foreshad-

---

[38] Japan, Gaimu Sho, *Waga Gaiko no Kinkyo*, No. 10, Sato Naikaku Sori Daijin Shisei Hoshin Enzetsu, Shiryo, p. 5: foreign policy portion of the prime minister's major policy speech to the 51st Regular Diet, 28 January 1966.

[39] *Mainichi Shimbun*, 16 September 1967, morning edition, pp. 1 and 3; evening edition, p. 1.

owed the future. The Japanese foreign ministry spokesmen said it was utterly out of the question for the time being. At the same time, Secretary of State Rusk told Foreign Minister Miki in Washington that it was inopportune to discuss the return of Okinawa. Secretary of Defense Robert McNamara told Miki that Okinawa was the key to the American policy of military encirclement of the Communist bloc. The Japanese chief cabinet secretary speaking for Prime Minister Sato rejected any idea of Japan being a party to the encirclement of China.

On his return to the United States, Senator Mansfield presented his views in a report to the senate foreign relations committee. As a leading exponent of letting American allies take greater responsibility for their own defense and reducing American intervention in other countries' affairs, he expressed a very important point of view that was to be incorporated in the Nixon Doctrine, as it had been in Truman's and Eisenhower's Asian policies in their conciliatory phases. Mansfield proposed replacing "military confrontation" with "economic interplay" and urged greater self-reliance for Japan and other Asian countries.[40] In fact, self-reliance had been promised by Japan in the first security treaty of 1951, a condition which the United States still waited in vain to see achieved.[41]

In 1968 upon the agreement for the return of the southern islands by the United States, the director general of the Administrative Management Agency, Kimura, told the Japanese cabinet that it was time to raise actively with the Soviet Union the question of the return of the northern islands. Foreign Minister Miki said the northern islands were in a different class from the southern and southwestern islands which could be handled with regular diplomacy. However, he thought progress would be possible with a popular campaign and patient diplomacy. In consequence, the prime minister in his upper house election speeches in July said that after Okinawa he would like to see Kunashiri and Etorofu returned.

In August 1968, the Japanese government amended the law for organization of the prime minister's office, which was responsible for matters in the occupied islands, so that the officially sponsored Southern Compatriots' Protective Association changed its name to the Special Areas Compatriots' Protective Association to include evacuees from the Kuriles and the Okinawans. The director general of the prime minister's office then visited Hokkaido to observe conditions in the area of the northern islands. He also conferred with former inhabitants

---

[40] *New York Times*, 1 October 1967, pp. 1 and 3.

[41] See Preamble, paragraph 5: "Japan will itself increasingly assume responsibility for its own defense"—a phrase significantly missing from the 1960 Security Treaty.

of the islands who had been expelled by the Russians and were now living at Nemuro on Hokkaido.

The cabinet formed a liaison council of various ministries concerned with northern territorial problems such as records, property, and family registers of the former inhabitants. On 19 October, a popular rally was held by the compatriots' association to promote the return of the northern territories. Sixteen hundred persons assembled in Tokyo including the director general of the prime minister's office and representatives of the Liberal Democratic party, Democratic Socialists, and the Buddhist Komei party. As a result of the rally, an executive committee was formed by thirty-eight organizations under Shunichi Matsumoto, who had been the chief Japanese diplomatic negotiator in the restoration of relations with the Soviet Union in the mid-1950s.

In 1969 Japanese Foreign Minister Aichi did not limit himself to the return of Okinawa to Japan, but made efforts for the return of the northern territories from the Soviet Union. After his visit to the United States in September, he returned via the Soviet Union and talked to Prime Minister Kosygin. Aichi again repeated Japan's claims to the southern Kurile Islands of Kunashiri and Etorofu. He used the United States' promise to return Okinawa to suggest that it was an opportune time for the Soviet Union to return the northern islands. The Russian prime minister responded as before that the territorial question was already settled and there was no point in reopening the issue as he thought it better to leave things as they had been settled since the Second World War. Aichi said Japan was ready to negotiate as often as necessary to insure the eventual return of the territory and could see no reason to concede the southern Kuriles to Russia.

By emphasizing the desirability of preserving the territorial status quo reached after the Second World War, Kosygin indicated that the Soviet Union was concerned with making legitimate the postwar boundaries drawn in Europe and on the borders of China. He was unwilling to negotiate any changes with Japan which might weaken Russia's hand with repect to Germany or China as well as other states which might harbor grievances on such a score. The Soviet officials have not been willing to discuss the territorial question although they have discussed and negotiated the issue of the fishing rights near the islands and the vexing seizure of Japanese boats and fishermen.

The issue of the northern islands was not as important to Japan as Okinawa where many former Japanese subjects wished to be again part of Japan. Nor did it represent the military protection or threat seen to be involved in Okinawa. The islands did have a threatening character because of Russian bases and forces to the north, but this threat would remain even if the islands were returned.

Both Japan and the Soviet Union have used the issue of the northern islands as a means of pressure on each other. The Japanese leaders were not above using the issue as a means to deflect attention from American bases and to pose as a champion of Japanese nationalism by demanding return of Russian-held territory. The Russian leaders could use fishing rights, capture of fishermen, and their obstruction of an essential Japanese industry to squeeze some concessions from Japan. This problem has tended to be handled in isolation from the generally improving relations and trade between the two countries and even has permitted some steps toward joint exploitation of resources in the former Japanese territory now held by the Soviet Union.

As the Mansfield proposals suggest, it is likely that a solution to the northern territories dispute will only be resolved in the context of some more general settlement dealing with Japanese, American, Chinese, and Russian defense relations. For example, the American abandonment of the containment policy and its detente with China provides an incentive for the Soviet Union to construct an entente with Japan which will involve the long-stalled peace treaty negotiations. These in turn will require settlement of the northern territories issue.

The Nuclear Option

A major part of Japan's defense against the Soviet Union and China has been provided by the American "nuclear umbrella" which obviates Japan's "self-reliant defense." This nuclear defense is to be found in the American security guarantee which includes protection not only against conventional attack but also against nuclear attack. This has been made clear by both official American as well as Japanese pronouncements. Any nuclear power threatening or attacking Japan therefore would risk nuclear retaliation if it used such weapons even though Japan itself has none. As a consequence, Japanese leaders consider Japan fully protected by the security treaty against nuclear threats or attacks and have never made any official statement indicating any doubt about the efficacy of this protection. This American umbrella makes nuclear weapons for Japan unnecessary.[42] Nor is it necessary for the United States to bring them into Japan. Intercontinental ballistic missiles (ICBMs) in the United States or nuclear missiles on Polaris submarines are probably sufficient to deter threats or attacks on Japan.

Japanese government policy has been strongly in favor of general nuclear disarmament which has been supported by all political parties and public opinion. Ever since the question arose with the arming of

---

[42] Japan, Sori Fu, *Nihon no Anzen o Mamoru ni wa—Anzen Hosho ni Tsuite no Seifu no Kangaekata*, June 1969, p. 20.

Japan with Honest John missiles under the Hatoyama Cabinet, Japan has refused to permit the United States to bring nuclear weapons into Japan. Despite the strict limits on Japanese defense, the government has never regarded nuclear weapons as forbidden by the constitutional strictures. Since 1955, the chief reason for opposing their introduction has been that the government did not consider them necessary. Hatoyama and his successors have continued to insist that the United States must not introduce them into its bases in Japan. However, even Prime Minister Hatoyama believed such weapons were legitimate defensive weapons in case of dire necessity.

Like its predecessors, the Sato Cabinet expressly disclaimed any nuclear ambitions. On 19 February 1966, Foreign Minister Shiina told the House of Representatives budget committee, "Setting up nuclear bases in Japan or participating in any Asian multilateral nuclear force does not exist in any plan at present, nor is there any intention of participating in such a thing hereafter."[43] On 27 January 1968, Prime Minister Sato in his policy speech told the Fifty-Eighth Diet:

> We ardently desire to stamp out nuclear weapons. We do not venture to possess them ourselves and are determined not to permit them to be brought into our country. Following the example of the United States and the Soviet Union, however, Britain, France, and Communist China have tried to pursue their national interests supported by nuclear weapons.
>
> Therefore, we are striving for the present for quick conclusion of a just treaty for preventing the spread of nuclear weapons and must bend all our strength to achieve nuclear disarmament through international negotiations. We must create proper international conditions where human reason will control nuclear weapons and stimulate world opinion so as to make impossible possessing countries which will use them or threaten to use them.[44]

On 12 February 1968, the opposition Socialist, Komei, and Communist parties took advantage of the government's strong stand and introduced a resolution in the Diet to forbid both nuclear and non-nuclear weapons in Japan. The government then put forward a counter-resolution which included its long-supported three non-nuclear principles (not to make, not to store, and not to let others introduce nuclear weapons); the elimination of nuclear weapons everywhere; the use of nuclear energy for peaceful purposes only; and the dependence on the nuclear deterrent of the United States under the security treaty.[45] The ruling and opposition

[43] *Asahi Nenkan 1967*, p. 308.
[44] Japan, Gaimu Sho, *Waga Gaiko no Kinkyo*, No. 12, October 1968, Shiryo, p. 4.
[45] *Asahi Nenkan 1969*, p. 270.

parties blocked each other's resolutions and refused to compromise but both sides managed to champion a non-nuclear position in the process, a stance which was certain to be popular.

In February 1969, the question was raised in the Diet whether calls by Polaris submarines armed with ICBM's constituted bringing nuclear weapons into Japan.[46] Both the prime minister and foreign minister replied that there was no legal obstacle to prevent the submarines putting into port but the government opposed such action out of deference to the popular revulsion against even permitting movement of nuclear weapons through Japan. In case of illness on board a ship carrying nuclear weapons a temporary exception could be made without requiring prior consultation. The foreign minister then amplified this explanation to say that Polaris submarines would not be permitted to enter Japanese harbors for provisioning or rest of the crew as in the case of non-nuclear submarines.

In March 1969, the prime minister in debate in the House of Councillors budget committee said that Japan could possess strategic nuclear weapons for defense.[47] However, the chief cabinet secretary hastened to explain that there was no change of the policy not to permit their introduction for the present even in the event of prior consultations or of an American request to introduce them.

The United States and the Soviet Union were the principal sponsors of the Nuclear Nonproliferation Treaty, which represented another high point of superpower cooperation and the desire of the Johnson administration to achieve detente with the Soviet Union. This treaty was ostensibly intended to prevent the spread of nuclear weapons by obligating nuclear armed-countries not to transfer weapons or weapon technology to non-nuclear armed countries and obligating the latter not to make or receive them.

The Soviet Union's motive in sponsoring the treaty was its desire to see West Germany and Japan, the two most feared nations able to acquire nuclear weaponry, bound into an agreement of self denial. The United States, for its part, wanted West Germany and Japan to sign the treaty so America could demonstrably display its good intentions to the Russians. Surprisingly, this was one of the few non-commercial issues on which Japan failed to follow the American suggestion immediately. The decision was taken because Japan's policy has always been to keep the nuclear option open but to oppose the introduction of nuclear weapons when they were not needed. The new treaty would foreclose this option. Even more surprising was the rejection of the treaty by

---

[46] *Asahi Shimbun*, 4 February 1969, evening edition, p. 1.
[47] Ibid., 12 March 1969, p. 1.

the opposition parties. They regarded themselves as the great champions of nuclear disarmament but objected to the treaty on the grounds that it did not require any disarmament by the nuclear armed states, that it provided no effective security guarantee to the states foregoing nuclear armament, and that it did not bind France or China which refused to sign it. As the Chinese government leaders charged, it would have the effect of confirming the nuclear superiority of the two superpowers and of perpetuating their global domination. It would not prevent proliferation among those countries which rejected it.

Japan had an American defense guarantee and a policy of non-nuclearization, but it was another matter to promise not to acquire nuclear arms for a period of twenty-five years just to bow to a current American policy of appeasing the Soviet Union. Even though the treaty provided for withdrawal from the treaty obligation on three-months notice if a country's supreme interests were jeopardized, such an action would emphasize the possibilities of nuclear armament and magnify the fears of revival of Japanese militarism which the government had tried to erase over the past twenty years.[48] Changing conditions in East Asia raised the possibility that the security treaty and the security guarantee might disappear in the near future as well.

The United States consulted with Japan in the final stages of preparation of the treaty before the Geneva Disarmament Commission with a view to gaining its cooperation and adherence to the treaty. The Japanese avoided the sensitive topic of the surrender of its nuclear option to press for disarmament by the superpowers and for assurance that the peaceful application of nuclear energy would be shared fully by the non-nuclear armed states. In February 1967, Foreign Vice-Minister Shimoda announced that the prevention of non-nuclear weapons states from conducting peaceful nuclear explosions would affect the acceptability of the treaty. However, in April, Foreign Minister Miki consulted the opposition parties in an effort to gain their support for efforts at improving the text of the treaty. He also sent representatives of the government to West Germany, Italy, Sweden, and India to discuss the provisions for insuring access to the peaceful uses of nuclear energy. Even the head of the United States Disarmament Agency and chief American representative at Geneva, came to Japan to consult with the Japanese authorities. He promised to send experts to Japan to explain it fully upon presentation of the final version of the text at Geneva.

Japan could not reject the treaty outright and risk antagonizing the United States nor could it freely state its desire to keep open its nuclear

---

[48] Even the Canadian prime minister rather tactlessly referred to future Japanese militarism in Singapore prior to a visit to Japan. Vancouver *Province*, 2 June 1970, p. 5.

option. Japanese demands therefore included equal obligation (to disarm) by both nuclear weapons and non-nuclear weapons states; extension of a security guarantee to non-nuclear weapons states; equality in research and development for peaceful purposes; equality in provision for peaceful explosions; equal treatment in the matter of safeguards; and reconsideration of the treaty every five years. On 27 January 1968, Foreign Minister Miki told the Diet: "Equality of opportunity in the utilization of nuclear energy for peaceful purposes must be absolutely secured."[49] The treaty was later modified to include a provision for review in five years, as originally requested by Japan and the preamble pledged to refrain from threat or use of force which had been already agreed to by most potential signatories under the United Nations Charter. Britain, the Soviet Union, and the United States sponsored a Security Council resolution pledging to protect the non-nuclear armed signatories, but this was no more binding than obligations already assumed by them as members of the Security Council and which had proved ineffective in the past. Also, in 1969, the United States and the Soviet Union began lengthy bilateral talks on checking or limiting the nuclear arms race between them.

An important aspect which caused great difficulty after the treaty was presented to the United Nations was the provisions for inspection of the non-nuclear armed states to insure compliance. In Japan, it was feared that inspection by the International Atomic Energy Agency might result in the loss of industrial secrets or expensive interference in peaceful uses of nuclear energy.[50] However, after several years it appeared that these fears were almost solved through separate agreements under negotiation with the agency. According to the treaty, the nuclear armed states were not subject to inspection although the United States and Britain agreed to voluntarily open some of their peaceful nuclear industry and research to international inspection.

The Japanese foreign ministry was the strongest advocate within Japan of signing of the treaty. It argued that Japan's policy of nuclear disarmament required support of the treaty if doubts were not to be raised about its peaceful foreign policy. It would be better to raise further questions as a signatory before ratification than be isolated from the participants and subject to suspicion. Besides this, as a non-participant, Japan would have no claims to share in nuclear technology

[49] Japan, Ministry of Foreign Affairs, Public Information Bureau, *Foreign Relations and Mutual Respect*, Foreign Policy Speech by Foreign Minister Takeo Miki at the 58th Ordinary Session of the National Diet on 27 January 1968, Japan Reference Series, No. 4-68, 1968, p. 8.

[50] Japan, Gaimu Sho, Kokunai Hokoku Ka, *Kaku Heiki Fu-Kakusan Joyaku*, 1970, p. 8. Japan, Naikaku Kambo, Naikaku Chosa Shitsu, *Chosa Geppo*, "Nihon no Kaku Seisaku to Gaiko," No. 150, June 1968, pp. 1–12.

and development with the signatories. If it antagonized the United States by refusal to sign, Japan might be subject to sanctions as it was almost wholly dependent on America for enriched uranium fuel and major aspects of its own nuclear industrial development.

In July and again in November 1969, the debate within the ruling Liberal Democratic party indicated that there was fear for Japan's own security by foregoing the nuclear option, as well as perpetuating the inequality between the weapons and non-weapons states. The party, however, decided that, on balance, signing was preferable to being left out. In February 1970, after West Germany signed and the treaty was about to go into effect, Japan finally signed.

Three years later, neither West Germany nor Japan had ratified the treaty. Both countries continued to raise objections about its numerous unequal aspects.[51] However, after it had gone into effect for many signatories, the Nixon administration concentrated on its policy of detente with the Soviet Union, and the United States eased its pressure on Japan for ratification and surrender of the nuclear option.

Defense Alternatives

In the 1970s a few defense alternatives for Japan appear to be possible. One alternative might be for Japan to continue to rely upon the United States for defense assistance against a major antagonist. This would permit it to continue its traditional defense policy of relying upon the American guarantee and the security treaty which would permit Japan to feel secure with a small but efficient and modernized defense force. Even if American bases were placed on standby status, or if they were shared by Japanese and American forces, this might be a feasible policy. It is one policy strongly supported by the Liberal Democrats and important elements such as big business. If Japan's economic expansion should resume at the high rates of the 1960s, its gross national product might double before the end of the 1970s. This would make increased defense expenditures easy to undertake without curtailing either growth of the economy or welfare services. If Japan were to double or triple its present rate of expenditure, whether in terms of the budget or of the gross national product, and not just double the absolute amount as under the Fourth Defense Buildup Plan, it could follow another alternative and build up its defenses on a scale comparable with Britain, France, or West Germany. It then would need only a slightly greater expenditure to equal the defense effort of China. Such growth might possibly some day enable Japan to rearm on the scale of the superpowers, the United States and the Soviet Union, if it felt sufficiently threatened or acquired ambitions to change the status quo.

[51] *Japan Times*, 4 February 1970, p. 11, "Government Statement on Nuclear Pact."

Probably the only circumstances that would impel the Japanese government to change its present policy of a modest self-defense force would be an increased security threat and a reduced willingness of the United States to protect Japan, or a reduced credibility that it would do so. This would induce Japan to increase its defense effort more on the scale of other countries of the same relative economic strength. Probably only a refusal or inability of the United States to continue its guarantee of Japan's defense and a much increased threat from its neighbors would induce Japan to try to equal or surpass China in defense expenditures.

If domestic political change produces a less conservative government, it might pursue another alternative and move in the direction of neutralism. This would lead to replacement of the security treaty and removal of the American military bases which would improve relations with China, but this would probably not lead to increased defense expenditures, although even this might be possible.

There is a strong fear of Communism and a pro-Taiwan sentiment among some of the conservative leaders of the Liberal Democratic party which resembles the similar fear which has dominated American policy for so long. These men would probably favor the traditional Japanese strategy of maintaining dominance in South Korea and Taiwan as a protection of Japan's flanks and buffer zones for the Japanese islands. This sentiment is similar to the policy followed by the United States in recent years. Should the United States decide, at least tacitly, to withdraw its support of Taiwan, then Japan would have to decide if it wanted to take on the task of supporting it and how it would do this even though Japan is more concerned with preserving a non-Communist regime in South Korea than in Taiwan. This would create a dilemma as those Japanese leaders have also favored the policy of keeping Japan's defenses small and relying on American support. The abandonment of Taiwan involves the fear of the "domino theory"—that if the line against Communist expansion is not held at one point it might give way at other places as well.

It is most likely that the Japanese government will follow the American lead even though it has more at stake than the United States in the preservation of non-Communist regimes on its flanks. Unless some much greater nationalist upsurge occurs in Japan, it seems unlikely that Japanese leaders of a pro-Taiwan persuasion could induce the Japanese government to take on any overseas commitment to preserve the Chinese Nationalists.

To deflate the campaign against the Japan-United States Security Treaty and the charges of a revival of Japanese militarism in 1970, Prime Minister Sato and Defense Director General Nakasone made a great effort to explain the limitations on Japan's defense policies and their peaceful nature. They emphasized the civilian control of defense and the non-nuclear principles. While reaffirming the cooperation with their great power ally, they sought to render this less threatening by enunciating what was claimed to be a new policy of merely supplementing Japan's own efforts with American assistance.[52] This was contrasted with the earlier policy of relying on American assistance and merely supplementing it with Japanese forces. This approach had the merit of appealing to nationalist sentiment which desired greater independence of the United States and to the desire for a greater international status. It also was designed to mollify Chinese and domestic critics by providing less ground for their fears and hostility.

In support of this Nakasone approach, the American Undersecretary of State, U. Alexis Johnson, told the United States senate, "The United States has no forces, either ground or air, in Japan that are directly related to the direct conventional defense of Japan."[53] He said that the American bases and forces in Japan were there to meet commitments in South Korea, Taiwan, the Philippines, and Southeast Asia. This statement supported Japan's contention that it was mainly responsible for its own defense.

When Japan's first Defense White Paper was issued in October 1971, spelling out in detail the type of forces which Japan had, it reiterated a non-interventionist self-defense policy, a non-nuclear one, and one aimed at peace.[54] The Defense White Paper also eschewed the acquisition of strategic missiles, bombers, or assault aircraft carriers. The paper insisted that Japan would not send its forces abroad and would not even acquire tactical nuclear weapons. These were the guidelines for the 1970s.

In July 1971 when American Defense Secretary Laird visited Japan, he stated that he saw no need for Japan to arm itself with nuclear weapons in the 1970s or beyond.[55] The continued American nuclear guarantee made this unnecessary.

Thus, up to the end of the Sato prime ministership, Japan's security policies remained substantially unaltered. Cooperation was continued with the United States while a limited defense effort was maintained together with a policy designed to prevent fears on the part of its neighbors and the domestic opposition. This policy was to meet serious questioning only with the disturbance to the alignments of the major powers in the area, with the outbreak of a kind of economic war between Japan

[52] Kobun Ito, "Japan's Security in the 1970s," *Asian Survey*, Vol. X, No. 12 (December 1970), pp. 1031-36.
[53] Vancouver *Province*, 24 August 1970, p. 3.
[54] Japan, Boei Cho, *Nihon no Boei: Boei Hakusho* (Okura Sho, Insatsu Kyoku, 1970).
[55] *Japan Times Weekly*, International Edition, Vol. XI, No. 29 (17 July 1971), p. 1.

and the United States over trade and currency questions in late 1971, and with the improved relations between the United States and China in early 1972.

Greater self-reliance was demanded of Japan by the Nixon administration and Japan claimed, in fact, to be more self reliant in its defense. The decision to proceed with the Fourth Defense Buildup Plan in 1972 involved the intention to increase defense expenditures at about a rate of 13 percent a year. While scarcely likely to bring Japan within range of the military power of a country such as China or even of the major Western European states, it will give it more effective naval and air power which could contribute to its defense needs in the region and its potential military influence in the future. This is likely to enhance Japan's regional and international status even if it continues its self-denying limited defense concept. The differing nature of Japan's forces (air and naval) and of China's forces (land and nuclear) may reduce the likelihood of clashes. Japan's capabilities also resemble those upon which the United States relies in the region.

7

Economic Liberalism

JAPAN HAS PURSUED its goal of prosperity by promoting its trade and investment throughout the world concentrating on the leading industrial countries, particularly the United States. After the Second World War, a general expansion in world trade benefited Japan greatly as it again became a major trading nation. Its economic expansion was also given impetus by the trend in the world toward freer trade and economic liberalism, in which the United States took the lead by advocating lower tariffs and reduced barriers to trade and investment.

Japan moved much later than North America or Western Europe to liberalize its trade and exchange restrictions in its efforts to strengthen its own economy while preventing a serious imbalance in its international payments position. It also had a long tradition of strict controls over foreign investment which yielded only slowly under Ikeda and Sato to permit more foreign business to enter Japan. At the same time, however, Japan was anxious to be accepted as one of the major industrial states on the same basis as countries such as Britain or France. This desire required that Japan deal in trade and investment with other countries on a reciprocal basis. It had further to go in allowing foreign investment in Japan and ran into resentment when it did not approach foreign standards.

Under Prime Minister Ikeda, Japan's plans for liberalization of foreign trade and investment in its domestic markets were slowed by unfavorable economic conditions in the early 1960s. Under Prime Minister Sato in the mid-1960s the sharp improvements in world trade redounded to Japan's advantage to give it one of the highest economic growth rates in the world and to place it in a strong international financial position. This improvement in the world economy in the mid-1960s provided the means by which Japan was able to make progress in its aim of liberalization of its foreign economic policy. Japan moved to reduce foreign tariffs and accelerated its program of easing the entry into Japan of foreign investment as well as foreign products, which previously had been excluded or sharply limited. Japan's commitment to freer trade and investment can be found in its official foreign policy statement under Sato:

> To develop free trade in the world, we have striven to mitigate various countries' trade restrictions under the General Agreement on Trade and Tariffs as well as bilateral negotiations. Furthermore, to prevent introduction of restrictions, our country must fully solve the problem of import liberalization. Also, it is necessary to make efforts in accord with the principle of economic liberalism which animates some countries in even freeing capital transactions. [1]

The recognition of Japan's efforts to liberalize its economic activities came at the time Japan was accepted as a full member of the Organization for Economic Cooperation and Development. Originally this organization had been formed to carry out economic recovery of Western Europe after the Second World War, but after this was accomplished it undertook to supervise its members' policies of aid-assistance to newly independent states. Besides joining this organization, Japan also agreed to undertake the responsiblities of advanced status in the International Monetary Fund group of states by liberalizing financial and currency transactions. It was, henceforth, under considerable pressure from OECD partners to reduce trade and investment restrictions to the level of the other members. On 25 January 1965, Foreign Minister Shiina in the new Sato Cabinet said in a speech in the Diet: "It [1964] was a year of deep significance when we achieved the position of an advanced industrial country in the international economy and international society. At the same time our country as an advanced industrial country undertook heavy responsibilities for the world economic system." [2]

Balance of Payments

As can be seen in table 7.1, Japan's balance of payments, which includes foreign trade, services, and capital transactions, was unfavorable in the early 1960s. This was during the Ikeda prime ministership when Japan was constantly appealing to the United States to increase its purchases from Japan in order to ease the strain on Japan's trade balance. At

[1] Japan, Gaimu Sho, *Waga Gaiko no Kinkyo*, No. 13, 1968, part 1, p. 95.
[2] Japan, Gaimu Sho, *Waga Gaido no Kinkyo*, No. 9, 1964, Dai Yonjuhachi Kai Tsujo Kokkai ni Okeru Shiina Gaimu Daijin no Gaiko Enzetsu, 25 January 1965, documents, ı. 11.

TABLE 7.1
JAPAN'S BALANCE OF INTERNATIONAL PAYMENTS, 1961-72
(IN MILLIONS OF DOLLARS)

Year	Exports	Imports	Trade Balance	Payments Balance
1961	4,149	4,707	−558[a]	−982[a]
1962	4,861	4,460	401	−48
1963	5,391	5,557	−166	−780
1964	6,704	6,327	377	−480
1965	8,332	6,431	1,901	932
1966	9,641	7,366	2,275	1,254
1967	10,231	9,071	1,160	−190
1968	12,751	10,222	2,529	1,048
1969	15,679	11,980	3,699	2,119
1970	18,969	15,006	3,963	1,970
1971	23,566	15,779	7,787	5,797
1972[b]	30,160	21,188	8,972	6,660

NOTE:[a] The excess of imports or outpayments over in-payments is indicated by a minus sign.
NOTE:[b] Estimates of ministry of trade, *Japan Times Weekly*, Vol. XIII, No. 6, 18 February 1973, p. 9 and Vol. xiii, No. 4, 27 Jan. 1973, p. 8.
SOURCE: *Asahi Nenkan 1971*, p. 377. ibid, 1973, p. 311.

this time Japan was also reluctant to fully relinquish its currency and trade restrictions by which it could keep the situation under control. The American leaders' reply to these appeals was that the adverse balance was a small price to pay for supporting the free world and helping the United States which bore most of the burden.

After 1964, there was a dramatic change in Japan's balance of payments position when a surplus on trade account and a surplus on overall payments appeared and became quite large, especially in terms of the value of exports over imports. Now it was the United States that began to demand, with greater insistence, that Japan buy more from the United States, particularly by permitting the entry of foreign goods.

In 1965, there was an overall surplus in payments of nearly $1 billion in Japan's favor and in the following year it even exceeded that amount. In 1967, imports drew close to exports to reduce the trade surplus and the large out-payments on capital account pulled the balance back into an unfavorable position again. After that single setback, the payments surplus was back to more than $1 billion in 1968 and nearly double that amount in the next two years. For 1972 it was almost $7 billion.

Balance of Trade

When trade exports and imports after 1963 are compared, Japan consistently showed a surplus of exports. This increased about fivefold in 1965 over 1964 and then in 1966 it showed an even larger increase. In 1967, imports were brought up closer to exports, but then the surplus

TABLE 7.2
JAPAN'S TRADE WITH THE UNITED STATES
(IN MILLIONS OF DOLLARS)

Year	Exports	Imports	Trade Balance
1950	181	421	−240
1955	456	774	−318
1960	1,102	1,554	−452
1965	2,479	2,366	93
1966	2,969	2,658	311
1967	3,012	3,212	−200
1968	4,086	3,527	559
1969	4,958	4,090	868
1970	5,940	5,560	380
1971	7,495	4,978	2,517
1972[a]	8,856	5,848	3,008

NOTE:[a] The 1972 estimates are those of the Japanese ministry of finance, *Japan Times Weekly*, Vol. xiii, No. 5, 3 February 1973, p. 9. American figures show a larger trade gap—projected at about $4,300 million, *Japan Times Weekly*, Vol. xiii, No. 2, 13 January 1973, p. 12, editorial.

SOURCE: *Asahi Nenkan* 1954–1973, passim.

doubled and tripled in the next two years. A significant portion of this surplus was due to the excess of exports over imports to the United States.[3]

From 1965 to 1967, Japan showed a favorable trade balance which was not extremely large, although it was a surplus rather than the usual deficit. It increased thereafter to the consternation of American officials. American trade figures also showed a much larger gap than those of Japan as shown in table 7.3.

In 1969, the United States Deputy Assistant Secretary of Commerce, Robert McLellan, noted the steep increase in Japanese exports over imports to the United States although he gave a figure different from those in table 7.3.[4] The American Secretary of Commerce, Maurice Stans, predicted an even larger surplus of $1.5 billion for 1969.[5] The actual figure proved to be not too far from his estimate.

On 22 October 1969, the American Ambassador to Japan, Armin Meyer, and Undersecretary of State, U. Alexis Johnson, told a meeting of American state and Japanese prefectural governors in Cincinnati:

> [Last year] Japan sold over a billion dollars more to us than we sold to Japan, which, taken together with our other expenditures in Japan and the billions of dollars in long- and short-term loans,

[3] This amounted to $3,850 million from 1965 through 1969. United States-Japan Trade Council, *Some Questions and Answers on U.S.-Japan Trade Relations and Japanese International Economic Policies* (Washington, D.C., 1971), p. 5.

[4] *Japan Times*, 11 October 1969, p. 8.

[5] Ibid., 9 October 1969, p. 1.

TABLE 7.3
UNITED STATES TRADE WITH JAPAN
(IN MILLIONS OF DOLLARS)

Year	Exports	Imports	Trade Balance
1965	2,041	2,401	−359
1968	2,924	4,044	−1,120
1969	3,462	4,849	−1,387

SOURCE: United States—Japan Trade Council, *United States and Japan: A Comparison of Trade and Economic Data*, Washington, D.C. 1969, table 6, and ibid., 1970, table 7.

our financial institutions have outstanding in Japan, probably has more of an adverse impact on our international financial situation than our relations with any other single country in the world.[6]

In terms of trade, the impact of Japan on the United States was becoming as great as the impact of the United States on Japan. In 1969, the $9 billion two-way trade between Japan and the United States was the largest bilateral trade in the world with the sole exception of the trade between the United States and Canada. The sharp increase in Japanese exports to the United States was caused partly by the rising cost of production in the United States in which increases in wages were not offset by sufficient increases in productivity.

Japan became one of the chief members of the major trading countries involved in the multilateral negotiations that led to one of the largest moves toward freer trade through tariff reduction ever recorded in history. With the United States, Britain, and the European Common Market, Japan became a member of the steering committee at the negotiations held at the headquarters of the General Agreement on Trade and Tariffs in Geneva. However, the entire attempt at a massive tariff reduction looked as though it would fail as talks dragged on from 1963 to 1967 without any significant agreement. The expiration of the American Trade Expansion Act in June 1967 threatened to remove the legal basis for American participation in large-scale tariff reductions by withdrawing the American president's authority to make extensive tariff cuts. The pending expiration of the act stimulated furious last-minute negotiations in which Japan played an important role in support of American efforts.

Many of the participants advanced the dates on which the agreed successive tariff cuts were due in order to help the United States ease its adverse balance of payments, which became increasingly unmanageable as the Vietnam War progressed and inflation ran rampant in the United States and in the whole world's economy. Japan advanced its application

[6] Ibid., 24 October 1969, p. 4.

of tariff cuts further in 1970 and 1971 to help the American financial position, and by early 1971 its tariffs averaged slightly less than those of the United States so that it had reached a level which compared favorably with other advanced countries.

As Japan was anxious to expand its exports, the reduction of tariffs in other countries, which tended to be high on Japan's manufactured goods, was beneficial to Japan. It also imported comparatively few of these high-cost items itself or barred them·through quotas and other restrictive regulations. Also, Japan, like the other advanced countries, protected its farmers by reducing competing food imports through tariffs or quotas, but it did take part in a grain agreement. Under the agreement Japan was obliged to ship wheat to developing nations. But such shipments would deplete the Japanese domestic supply and force the country to buy wheat from abroad. To get around the impasse, Japan agreed that it would ship fertilizer and agricultural implements rather than wheat.

Japan's chief trading partners, especially the United States, continued to be dissatisfied with Japan's efforts even though Japan's tariffs in general had become fairly liberal. The chief reason for this dissatisfaction was that Japan continued to exclude some products, such as automobiles, by one means or another.

The currency crisis in May 1971 highlighted the need for adjustment in exchange rates. Canada, West Germany and some of the countries closely linked to West Germany by trade began to let their currencies appreciate in terms of the American dollar. Although refusing to revalue the yen, the Japanese government was under strong pressure to do so. Suddenly, on 15 August 1971, without consultation with any of its allies or trading partners, the United States imposed a 10 percent surcharge on all dutiable imports into the United States in an attempt to reverse the unfavorable American balance of trade which had begun in 1970. President Nixon also abrogated the agreement to maintain a fixed gold value of the dollar by refusing to redeem United States dollars with gold as originally agreed at Bretton Woods in 1944—the agreement which made dollars the basic currency in world trade. The result was intended to make foreign exports to the United States more expensive and to force the appreciation of foreign currencies, thus making American exports cheaper abroad. This move threatened a sharp setback for Japanese, Canadian, and other foreign businesses whose major market was the United States.

In an effort to hold the yen at its former dollar value, the Bank of Japan bought nearly $3,900 million on the foreign exchange market in the second half of August 1971 before the Japanese ministry of finance on 28 August finally let the yen float.[7] The Bank of Japan then held

[7] *Japan Times Weekly,* International Edition, Vol. XI, No. 36 (4 September 1971), p. 1.

the rate at about 7 percent above its old value. The other currency which the United States wished to see valued upward was the mark, which rose about 11 percent above its former fixed value. In the initial currency revaluations, the American Treasury Secretary, John B. Connally, said that the currency revaluation had not been substantial enough to warrant removal of the surcharge.[8] He was also adamant that quotas and other trade barriers had to be removed as well as more substantial revaluations and a fairer sharing of defense costs.

When international agreement on revaluation finally was reached in December 1971, Japan made a severe adjustment in its currency amounting to a 16.6 percent upward valuation in relation to the United States dollar. Partly because of the panic in Japan among businessmen, imports were reduced but exports continued at the same high rates as before with the result that the trade surplus became even greater in 1971.

Among the barriers to trade which have been most important and most frequently the subject of negotiations were tariffs. As Japan depends upon foreign sources for most of its raw materials and fuel, as well as a significant proportion of its food, it has a strong incentive to keep the cost of essential items such as these at a low level. As a result, importations of such items have little or no tariff applied to them. Despite the obvious advantage to world trade and to individual countries by removing restrictions to commerce—to say nothing of the benefit to consumers—the drive to protect one's own high-cost agriculture or industry appears to be almost irresistible.

The weak sectors often can muster great political strength by appealing to nationalist sentiment in a country's domestic affairs to exclude or seriously restrict the entry of foreign goods. Despite the damage done in the era of tariff retaliation in the 1930s and the unfavorable influence on world trade of exclusive trading blocs, there continues to be a dynamic struggle between the forces of protectionism and the proponents of freer trade. The American steps to loosen the tie of the dollar to gold and the temporary 10 percent surcharge of 1971 were at least partially a protectionist reaction to the growing protectionism of the European Common Market which increasingly excluded American agricultural products through the application of high tariffs. American retaliation was also aimed at compelling revaluation of West German and Japanese currencies to make American exports more competitive in foreign markets and to reverse the balance of trade deficit in the United States.

Restrictions on Foreign Investment in Japan
In the mid-1960s, the favorable American balance of trade that helped the United States make large military expenditures and capital investment began to be reduced. In 1964 the surplus on trade account was \$6.7

---

[8] Vancouver *Sun*, 2 October 1971, p. 21.

billion, in 1965 it was $4.8 billion, and in 1966 it shrank to $3.5 billion. By 1970, there was an adverse balance—for the first time in the century—of $2.2 billion in excess of imports over exports. Other unfavorable developments tended to threaten further protective measures by the United States that would limit rather than extend freer trade.

When Japan became a full member of the Organization for Economic Cooperation and Development in 1964, considerable pressure was exerted by the organization to withdraw or reduce restrictions on capital movements to and from Japan in order to conform to the organization's rules. Although Japanese leaders such as Prime Minister Ikeda, heads of business federations, and foreign ministry officials hoped Japan would make the necessary adjustments which were in its long-run interest, it was difficult to hurry the process as demanded by OECD, especially in the sensitive industries which were apt to be where foreign businessmen particularly wanted entry.

Japan was allowed eighteen reservations under the revised liberalization code of 1964. This was almost tantamount to allowing it into the organization without fully undertaking the obligations of membership, at least until it was ready. However, Japanese officials feared to move too quickly in areas in which they thought Japan did not have sufficient international competitive power.[9] On 21 December 1965, the Japanese section of the OECD's business and investment advisory committee recommended a plan for Japanese capital liberalization as an aid to Japan's prosperity. The chairman of the Liberal Democratic party foreign policy committee and member of the House of Councillors, Morinosuke Kajima, expressed the common Japanese fear of foreign capital which, once entrenched in Japan, could not easily be dislodged or controlled. He even feared that once important foreign producers were established in Japan, national boundaries which protect Japan from huge foreign corporations with superior technology and marketing networks would be swept away.[10] Nevertheless, he moderated this view to conform to the necessary degree of foreign cooperation. He stated that Japan should bring its level of liberalization of capital to that of Western countries, as requested by OECD, but the period of adjustment should be three to five years from 1967 and timed according to Japan's judgment and initiative.

In July 1967, the Japanese government finally announced its five-year program of capital liberalization. In this program, Japanese industry was divided into three categories. Included in the first category were

[9] Noritake Kobayashi, "Some Organization Problems," *Joint Ventures and Japan*, ed. Robert J. Ballon (Tokyo: Charles E. Tuttle, 1967), p. 99.

[10] Morinosuke Kajima, *Modern Japan's Foreign Policy* (Tokyo: Charles E. Tuttle, 1969), pp. 255–56.

those industrial lines in which foreign capital investment would be automatically approved up to 100 percent, or in wholly-owned foreign subsidiaries. The second category permitted investment in joint ventures of as much as 50 percent of foreign capital and these would be automatically approved provided there was no foreign management or control. The third category of industries were those that would be approved only on a case-by-case basis, if at all. [11]

Japan entered upon implementation of this program at a slow pace and naturally it liberalized more in the less sensitive areas initially. It was considered that those industries in the category open to complete foreign ownership not only were strong enough to stand up to foreign competition, but also some industries were unlikely to attract any foreign capital in large amounts.

In 1967, in the first round of capital liberalization, only seventeen industries in the first category of one hundred percent ownership, were approved. Thirty-three in the second category—50 percent foreign ownership—were approved. International response was negative and a second round was implemented in March 1969. On 1 September 1970, a third round was effected and a fourth on 4 August 1971. By this time, 228 industrial lines (about 30 percent of Japan's industry) were opened to up to full foreign ownership. Most of the remainder were limited to 50 percent ownership and only seven lines remained closed—oil refining and sales, electronic computers and computer peripheral equipment, data processing, leather products, retail chains of more than eleven stores, agriculture-forestry-fishery enterprises, and real estate. [12] The limit on cumulative foreign share holding in already existing Japanese enterprises was up to only 25 percent. The more open categories applied to new joint ventures or new wholly owned firms.

The OECD and the United States government remained dissatisfied with the Japanese effort even though plans for a further fifth round within a year or two were mooted as soon as the fourth round was announced. By announcing that all industry would be open to some degree of foreign participation, the Japanese government hoped to complete the liberalization program in capital investment but business counter-pressure in Japan was too strong.

In 1967, the European Common Market tended toward protective tariffs, and economic difficulties attendant on the Vietnam War began

[11] Herbert Glazer, *The International Businessman in Japan* (Tokyo: Sophia University in cooperation with Charles E. Tuttle, 1968), pp. 34-42. Noritake Kobayashi, "Through Japanese Eyes," *The World of Japanese Business* by T. F. M. Adams and N. Kobayashi (Tokyo and Palo Alto: Kodansha International, 1969), pp. 229-57.

[12] *Japan Times Weekly*, International Edition, Vol. XI, No. 32 (7 August 1971), p. 1.

to occur in the United States. Similar to the situation which had occurred under the Kennedy Administration when a special levy was considered on cotton textiles, special levies on some imports were again urged in the United States. In October 1967, the Emergency Committee for American Trade with about fifty prominent business leaders as members was organized by former Undersecretary of State George Ball. The committee aimed at promoting freer trade and economic relations by pressing for removal of Japanese trade and capital investment barriers. In 1971 the committee argued that if Japan reduced her high levels of protectionism, the American president might be inclined to reciprocate by removing or lowering the 10 percent surcharge. While reducing barriers to American imports would help the American balance of payments, the freer movement of American investment would worsen the balance by increasing the outflow of capital, which was the largest source of imbalance in payments of the United States. However, it did facilitate the invasion of the large American firms into Western Europe and Canada, and it was only in Japan that they were still excluded.

The American government began to press more vigorously than before for entry of foreign investment into Japan and also for the elimination of Japanese import quotas to protect Japanese agriculture and industry. The Emergency Committee for American Trade was alleged to have urged the American cabinet secretaries to threaten Japan with retaliation at the Joint United States-Japan Trade and Economic Affairs Committee.[13] Japan was reluctant to permit foreign firms to acquire ownership or control of Japanese companies. Part of this reluctance stemmed from the mid-nineteenth century when foreign states dominated Japan's foreign trade and imposed rigid treaty tariffs on Japan. Japan continued to fear foreign ownership and control, especially in those industries it considered essential to its economy. Although a great deal of foreign investment has been put into Japan in recent years, especially in the form of loans, share ownership in Japanese firms has been strictly limited. Only 8 percent foreign ownership of a Japanese firm's stock was permitted without approval of the Foreign Investment Council but in the case of utilities, banking, and mining this was limited to 5 percent. Even when a new joint venture promised to introduce new techniques, foreign ownership was limited to 49 percent to prevent foreign control.[14]

A major cause of unremitting American dissatisfaction with Japanese liberalization measures was that the lines in which American business wished to invest tended to be the last liberalized. However, even in

---

[13] *Nihon Keizai Shimbun*, 14 August 1969, evening edition, p. 3.

[14] G. C. Allen, "Japan's Place in Trade Strategy," *Trade Strategy and the Asian-Pacific Region*, ed. Hugh Corbet (Toronto: University of Toronto Press, 1970), p. 69.

these areas Japan finally began to yield in the early 1970s, and the Japanese government promised to open one of the most sensitive areas, the computer industry, to foreign capital. To reduce American pressure in 1971, Japan liberalized imports of peripheral components expected to amount to half of the total value of computer imports. Banking, securities dealing, and whisky distilling, which foreigners desired to enter, continued to be limited to 50 percent ownership despite the hope of some Japanese government leaders allowing full ownership in 1971.

Despite Japanese protectionism, there were more American firms in Japan than Japanese firms in the United States. This probably reflects the attractiveness of the Japanese market and low Japanese labor costs as well as entrepreneurial initiative which was high among American businessmen. The comparative freedom of entry for Japanese business-men to the United States did not offset the difficulties they found in operating in a foreign cultural environment when they lacked the necessary self-confidence. Having relied on the large Japanese trading firms to represent them abroad for so long, Japanese entrepreneurs were not prepared to enter directly into manufacturing in the United States.

Quota Restrictions

Quota restrictions were an important barrier to foreign business with Japan. In 1962 and 1963 under Prime Minister Ikeda, the Japanese government had removed limitations, to an important extent, on the fixed quantities permitted to be imported, but for the balance of the decade there was relatively little progress toward removing the remaining quotas. The Japanese government officials claimed that of those items that were controlled in 1959 about 93 percent were decontrolled in the 1960s. However, it was precisely in the items still controlled that businessmen desired to sell more. A few important items which were not on the Japanese control or quota list of 1959 were outside this percentage. Even in 1964 when quotas were removed from automobiles the tariff and commodity taxes still continued to exclude them.

As can be seen in table 7.4, Japan restricted more imports than did other major trading states, as shown in GATT records. The industrialized states began to argue for the elimination of Japanese import quotas after the success of the Kennedy Round and a schedule of capital liberalization. Canada, Australia, and New Zealand wanted to gain entry for their agricultural products if not to gain some preferential treatment in the Japanese market. The United States, which was Japan's major trading partner, was anxious to increase its exports to Japan by reducing Japanese protective barriers to its products.

At the twenty-fifth meeting of the GATT participants at Geneva, it was agreed to have preparatory talks on such Japanese quantitative

TABLE 7.4

RESTRICTED IMPORT QUOTAS OF INDUSTRIALIZED COUNTRIES

Country	Industrial	Agricultural	Total Quotas
Japan	52	68	120
France	31	39	70
Denmark	2	63	65
Norway	1	50	51
West Germany	21	22	43
Austria	5	36	41
Italy	12	14	26
Britain	8	14	22
Benelux	6	12	18
Canada	1	3	4
Sweden	0	2	2

NOTE: Japan's figures were as of 1 April 1969 and the others according to GATT records.

SOURCE: Keidanren, *Nichi-Bei Keizai no Sho Mondai* (Tokyo: Keidanren, 1969), p. 122.

restrictions on imports, which were later held in November 1968. At the meetings, the American officials insisted that the Japanese quota restrictions were in violation of GATT requirements and must be rectified immediately. The Japanese said that their internal political and economic situation made complete and immediate liberalization impossible, but it did not foreclose eventual compliance. The United States then asked to open talks as soon as possible and Japan agreed. However, before these further meetings were held, the Japanese cabinet, on 17 December, announced: "We would like to consider imports that are restricted both quickly and fully. We have decided to carry out liberalization to a substantial degree in the next two or three years."[15] This was in accord with the procedure initiated in November 1960 at the seventeenth meeting of GATT members at which it was agreed that each country with residual import restrictions would report annually to the GATT secretariat. At the request of any country affected by these restrictions, bilateral negotiations would have to be undertaken. If the negotiations proved fruitless the exporting country could take counter measures.

Under Sato, Japan's major trading partners in order of importance were the United States, Australia, and Canada. The United States absorbed about 30 percent of the total Japanese trade. Therefore, major concessions by Japan would have to be worked out with the United States first as it would probably have the greatest impact. As well, any concessions to a Western European country would be difficult to deny to the United States, especially as most favored nations clauses of commercial treaties made differential treatment difficult.

[15] Keizai Dantai Rengo Kai, *Nichi-Bei Keizai Kankei no Sho Mondai* (Tokyo, 1969), p. 121.

The Japanese government was determined to insure that any concessions it granted would be balanced, as far as practicable, by reciprocal concessions by the other party to remove its restrictions against Japan. In addition, Japanese officials were pressed by their own textile industry not to continue and certainly not to increase the "voluntary" restrictions, which they had been forced to accept on threat of imposition of import restrictions by the United States. Although both Japan and the United States threatened to submit the matter to GATT, neither country did so nor did either country submit it to its own national legislature. Both hoped to induce the other to give way without resorting to either national or international authoritative bodies before which they would be exposed to the interference of domestic opposition or international attention.

In 1968, by Japanese reckoning, the United States was restricting the importation of thirty-eight types of textiles, seventeen kinds of steel, and eighteen other items through the indirect and unofficial (but officially arranged) Japanese voluntary quota system. Another source of discontent for Japan was the manner in which some American tariffs were levied, not on the import price but on the American sales price or in some cases on the price in the producing country.[16] Also, the "buy American" campaign in the United States, which was intended to reduce imports and ease the pressure on the unfavorable balance of payments, was objected to as being a form of protectionism contrary to the principle of free trade that both countries upheld.

In 1968, rather than a frontal attack on the whole range of Japanese quota restrictions, the United States worked out and presented to Japan a list of some thirty-eight items centering on agricultural products and electronic equipment, such as computers, which the United States wished to export to Japan. These were items that Japan feared to decontrol because of the possible impact on its domestic industry and agriculture as well as the political pressure stemming from the respective sectors of the economy. American officials and businessmen became increasingly impatient with Japan as their trade position deteriorated at the end of the 1960s and early 1970s. For more than a decade Japan had liberalized the least contentious items and held back on the desired ones. American business competitors' doubts about Japanese sincerity to liberalize tended to increase.

Officials in the Japanese foreign ministry and many leaders of the major business association, the Federation of Economic Organizations, felt there was no alternative to substantial liberalization if Japan were to continue to expand its trade. Much of its essential raw materials

---

[16] David R. Francis, "Nontariff Trade Barriers Hardest to Crack," *Christian Science Monitor*, 24 July 1971, p. 10. Congress has refused to approve legislation permitting elimination of tariff on the American selling price.

came from the industrialized countries which Japan could not afford to alienate through protectionist policies, even if the offending nations practised protectionism themselves. The protective attitude of the Japanese trade and finance ministries as well as the protected industries themselves were a potent counterforce which slowed progress on the desired long-range goal in Japan just as it had done in America. Temporary economic difficulties in both countries added to the insistent demands for protective relief which were finally to produce the Nixon 10 percent surcharge that startled the world in August 1971. Japanese government officials as well as businessmen were also heirs to a long tradition of formal and informal guidance and control which had facilitated and protected Japan in its struggle against the strong Western powers during the process of industrialization. They were also culturally attuned to a greater degree of group collectivism than Western businessmen and officials and probably did not appreciate the extent to which they had fallen behind the freedom of trade in Western Europe and the United States.[17]

The result of the need to liberalize was that Japanese leaders quite sincerely intended to push ahead with liberalization of import quotas and they were galvanized into greater action by pressure from foreign sources in 1968. However, the American hope of immediate and substantial relief at the December 1968 Japanese-American meeting was doomed to disappointment. Japanese officials considered liberalizing about one-half of the thirty-eight items proposed by the United States, and those were principally industrial products.[18] It should be remembered in this connection that all industrialized countries engaged in extensive protection of their own agriculture and that this sector of the economy is the worst offender against free trade principles.

Japan made few concessions on agricultural products and gave some qualified agreement on computer imports, although Philip Trezise, the American delegation leader, confessed to being "personally disappointed" at the result.[19] Despite the efforts of the Japanese Foreign Vice-Minister, Haruki Mori, the finance, agriculture, and trade ministries prevented any further concessions. Argument arose over aircraft radar, which Japan contended was exempted by article XXI of GATT as war materiel which could be controlled for the sake of security.

In May 1969, the first important Japanese business mission to the United States during the Nixon administration took place. The mission visited the southern cotton-producing states where the textile industry was particularly hostile toward Japanese competition. The mission was

---

[17] Allen, "Japan's Place in Trade Strategy," pp. 68–69.
[18] Asahi Shimbun, 6 December 1968, p. 1.
[19] New York Times, 29 December 1968, p. 6.

led by Masao Anzai, president of the Showa Denko Company and prominent leader of the Japan Federation of Employers' Organizations. The mission also visited Washington where it thought that the new administration considered Japan a major economic power which had to accept its responsibility to liberalize trade as well as capital. [20]

The United States Secretary of Commerce, Maurice Stans, told the Japanese business delegation that he found it hard to understand restrictions on capital transactions when Japan was eager to carry its economic expansion even further. Anzai replied that insistence on voluntary restrictions in textiles was a form of controlled economy contrary to the tradition of economic freedom in the United States and he feared it would lead to shrinkage of world trade. The deputy chief of the mission, Toyosaburo Taniguchi, chairman of the Toyo Spinning Company, said the American textile industry had failed to develop in accordance with the times. To depend on import restrictions was to weaken its essential character. Stans was unable to accept this view. He said that the voluntary Japanese restrictions on textile exports were intended to insure an orderly market and avoid import restrictions which might be imposed by Congress.

On his visit to Japan later that same month, Stans made a strong plea for prompt relaxation of Japanese investment controls on the basis of reciprocity. He also referred to the enormous surplus with the United States in trade and Japan's responsibility as the second largest producer in the free world. More important was the strong stand he took on the need for continued voluntary restriction on textile exports to the United States. [21]

While Japanese steel manufacturers agreed to hold their exports to 4.4 million tons, a level which had been reached the year before, the textile producers pressed for removal of the voluntary quotas which were also opposed by the ministry of trade. When the Japanese Foreign Minister Aichi visited Washington on 3 June 1969, to participate in a discussion on the return of Okinawa, he talked to Stans, who at this time took a less insistent position. Stans said that he wished to avoid the necessity of restrictive legislation in the United States and proposed to consider the voluntary quotas further at the September meeting of GATT. [22] Aichi maintained that the voluntary restrictions were irrational but avoided a sharp exchange with the secretary.

In October, talks on import quotas by Japan were finally resumed

[20] *Asahi Shimbun*, 30 April 1969, evening edition, p. 1.
[21] Secretary Stans's attitude in Japan was criticized by the American author, Frank Gibney, as "ham-handed pressure" which drew an equally blunt reply. *Japan Times*, 8 October 1969, p. 2.
[22] *Asahi Shimbun*, 4 June 1969, evening edition, p. 1.

in Tokyo. The American mission, which was led by Philip Trezise, did not limit itself to any particular items for decontrol but pressed for the removal of all quantitative import controls under the more insistent Nixon administration.[23] Haruki Mori, the Japanese delegation leader, attributed this greater pressure to the strong gains in trade which Japan continued to make with the United States. Trezise was reported to have told the Japanese delegation leaders that Japan was the only industrialized nation in the world with a favorable balance of payments that still maintained quotas on imports.[24] He estimated that the 1969 Japanese trade surplus would be $4 billion and the 1970 surplus would be $5 billion—figures that could not be tolerated without retaliation by the United States Congress.[25]

In its economic report of December 1969, the Japanese foreign ministry indicated support for further liberalization. The ministry urged completion within a few years of decontrol of trade and capital transactions which had been underway since 1960. It affirmed that residual import restrictions were in violation of the rules of GATT and that their elimination would curb price increases in Japan as well as stimulate modernization of Japanese industry. Japan, it thought, should aim at reducing its restrictions to the levels of Italy and Britain. It also advised the removal of non-tariff barriers such as the commodity taxes on coffee and cocoa. This was implemented later and marked a major agricultural concession. Foreign capital investment liberalization was urged to bring in needed technology to spur Japanese industry. The ministry also recommended that the number of industries in which foreigners could invest freely should be increased to keep pace with countries overseas.[26]

As pressure mounted between Japan and the United States over voluntary quotas on textile exports from Japan, the Japanese government was urged to make concessions on freeing trade quotas further. When Donald Kendall, president of the Pepsi Cola Company and chairman of the Emergency Committee for American Trade, came to Japan in March 1970, he pleaded for freeing some of the restricted items, even if GATT gave a waver to permit quotas on them. After the Washington conference on voluntary textile quotas failed to reach agreement, the Japanese Minister of International Trade and Industry, Kiichi Miyazawa, also urged the liberalization of quotas on Japanese imports and foreign

[23] *Japan Times*, 10 October 1969, pp. 1 and 4.
[24] He must have been misquoted. GATT reports show virtually all industrialized states have import quotas.
[25] These amounts must refer to the total of several years from 1965 in the trade surplus with the United States. The actual cumulative total by 1970 was $3,850 million. Vancouver *Sun*, 14 October 1969 and "Some Questions and Answers," p. 5.
[26] *Japan Times Weekly*, International Edition, Vol. IX, No. 52 (27 December 1969), p. 8.

capital investment. He suggested advancing the dates of those items already scheduled for decontrol. In early September 1970, the Japanese cabinet conformed to these proposals by advancing the decontrol dates. Some ninety controlled items were to be reduced to less than forty by the end of September 1971, and eight items were freed immediately. Of the remaining ninety, ten more were due to be decontrolled by the end of the year, twenty by the end of March, and twenty more by the end of September 1972.[27] The remaining forty would leave Japan at a level comparable with West Germany.

Automobile Confrontation

The automobile was one product which caused particularly bad feelings between Japan and the United States. The American automobile manufacturers pressed hard to obtain entry for their products in the Japanese market and desired to bring in capital to establish their own subsidiaries or joint ventures. However, Japan's high tariff and commodity taxes virtually excluded foreign cars and car parts. In fact, no foreign manufacturer was allowed to make cars in Japan. On the other hand, Japan had free access to the American and other foreign markets. This situation was bound to produce serious friction and, in fact, did produce strong pressure for Japan to liberalize its import restrictions on automobiles.

Although Japan feared the competitive power of the foreign manufacturers such as Ford, General Motors, and Chrysler, its own industry appeared to be very strong and growing stronger. In 1967, the Japanese automobile industry was second only to the United States in output of cars, and it resembled the powerful American industry in its makeup. Passenger cars made up 70 percent of its output compared to 80 percent of the American automobile production. Its competitive strength was suggested by the average yearly increase in production of 23 percent in the last half of the 1960s. Nevertheless, Katsuji Kawamata, the president of the Japan Automobile Industry Association and head of Nissan Motors, one of the largest automobile manufacturers in Japan, expressed Japanese businessmen's fear that the introduction of the American "Big Three" into Japan would utterly ruin or assimilate Japanese automobile manufacturers.[28] Japanese officials, especially those in the ministry of trade, were strongly disposed to protect their own industries.

[27] *Japan Times Weekly*, International Edition, Vol. X, No. 38 (19 September 1970), p. 8. Actually by April 1972 Japanese quotas were reduced to 33 items when the United States was restricting 21% of all industrial imports as compared to 8% in Japan, 4.3% in the European Market and 0.4% in Canada.

[28] "Opposition to Arguments for the Liberalization of Passenger Cars. . . . Is It All Right to Be Made into a Colony?" *Asahi Janaru*, Vol. X, No. 30 (21 July 1968), pp. 86–88.

The American government represented its industrialists when it pressed Japan at the Sixth Joint Economic Affairs Committee of the cabinet ministers of the two countries to convene a meeting to discuss the automobile question. Japan was unable to refuse, but tried to diminish the impact of the meeting by keeping it informal and by holding it at the Tokyo headquarters of the Federation of Economic Organizations, the leading business association in Japan. The Japanese group was headed by Kawamata, and included officials of the foreign, finance, trade, and home ministries as well as leading businessmen. The American group was headed by a government representative, Philip H. Trezise, who was to be the chief American negotiator on liberalization issues in the succeeding five years. His group contained officials from the commerce department as well as executives of the Ford Motor Company.

As was to be expected, the American side asked the Japanese to lower the high tariff, the sales tax on large passenger cars, and the local car tax. They also wanted quantitative restrictions or quotas to be removed on the importation of automobile engines and chassis into Japan. In addition, they wanted American car manufacturers to be permitted to invest in automobile manufacturing in Japan—the most sensitive area of all.

The Japanese resisted all these demands diplomatically, pleading that the tariff was to be lowered under the Kennedy Round agreement. The high sales and automobile taxes would remain because they were based on the ability to pay. This did not discriminate against American cars as such but it did have the effect of excluding the large American-made automobiles. The Japanese asserted that they could not compete if engines and other parts were liberalized or if foreign investment was permitted.

As Japan's industry grew in strength under the Sato Cabinet and its automobiles continued to flood the foreign markets, Japan could not reasonably continue to exclude foreign automotive products from its own market. This was acknowledged by Japan's business leaders, such as Kogoro Uemura, the president of the Federation of Economic Organizations, as well as by the government leaders in the cabinet. However, it was difficult to reorient officials and businessmen who were accustomed to a comparatively fragile Japanese economy easily damaged by any change in the economic situation from abroad.

In 1968, the Japanese government was compelled to act despite the hesitation of many officials and businessmen. On 11 June, it announced that the tariff on cars would be reduced and that quantitative restrictions on imports would be eased. The tariff was to be cut in half and large-model cars and used cars were to be permitted entry. Rather than being satisfied, the United States immediately pressed for an even greater degree of liberalization, and the American government threatened to appeal to

GATT. Japan then agreed to increase engine imports to 30,000 a year starting in 1969. As the American manufacturers had only approached Japanese firms informally in an effort to plan joint ventures, the Japanese action went even further than the Americans had requested. Japan next agreed to increase engine imports to 50,000 in 1969 and by 1971 to allow 90,000 to 95,000 engines to be imported. In August 1968, the Japanese government said that the importation of engines and parts would be completely freed of quantitative restrictions by the beginning of 1972 if economic conditions continued to be favorable. Chassis with engines would be permitted entry in the fall of 1968, and the government would be willing to consider participation of foreign makers in the assembly of these imports.

It was direct American participation in the manufacture of automobiles in Japan through investment (capital import) that was most feared by the Japanese manufacturers. The concessions to ease import quotas in 1969 was designed to dampen the American diplomatic pressure but not to allow capital investment on the part of the American automobile manufacturers. The American industry complained to the American state department in 1969 that Japanese capital restrictions were contrary to the treaty of commerce between Japan and the United States. Within Japan, the Japanese automobile manufacturers had pledged to each other not to collaborate with the American Big Three except to a limited extent in the use of American car components and cooperation in car sales.

The common front of the Japanese industry was broken in May 1969 when Chrysler announced plans to invest in Mitsubishi Motors. Vice-President Makita of Mitsubishi Heavy Industries, which owned Mitsubishi Motors, said they planned to import engines, fabricate cars in Japan, and export completed models once capital liberalization was undertaken. In September 1969, the Japan Automobile Industry Association said that it would not object to fifty-fifty joint ventures after 1971. In October 1969, the ministry of trade then announced that joint enterprises would be permitted from October 1971, even though a few months earlier the Japanese industry had hoped that capital liberalization could be held off until 1974.

The Japanese capitulation, however, was far from complete. The government intended that the introduction of foreign capital should be at a moderate pace to prevent any undue disruption of the domestic market for the Japanese producers. Therefore, the Foreign Investment Council of the finance ministry approved the application of Chrysler to participate in Mitsubishi Motors because the strong Japanese firm was not likely to be easily dominated by its foreign partner. Chrysler was permitted to acquire 15 percent of the Mitsubishi Motors stock by 30 September 1971 and to purchase a further 10 percent in each of the next two years. Similar arrangements were planned by General Motors and Isuzu as well as by Ford and the Toyo Kogyo Company. The Japanese authorities did not yield to the American desire for wholly owned subsidiaries. Also, they did not intend that the Japanese partners in joint ventures should be subordinate to the foreign partners but, rather, that the Japanese partners should retain control. The firms General Motors and Ford were considering as partners were weaker than the major Japanese manufacturers of cars, and this weakness gave the Japanese finance and trade officials some hesitation about the proposals. However, approval was finally given.

The Japanese government program limited foreign participation in automobile manufacturing joint ventures to 50 percent for new firms. To invest in an existing firm, a single foreign investor was normally limited to 7 percent of the stock and foreign holdings could not exceed 25 percent in total. Although the Americans were far from satisfied, the Japanese had made major concessions and had moved substantially in the direction of liberalization at the behest of three of the world's strongest international corporations.

Textile Confrontation

The conflict between Japan and the United States in 1970 and 1971 over the so-called voluntary quotas on textiles proved to be the most severe clash Japan had with any country since regaining its independence in 1952. The conflict was due more to what it symbolized than to any damages to the textile trade. Textiles were, in fact, a declining industry for Japan and consequently of diminishing importance. In 1969, foreign textile imports to the United States constituted only 8.5 percent of the textiles and textile products consumed in the United States, and in terms of dollar value only amounted to 4.2 percent of the American market. Of the textile imports to the United States, Japan was responsible for only about half but it was Japan that bore the brunt of American fears of low-cost foreign imports despite the relatively minor importance of the trade.

An economic slowdown in the world economy in 1970, similar to that of 1961, stimulated strong demands for protection from both manufacturers and workers in the United States. Japan already had been subjected to voluntary quotas on cotton goods during the Ikeda regime and these were still in effect and firmly entrenched by international agreement arranged through GATT. The American textile industry was anxious to obtain similar restrictions on woolen and synthetic textiles but the Japanese industry was equally eager to forestall such a move.

President Nixon's need for retaining valuable political support, which represented the textile industry, was an added factor in what was an almost classic case of international trade conflict. The president's frustration in seeking Japanese accommodation over textiles may well have precipitated his 10 percent surcharge of 15 August 1971.

When Nixon took office in 1969, he was reported to have promised to obtain Japanese agreement to voluntary quotas on woolen and synthetic textiles. As a result, the Secretary of Commerce, Maurice Stans, was sent to Japan in May 1969 to seek voluntary restraints on the part of the Japanese industry on these products. At the July meeting of the Joint Economic Affairs Committee of cabinet ministers of both countries, both Stans and the United States Secretary of State, William Rogers, repeated their demands for voluntary quotas in order to prevent the American government again legislating restrictions on Japanese textile imports. The Japanese industry was strongly opposed to any further voluntary restrictions and sent a mission to the United States to investigate the damage alleged by the American producers. After their investigation they reported that they found virtually no evidence of injury to the American producers.

When Prime Minister Sato went to Washington in November 1969 to finalize the agreement for the return of Okinawa, no formal statement was issued concerning textiles. However, President Nixon was reported to have urged the prime minister to obtain an agreement from the Japanese textile manufacturers to voluntarily restrict woolen and synthetic textile exports to a substantial degree. The prime minister was said to have stated that he would take steps to solve the problem *(zensho suru)*. The president interpreted this as a commitment by the Japanese. But the prime minister thought all he had agreed to was to try to persuade Japanese industrialists to accede to American wishes. He did not intend to force compliance and the Japanese industry interpreted this to mean that only moral suasion was being applied. The industrialists were not inclined to go very far to meet the American demands.

In early 1970, intergovernmental proposals were exchanged which dealt with categories of wool and synthetic items to be restricted for a period as long as five years. The Japanese industry was opposed to any lengthy controls and wanted a flexible system such as one in which unfilled quotas in one category could be transferred to another. The American industry wished to set strict limits by categories with quick application of stoppage in case these were approached. The Japanese textile manu-facturers organized their own lobbying group to resist pressure. Even the eloquent arguments of the Minister of Trade Miyazawa were of no avail when he met with the lobby. To the persuasion of Japanese officials was added the advice of the Emergency Committee for American Trade which aimed at preventing American protective measures by inducing Japanese businessmen to observe moderation and discretion in their exports to the United States. The committee sent its chairman, Donald Kendall, to Japan to propose a one-year temporary agreement while damage was being assessed. The secretary-general of OECD, Oliver Long, was also greatly concerned over the threat of American protective legislation which was pending in the United States House of Representatives under the ways and means committee chaired by Wilbur Mills. This move threatened to reverse the trend toward freer trade among the advanced industrial states. Long proposed an international working party from GATT to provide selective export controls for a short period on synthetic and woolen textiles with a temporary arrangement between the United States and Japan in the interim. Even the Japanese ministry of trade urged an international approach of this nature. The Japanese textile producers, however, were not prepared to accept any of these proposals, and consequently these efforts were unsuccessful.

In October 1970 when Prime Minister Sato went to New York to attend meetings of the United Nations, he stopped in Washington to meet President Nixon, and they announced that government negotiations would be undertaken to resolve the differences. This time the Japanese Ambassador to the United States, Nobuhiko Ushiba, held talks with the special assistant to the president, Peter Flanigan, but still no solution was reached. Meanwhile the bill proposed by Wilbur Mills to enact protective legislation against textile imports failed to pass Congress.

In March 1971, the Japanese textile industry undertook to implement its own voluntary quota plan for three years and to keep textile export increases within 5 or 6 percent annually. However, the American industry did not regard this as sufficiently restrictive. When the president used own power to restrict imports by the 10 percent surcharge in August, the Japanese government decided to compel its industry to conform to a solution satisfactory to the United States. The president's envoy, David Kennedy, and the new Japanese Minister of Trade, Kakuei Tanaka, finally reached agreement in Japan, and they signed a memorandum on 15 October 1971 in Tokyo. The result was a compromise; it limited the period to three years, as the Japanese had wished, but generally required fixed limits by categories of textiles which could not be exceeded. Japan's agreement resulted in the end of the surcharge against it.

Since the Second World War, freer trade has been a source of prosperity and strength so that any trend toward protectionism is bound to injure all countries involved in much foreign trade. This is even more true for Japan than it is for the United States because Japan is more dependent on foreign trade and, in fact, has a much larger percentage of its trade with the United States than the United States has with Japan. In any economic confrontation between the countries, Japan is therefore comparatively weak. A significant amount of Japan's exports were affected by the Nixon surcharge. Of its exports 94 percent, or more than $5 billion, were subject to the surcharge which amounted to $2.5 billion.[29]

However protectionist Japan may have been under the Ikeda Cabinets or the early Sato Cabinets, it has substantially liberalized the entry of foreign products and investment to Japan. After the Kennedy Round, Japan's tariffs averaged 9.5 percent compared to the American level of 9.6 percent. The Japanese government carried out final tariff cuts nine months in advance, on 1 April 1971, and reduced its tariffs on thirty categories of food and consumer goods below the levels agreed in the Kennedy Round in April and June 1971. In addition, less than 4 percent of Japan's imports are limited by quotas and the number of items is being reduced further. Restricted items were reduced to about thirty items on 31 March 1972 while the United States ostensibly had restrictions on only five items; there were said to be as many as eighty products on which Japan "voluntarily" limited exports under American pressure. These, of course, were equivalent to American quotas.

Although Japan has been slow to meet international trade and investment demands for liberalization, it has done so to a substantial degree at a time when the United States seemed to be moving toward protectionism. While the effect of such action has been minimized by negotiations, the arbitrary way that the action of 15 August 1971 was taken by the United States produced a psychological shock to Japanese leaders and signaled a new and less intimate relationship between the countries. This was, of course, even more serious when it was accompanied by unusual steps to improve relations between the United States and China in 1971 and 1972, again without consultation with Japan and without much willingness to keep it informed of the steps being negotiated with China. As Japan had been forced more or less into following the American anti-China policies, this placed Japan in a particularly embarassing position.

The Nixon surcharge and textile measures in 1971 seemed severe methods to deal with Japan just when it was making substantial moves to liberalize its trade. Multilateral negotiations and more diplomatic bilateral negotiations will probably not reduce the confrontation between Japan and the United States as long as the balance of trade of the United States is so adverse. Despite Japan's acceptance of liberalization in principle, and to a major extent in action, Japan only slowly realized the enormous economic impact of its trade and the need to keep it

[29] United States-Japan Trade Council, *What are the Facts About U.S.-Japan Economic Relations?* (Washington, D.C., 1971), p. 5.

under adequate control. This is required for the sake of its crucial relations with the advanced states on which its prosperity and related goals depend. The skill with which it handles these trade and financial problems may well be more important than any other in the years ahead.

8

Japan's Role in Asia

UNDER SATO, Japan became a leading power in Asia as it pursued its main goals of prosperity, security, and gaining recognition as a leading world power. This was done primarily through its programs of aid and trade. The expanding markets for its manufacturers and its access to the essential raw materials assisted its own economic development.

The grants, loans, and credits, which Japan classed as economic aid, to its non-Communist neighbors increased sixfold in the period 1963 to 1970. This aid not only promoted the business of those Japanese firms participating in the various aid projects but also made Japanese trade and investment more welcome abroad. The assistance which Japan gave did much to counter the effect of Asian sensitivity to the aggressiveness of Japanese businessmen and the fears by the Asians of Japanese economic domination. By virtue of its aid activities, which emphasized Asia, it was able to play a major role as an advanced industrialized state, which was recognized through its membership in the Organization of Economic Cooperation and Development. This aspect became increasingly important and by 1970 Japan was second only to the United States in terms of the amount of aid funds it was giving to the developing countries. In 1971, further evidence of Japan's growing stature in the Asian area were the requests for Japanese economic support from its communist neighbors, the Soviet Union, North Vietnam, North Korea, and Mongolia, each of which tried to improve relations and obtain Japanese economic assistance. The approach by these countries to Japan was, in part, to counter the improved relations between the United States and the People's Republic of China.

Japan's relations with its non-Communist neighbors reflected its policy of non-intervention and the avoidance of the use of military power, and this non-military role assisted Japan in reducing the fears of its neighbors. Its trade and aid provided a stabilizing influence on local regimes and was intended as a substitute for a regional military activity. However, Japan's communist neighbors still felt threatened by the American military bases in Japan and objected strongly to Japanese security cooperation with its great power ally. Besides contributing to Japan's prosperity, the increasing trade with such countries as China and the Soviet Union was intended to mollify them on security matters. Nevertheless, in trade negotiations China constantly pressed for a reduction of the security cooperation of Japan with the United States and urged that it break off recognition of Taiwan and abrogate the peace treaty with it.

Success in gaining recognition as a leading power followed from Japan's increased prosperity, security, and improved relations in Asia. It was attained through increased trade and investment in all of the countries of the region and it was augmented by Japan's participation in a number of regional conferences and institutions. Japan played a major role in the establishment of the Asian Development Bank and became a chief donor country. In the Southeast Asian Development Conferences, Japan

TABLE 8.1
JAPAN'S EXTERNAL TRADE, 1969-71
(IN THOUSANDS OF DOLLARS)

Country	1969	1970	1971
Japan's Total Trade	31,012,550	38,198,855	43,730,630
Principal Pacific Rim Partners			
United States	9,047,720	11,499,398	12,473,332
Australia	1,718,990	2,906,734	2,471,201
Canada	1,150,452	1,491,855	1,880,547
Principal Asian Neighbors			
Indonesia	633,130	952,333	1,307,302
Taiwan	786,874	1,013,210	1,374,217
South Korea	901,118	1,047,145	1,130,108
Philippines	943,648	987,182	978,599
China	625,343	822,696	901,360
Hong Kong	682,710	792,089	885,404
Soviet Union	729,810	821,970	873,147
Thailand	601,258	638,793	674,969
Singapore	378,531	509,573	621,881
Ryukyus	406,024	494,164	705,253
India	416,990	493,179	580,441
Malaysia	540,189	585,359	576,588

SOURCE: Japan, Gaimu Sho, *Waga Gaiko no Kinkyo* (Tokyo: Finance Ministry Printing Bureau, 1971), No. 15 (1971), pp. 480-93. Japan, Ministry of Finance, Customs Bureau, *Japan Exports and Imports, Country, By Commodity*, Jan.-Dec. 1971 (Tokyo: Japan Tariff Association, 1972), table 1. *Asahi Nenkan 1973*, p. 306.

established itself as a leader in the efforts to inaugurate more effective joint economic development plans. Also in the matter of military conflict in Indochina, Japan played a role in attempting to mediate the conflict caused by the American invasion of Cambodia.

Japan's trade with the Asian countries increased about threefold in the 1960s, but its trade with other parts of the world increased at an even greater rate. The result was a decline in the Asian percentage share of Japan's total trade from 30 percent in 1951 to 20 percent at the end of the Ikeda Cabinet. During the Sato Cabinet, the Asian share initially increased slightly and then grew at about the same rate as its global trade elsewhere. In the period of the mid-1930s, more than half of Japan's trade had been with its Asian neighbors, particularly South Korea, Taiwan and China. However, today these countries have less than one-quarter of Japan's trade. Now 40 percent of Japan's trade is with Canada, Australia, and the United States, almost the reverse situation of the prewar period. Japan is correspondingly more dependent economically on its neighbors on the Pacific rim than on its nearer Asian neighbors. Being less vulnerable economically to its Asian neighbors gives Japan some leverage in its dealings with them, but this is balanced, to some extent, by the likelihood that any security threats to Japan will come from Asia, and tension or warfare there is of great concern.

Growing Regional Relations

Among Japan's largest Asian trading partners, Indonesia, Taiwan, South Korea, and the Philippines, the two most important to Japan are Taiwan and South Korea. These countries are important not only because of their trade and investment but also because they guard Japan's two flanks from less friendly neighbors. Culturally and historically, Japan has had the most intimate relations with these countries, and it has been drawn into their political and ideological confrontation with the communist regimes which claim to be the legitimate governments over their respective territories. Japan's trade and investment in Taiwan and South Korea represent not only a means to pursue its own prosperity but also a stake in the legitimacy and viability of the respective non-Communist governments. Japan's ties with Indonesia and the Philippines are more purely commercial ones, but here too it has a stake in the viability of the two non-Communist regimes. Greater business accessibility is one reason and the support of ideologically friendly regimes helps promote Japan's leadership of the developing nations of the Southeast Asian region.

In terms of military power, Japan's most important neighbor is the Soviet Union, which is also rich in resources and raw materials, but Japan's trade with it is not much larger than it is with China. The comparatively small countries of Taiwan and South Korea surpass both the Soviet Union and China in trade with Japan. Thus, the Communist type of economy has thus far offered less in the way of markets or investment opportunities to Japan than the much smaller capitalist economies. Besides this, the hostility or suspicion toward and from Communist neighbors still severely restricts economic relations between the countries. With the lessening of the political division and tension between Communist and non-Communist states in the Asian area, these restrictions may become less in the future. The Soviet Union is eager for Japanese capital and equipment to develop Siberia but it fears the entry of Japanese technicians and enterprises into the country. For its part, Japan desires its raw materials but fears Soviet economic domination as well as its military power.

China Trade and Recognition

The system by which Japan has dealt with China since 1952 has been through unofficial trade negotiations which were established before Sato became prime minister. This system was regularized by the Liao-Takasaki Memorandum of 1962, which provided for trade over a five-year period with an annual negotiation of details under the sponsorship of Diet members of the Liberal Democratic party. These meetings were in addition to the "friendly trade" carried on directly with China by smaller Japanese firms at the spring and fall trade fairs held in Canton. From 1963 to 1966 the volume of trade brought about by the Liao-Takasaki Memorandum more than tripled, from $64.1 million to $204.3 million, while the volume of the friendly firm trade arranged in Canton increased even more rapidly from $72.9 million to $416 million in the same period. Thereafter, memorandum trade declined both relatively and absolutely. By 1970 it was back to the 1963 level of $70 million or 8.7 percent of the total China trade. The fall off in trade was due to Chinese retaliation for unfriendly action of the Sato government.[1] The friendly trade was permitted to increase so that the overall trade with China continued to grow, except in the years 1967 and 1968. The large Japanese trading firms established subsidiaries to enter into the friendly trade and to evade the reductions demanded by China in the memorandum trade.

The Sato Cabinet persisted in its policy of "separating economics and politics" by refusing to move toward accepting Peking as the legitimate government of China even though the reduced memorandum trade reflected China's pressure on the Sato Cabinet to adopt a more pro-China policy. In February 1965, Sato said in the House of Representatives that he was bound by the letter that had been sent by former Prime

---

[1] *Japan Times Weekly*, International Edition, Vol. XI, No. 8 (20 February 1971), p. 1.

Minister Yoshida promising the Taiwan government that the Japanese government would not permit export contracts, which were financed by Export-Import Bank credit, to China. This encouraged the Taiwan officials and businessmen who came to Japan in their lobbying of Japanese government and business leaders to the discomfiture of the Chinese leaders who became increasingly angry at Prime Minister Sato for not reducing Japan's ties with Taiwan in favor of recognizing their government.

Concommitant with the large scale participation of the United States in the Vietnam War and with the appearance of the Cultural Revolution in China, relations between Japan and China grew even worse. Japan put obstacles in the way of unofficial exchanges of persons with China, especially after the Red Guard movement in China in 1966. In July 1967, Red Guards arrested some Japanese residents, including businessmen and reporters, and accused them of spying; they did not release them until 1969. Although the Red Guard did this to nationals of other countries as well, it had the effect of increasing the friction between Japan and China.

In 1967, when the Japanese prime minister made a series of trips to South Korea, Taiwan, and South Vietnam and gave verbal support to American efforts in Vietnam, it produced hostility and suspicion in China but without adversely affecting Japanese trade negotiations. In 1967, when the Liao-Takasaki Memorandum lapsed, there was no invitation from China for the Liberal Democratic Diet members, Yoshimi Furui and Seiichi Tagawa, to meet with the Chinese for the annual political discussions that took place at the same time as detailed trade talks. Suddenly, in November 1967, an abrupt summons arrived from the Chinese with which the Japanese were unable to comply immediately and therefore the year ended with no trade agreement of any kind.

To ease the tension, the Japanese Chief Cabinet Secretary, Kimura, told Furui that the Japanese government would not necessarily hold to the Yoshida letter policy of denying long-term credit to China through the Export-Import Bank. Dietmen, therefore, were able to conduct their delayed negotiations in Peking in February 1968 in a more friendly atmosphere. This promise was not sufficient to ensure a sound relationship and they obtained only a trade agreement of less than half the usual amount and for a reduced trading year. However, to obtain even this agreement, the Japanese were compelled to join in issuing a communique denouncing the Japanese government for following American imperialism and regarding China as an enemy.

In contrast to the setback in memorandum trade, friendly trade was permitted to expand between the countries so that the overall trade in 1968 declined only slightly from the previous year. Nevertheless, trade continued to be the chief medium of indirect communication between the two governments because of the political talks that accompanied it, but the trade encountered increased difficulties from China, which indicated its increasing displeasure with the Sato Cabinet's policy toward it.

In 1968, as several times before, Japan sponsored the motion in the United Nations General Assembly that would require a vote of two-thirds majority of the members to enable the Peking government to occupy China's seat. This was done to cooperate with the United States in preventing Peking from obtaining the seat. In October 1968, when Liberal Democrat Diet member Tagawa went to Peking to ask for the extension of the memorandum trade agreement and the release of the detained Japanese, he received no satisfaction to his requests from Foreign Minister Ch'en Yi because of Japan's position in the United Nations regarding the China seat, and again the year ended without any trade agreement.

In February 1969, the political discussions were resumed between the countries when Furui and Tagawa were finally allowed to return to Peking. In their discussions with the Chinese they reaffirmed their agreement with Prime Minister Chou-En-lai's three political principals: not to view China as an enemy, not to obstruct normalization of Japan-China relations, and not to participate in the plot to create two Chinas. The Chinese rejected the Sato Cabinet's policy of separating economics and politics by permitting only trade with China and preventing restoration of diplomatic relations. China demanded the abrogation of the peace treaty with Taiwan and the cessation of diplomatic relations between the countries. It also declared the Sato Cabinet to be following a policy of aggression in Asia by cooperating militarily with the United States in connection with the security treaty.

At the same time, China's attitude to Japan changed considerably with the end of the Cultural Revolution and the large-scale withdrawal of American military forces from Vietnam. In late 1969, the detained Japanese traders and reporters were finally released from prison in China. However, the Japan-China trade talks, which resumed in November, were abruptly cancelled when the Japanese prime minister went to Washington and affirmed that the security of South Korea was "essential" and that the security of Taiwan was "a most important factor in the security of Japan." These statements drew a sharp reaction from China. Nevertheless, after the display of annoyance, the Japanese negotiators were permitted to return for trade talks again after a few months delay. Six weeks of talks on trade were necessary before agreement was reached on memorandum trade in April 1970, and the annual amount was again sharply reduced to indicate the displeasure of China toward Japan. The joint political communique following the talks denounced Japanese militarism in view of the Sato acknowledgment of the security of Taiwan being important to the security of Japan.

In April 1970, Prime Minister Chou-En-lai utilized a new technique to bring pressure on Japan when he announced four trade principles which would exclude from China those Japanese companies which carried on trade with the purpose of aiding Taiwan and South Korea, those companies which invested in Taiwan or South Korea, those companies which cooperated in the American policy of aggression in Vietnam, and those companies which cooperated in American-related joint ventures in Japan. Although Japanese officials denounced these criteria, some of the Japanese firms which were anxious for the trade, accepted the demands. Most of the major steel companies in Japan announced compliance with the terms at once. The subsidiaries of the big Japanese trading firms had already separated their organizations from formal control by the parent firms in an effort to insure continued participation in the friendly trade with Peking. However, the desire for large-scale plant exports and other big contracts beyond the capacity of the small firms made the major trading firms eager to gain access to China trade on the mainland for themselves.

In the following year, major Japanese firms began to discontinue their participation in the Japan-Taiwan Cooperation Committee and the Japan-South Korean Economic Committee which were composed of important businessmen and officials. These committees issued anti-China pronouncements and lobbied for the anit-Communist governments in Japan.

Within the Liberal Democratic party, pressure increased for recognition of China as a large number of party members in the Diet joined with the members of the opposition parties in the Dietmen's League for Promotion of Restoration of Relations with China. Outside Japan, more countries, led by Canada and Italy, established diplomatic relations with China which had the effect of increasing the pressure on Japan. The major change forcing Japan to reconsider its China policies occurred when Peking was given China's place in the United Nations in October 1971 and Taiwan was expelled. Japan was the only major state to co-sponsor the American motion, which required a two-thirds majority to expel Taiwan—a motion that was defeated. Although Japan joined the United States in favoring the seating of China, provided Taiwan was not expelled, the pro-China opposition parties in the Diet brought a nonconfidence motion against the Japanese foreign minister for Japan's unfriendly attitude in the United Nations toward China. This failed to pass but a dozen Liberal Democrats broke party discipline and abstained from voting in the protest against the government's China policy.

Pressed from abroad and within for Japan to modify its policy toward China, the prime minister moved from a position in which he was willing to hold ministerial talks with China, even though he refused to even consider breaking off relations with Taiwan, to a position in which he himself became willing to go to China. He said he was no longer bound by the Yoshida promise to prevent plant exports to China with Export-Import Bank funds, which Taiwan alleged were tantamount to economic aid. The minister of trade indicated that Japan had set aside more than $250,000 in the budget for the trade office which was maintained by the Japan-China Trade Promotion Council in Peking where some Japanese officials were dispatched on temporary leave from their official positions. However, the Chinese leaders were unwilling to invite Sato to Peking.

Japanese trade continued to increase even though there was little concrete progress in political relations. In November 1971, a mission of the most influential Japanese businessmen went to China for the first time but were told that such measures as opening an air service must wait for restoration of diplomatic relations. Prime Minister Chou was reported to have told them that while an independent country like Japan must have some defense forces, he feared imperialism by Japan if resource-rich neighbors were to industrialize in competition with it.[2] Apparently the Chinese leader feared the possible use of any strong Japanese military forces in the event of Chinese or other Asian economic rivalry with Japan. The Chinese still showed an interest in the same ship and plant exports which they had wanted while Prime Minister Ikeda was in power and which were frustrated by the pressure of Taiwan. However, they were hesitant about getting tied down to any long-term debts to Japan. Chinese officials indicated they would like to pay cash as they feared the possibility of future Japanese economic controls.[3]

Obstacles to Soviet Cooperation

Until 1972, the only Communist neighbor with which Japan had any formal diplomatic relations was the Soviet Union. Trade with it was only about as large as with its other close neighbors, as relations between the countries were hampered by suspicion and political strain which were evidenced in the failure of the countries to negotiate a peace treaty after the breakdown of treaty talks in 1956. Japan coveted access to Siberian oil, gas, iron, tin, copper, and coal but feared the possible arbitrary actions by the Russians such as violating contracts, not paying agreed prices, and excluding the Japanese from sufficient inspecting facilities on joint projects. Yet, by the early 1970s, the Japanese were participating in schemes for the importation of logs and lumber from the Soviet Far East and building port facilities at Nakhodka in the Russian Far East. However, the Russians proved to be very slow in negotiations,

[2] Ibid., No. 48 (27 November 1971), p. 2.
[3] *Christian Science Monitor*, 14 February 1972, p. 2.

as in the case of the contract for importing wood pulp and chips which took several years to negotiate. The potential for low costs and large supplies close to Japan was very tempting to Japan and it would reduce, to some extent, Japan's reliance upon the Canadian and American supply if only the Soviet Union could be induced to come to reasonable decisions on surveys, financing, and volume of raw materials for export.

The improved relations between the United States and China that brought about the Nixon visit to China in 1972 gave new impetus to the Soviet Union to be more conciliatory to Japan. In February 1972 when Andrei Gromyko, the Soviet foreign minister, visited Japan he agreed to reopen negotiations shortly on a peace treaty which had been stalled for almost sixteen years, mainly over the northern territories issue. Gromyko also told the Japanese he favored cooperation with Japan on the building of an oil pipeline from Tyumen in Western Siberia to Nakhodka. He proposed that the Japanese provide a billion dollars in credits to supply the pipe. However, doubts about the sulfur content of the oil and the reliance upon Russian construction made Japanese participation difficult, although Japan continues to have an interest in this scheme and alternative sources of oil and coking coal from Yakutia which might insure future supply and joint development if the two countries can reduce their suspicion of each other. The Soviet Union, however, continues to exclude most foreign business from its domestic development and has not forgotten Japanese, American, and British intervention in Russia during the Revolution. Russia, like China and some of the Southeast Asian countries, therefore, continues to have fears of Japanese direct participation in its development.

The possibility of joint development was improved as a result of the Nixon visit to Russia in 1972 when closer economic ties were agreed upon between the United States and the Soviet Union. Apparently the United States was offered the opportunity to participate in the Tyumen project as a result of a request by the American firms Gulf Oil and Bechtel. Japanese businessmen welcomed the American participation in the $3 billion development which would strengthen Japan's position vis-à-vis the Soviets and ease some of the economic strain between Japan and the United States. It would also reduce the likelihood of strain in relations between Japan and China.

Approaches to Other Communist Neighbors

In 1972, Japan's economic ties with its small Communist neighbors were strengthened. In January 1972, the Dietmen's League for Promotion of Japan-North Korean Relations sent a special mission to North Korea under a Liberal Democrat, Chuji Kuno, who negotiated an unofficial trade agreement with North Korea. The agreement proposed increasing trade between the countries from the 1970 total of about $58 million to more than $400 million by 1976. Although it was an unofficial agreement in which only one Liberal Democratic Diet member was involved and, unlike the China trade negotiations, did not have the tacit or informal support of the prime minister, it was the first trade agreement by North Korea with a non-Communist country. Prime Minister Sato disavowed any responsibility for this agreement in view of his government's commitment to the South Korean government as the government of all Korea.

It was the Japanese foreign ministry which took the initiative in developing trade with North Vietnam and Mongolia. In February 1972, a mission under Southeast Asian section chief Miyake went to North Vietnam to discuss plans for postwar reconstruction with Japanese assistance, which had been offered as early as 1966. There was only a minimum of trade between the two countries amounting to about $10 million based on an exchange of Japanese textiles and chemicals for North Vietnamese coal. The North Vietnamese did not demand diplomatic recognition or commercial treaties as did China and North Korea and were willing to participate in trade and aid.

As early as 1961, Japan had supported the entry of Mongolia to the United Nations even though there were no diplomatic relations between the countries. Mongolia had demanded war reparations from Japan which Japan was not prepared to consider at that time and as a consequence no progress was made on the question of diplomatic recognition, although Japan continued to support Mongolia's entry to the United Nations. In 1971, when a Diet group under Liberal Democrat Shigeki Nakajima went to the capital of Mongolia, Ulan Bator, the demand for war reparations was dropped by Mongolia. This visit was followed up by the foreign ministry. Kinya Niiseki, the Japanese ambassador to Moscow, negotiated with the Mongolian ambassador there, Nyamyn Luvsancultem. On 19 February 1972, establishment of diplomatic relations between the countries was announced, which was the first time Japan had established diplomatic relations with an Asian Communist country. After this Luvsancultem became the first Mongolian ambassador to Japan. Trade, aid, and diplomatic recognition by Japan of the smaller Communist states thus complemented some of the moves of the great powers, the United States, China, and the Soviet Union. The new ties across the gulf between the Communist and non-Communist states accompanied the loosening of those ties among the members of the two former blocs.

Japan's trade, military, and diplomatic links with its non-Communist neighbors were amplified by its investments, loans, and grants which were provided by both government and private industry. Much of the private arrangements consisted of the economic cooperation and aid carried on with the less-developed countries. The aid program of Japan

TABLE 8.2
JAPAN'S ASIAN TRADE AND AID
(IN MILLIONS OF DOLLARS)

Country	Trade 1970	Aid 1964-68	Aid 1970
South Korea	1,084.0	434.2	505.9
Indonesia	1,052.3	288.1	478.1
Taiwan	1,013.2	172.6	361.3
Philippines	979.7	347.8	505.9
China	835.4	none	none
Soviet Union	852.7	none	none
Hong Kong	810.1	24.8	411.4
Thailand	648.4	122.5	228.0
Malaysia	589.5	26.8	66.7
Singapore	537.4	8.2	155.7
India	515.5	351.2	116.7
Ryukyus	494.2	83.8	63.2
Pakistan	182.6	122.4	144.5
South Vietnam	133.1	3.5	(a)
North Korea	57.7	none	none
Burma	53.5	74.2	(a)
Ceylon	42.3	24.1	(a)
Cambodia	16.8	3.0	(a)
Laos	6.7	9.1	(a)

NOTE: (a) These Southeast Asian countries received a total of $77.8 million in 1970.

SOURCE: Japan, Ministry of Foreign Affairs, *Highlights of Japan's Foreign Aid*, 1969. Japan, Ministry of Foreign Affairs, *Japan's Economic Cooperation*, 1971, p. 31. Japan, Ministry of Finance, *Summary Report of Trade of Japan*, October 1971.

has been closely associated with the development of its trade while the aid program of the United States has strongly favored those countries to which it has given military assistance. The ostensible purpose of economic aid is to strengthen the weaker non-industrialized country to enable it to raise its standard of living, rather than benefit the trade or political objectives of the donor country. Under the Sato Cabinet, Japan increased the amount of aid it gave and it emphasized the humanitarian aspects. It avoided military aid and overt political pressure in line with its limited defense concept. However, Japanese non-military aid was concentrated on major trading partners of strategic importance to Japan as can be seen in table 8.2.

Japan's role as an Asian Donor State

As with other donor countries of economic aid, Japan under the Sato Cabinet only gave a small proportion of aid through multilateral arrangements or agencies sponsored by the United Nations. Most of its aid went directly to the country concerned. Only a small part of its government aid was in the form of grants which did not require repayment but until 1972 did have to be spent in Japan for Japanese items or through Japanese firms. The largest part of government aid was in loans and credits which had to be repaid with interest and only differed from ordinary commercial loans in the more favorable terms of interest and repayment. The private loans and investment aid were similar. They only differed from commercial business by providing Japanese government guaranteed repayment or by giving favorable terms to private firms to engage in approved projects which might not otherwise be supported. It was expected that this would stimulate the economies of the recipient country as well as benefit Japanese business and the immediate recipients of the goods and services involved.

In 1970, Japan was the second largest donor in the absolute amount of government and private aid provided in that year, with only the United States providing more. To determine the extent of the effort of donor countries, the gross amount of aid is compared with the gross national product of each country. As can be seen from table 8.3, which ranks the members of OECD for 1970, some of the smaller countries

TABLE 8.3
AID FROM OECD COUNTRIES, 1970
(PERCENTAGE OF GNP)

Netherlands	1.46	Italy	0.78
France	1.24	Canada	0.77
Belgium	1.23	Sweden	0.73
Australia	1.12	Austria	0.67
Britain	1.04	Switzerland	0.67
Portugal	1.02	Denmark	0.62
Japan	0.93	United States	0.61
West Germany	0.80	Norway	0.59

SOURCE: Organization of Economic Cooperation and Development, *Development Assistance*, 1971 Review, table 2, p. 144.

made greater efforts in terms of their productive ability. The Netherlands, one of the smaller donor countries, made the greatest effort by giving 1.46 percent of its gross national product in aid, Japan was seventh with 0.93 percent, and one of the richest countries, the United States, was fifteenth in terms of its ability to give aid by providing 0.61 percent of its goods and services.

In April 1969, Finance Minister Fukuda set a precedent at a meeting of the Asian Development Bank when he announced that Japan expected to double its aid to Asia within five years.[4] In May 1970, he pledged at the ministerial meeting on Southeast Asian development that the Japanese government took as its goal increasing aid to one percent of

[4]Kiichi Aichi, "Japan's Legacy and Destiny of Change," *Foreign Affairs*, Vol. XLVIII, No. 1 (October 1969), p. 33.

its gross national product. The large increases registered by Japan in absolute amounts of aid accounted for its rise to second place among the donor states, but its large increase in gross national product each year made it difficult to maintain the 1 percent goal. However, the 1970 increase of 44.4 percent over 1969 brought it almost to that level. Government aid has been about one-third of private aid instead of the reverse, which was recommended by the Pearson report to the World Bank in 1969. Grants continued to be a small proportion of government aid so that the major part of aid is loans which place a growing burden of repayment with interest on the less-developed countries and may be a source of future conflict.

Japan's four chief Asian trading partners, South Korea, Taiwan, Indonesia, and the Philippines, are recipients of the largest amounts of economic aid with the exception of India, where Japan has participated

TABLE 8.4

AID FROM MAJOR DONORS AMONG OECD COUNTRIES

(IN MILLIONS OF DOLLARS)

Country	1963	1965	1967	1970
United States	4,579	5,520	5,567	5,971
Japan	320	601	855	1,824
France	1,242	1,299	1,344	1,808
West Germany	605	726	1,140	1,487
Britain	720	1,028	875	1,259
Italy	321	266	285	725

SOURCE: Organization of Economic Cooperation and Development, *Development Assistance,* 1971 Review, table 2, p. 144.

in the multilateral and international group aiding India. Similarly, Japan has participated in international loans to Pakistan as well. Hong Kong, Singapore, and Malaysia are important trading partners but they are already relatively industrialized and well-governed so that they are more capable of absorbing Japanese capital and investment on regular commercial terms without much government encouragement. It is probably significant that there is more Japanese participation in manufacturing and processing in those places than in other parts of Southeast Asia.

The 1965 settlement of South Korean claims against Japan provided for $300 million in grants and $200 million in credits over a ten-year period. Some of this was intended to help the establishment of a steel mill at Pohang from 1971 to 1973, although most of the grant was to be used for promoting agriculture, forestry, and fisheries. The credits were provided through the Overseas Economic Cooperation Fund and were used in such projects as city waterworks, communications, dam construction, harbor expansion, bridge construction, and factory building. By the late 1960s, close to the agreed $300 million in private loans had been used for the export of Japanese plants and equipment to South Korea. South Korea has been rather fearful of Japanese control and only in the 1970s did it permit wholly owned Japanese subsidiaries to operate freely.

In 1965, the Sato Cabinet agreed to the yen equivalent of $150 million credits to Taiwan which was to be spent by 1974. These were used to finance projects such as the Tsengwen dam and the Kaohsiung harbor improvements. Communications and power distribution systems were also undertaken with these funds. Unlike South Korea, Taiwan welcomed Japanese subsidiaries and manufacturing enterprises even when wholly owned by Japanese companies. The increased Japanese aid funds after 1965 helped replace the decrease in American aid to Taiwan which continued its industrial output and foreign trade growth at rates comparable to Japan itself. This was a promising place for Japanese investment in manufacturing as a great deal of it was intended for export to third countries. Taiwan authorities were anxious to increase the Japanese stake in their economy to insure future political support for their hopes of preserving their political independence of the Peking government. However, Japanese investment in Taiwan began to decline in 1971 due to pressure to recognize China.

Japan's interest in Indonesia was concentrated on its natural resources, especially oil of which Japan bought three-fourths of its 1971 production. Japanese government and private companies were involved in the Indonesian oil industry with drilling rights off North Sumatra even though Japan was still dependent on American oil companies for most of its oil which came from the Middle East. Japan developed production-sharing arrangements with Indonesia in timber and nickel to insure future supplies of its required raw materials. It also purchased bauxite and natural rubber from Indonesia and handled a large share of its foreign trade.

Japan placed great importance on Indonesian resources and therefore it continued to support President Sukarno even when he was abandoned by other donor countries. Japan was eager to take steps to help Indonesia under his successor, President Suharto, and took one of its then rare initiatives in Asian neighbors' affairs to revive the consortium to finance loans to Indonesia in 1966. Government yen credits were used for commodity aid in the effort to contain inflation. Yen credits continue to be supplied to maintain project aid for communications, power plants, waterworks, and similar undertakings.

The Philippines is an important market for Japanese manufactured goods in addition to its importance as a source of timber, sugar, iron, copper, and chrome. Although the United States has a larger share of the trade and foreign investment in the Philippines, Japan has one-third of the Philippine's foreign trade and Japanese ships carry much of the trade of the Philippines with third countries. During the Ikeda Cabinet, some of the reparations goods had been unused, and Philippine economic and political leadership was unable to take full advantage of the Japanese aid to carry out permanent economic development because of the lack of continuity of leadership and failure to carry on adequate government development plans. Fear and suspicion of Japan prevented ratification of the commercial treaty, and Japanese business continued to operate under uncertain conditions there. As a consequence, Japan was reluctant to grant more development project assistance. However, Japanese government loans secured by reparations payments were made for the Cagayan line of the Philippine Railways and expansion of the telecommunications network. In 1969 yen credits were agreed upon to help build a north-south highway.

In the Philippines, Japanese private investment previously had been confined to loans to timber and mineral industries to insure extraction and future supplies. The Investment Law of 1967 in the Philippines eased the import of Japanese capital in the manufacturing industries with the result that there were several cases of participation in the processing of metals and the manufacturing of electric machinery which by 1970 involved about $10 million in securities and $33 million in loans. Unreported equity held by the Japanese is said to be as much as ten times the recorded amount.

Of Japan's four other principal non-Communist Asian trading partners, Thailand, Malaysia, Singapore, and Hong Kong, only Thailand has received considerable economic aid. In May 1969, the rather small special yen payments were all paid to Thailand by Japan, but a large part of the balance remained unspent. These grant-like payments were earmarked for the purchase of textile mills, freighters, and rails. In 1968, the Japanese government offered $60 million in yen credits for Thailand's second five-year economic development plan. In October 1970, projects for hydroelectric power, railways, telephone extension, and port improvements were agreed upon.

Private Japanese export credits to Thailand were running at the rate of $126 million in the fiscal year 1968 but in the fiscal year 1969 these dropped to $96 million. These credits were provided for ships, automobiles, textile machinery, electrical machinery, communications equipment, and other industrial machinery. Six of the ten automobile assembly plants in Bangkok were Japanese or joint Japanese ventures. Many components of assembled products continued to be produced in Japan as there was less pressure for manufacturing and processing than there was in Malaysia and Singapore. The Japanese were also involved in textile mills some of which were wholly-owned Japanese subsidiaries. The Thai Economic Development Board wanted more Japanese companies to come to Thailand, and by March 1970 registered Japanese investment there had reached $79 million. Despite the close economic ties fear of Japanese penetration resulted in an anti-Japanese boycott in November 1972 that indicated need for much greater care in dealing with Southeast Asia.

Japan actively participated in the economic development of Malaysia. In the late 1960s, Japan supplied some small grants in connection with the settlement of claims arising from the Second World War, and it extended some moderate amount of yen credits, amounting to $50 million, to assist local development plans in that country. In 1969, the private Japanese export credits to Malaysia amounted to $31 million, and in 1970 registered Japanese investment was $36 million. Malaysia provided certain essential raw materials to Japan, but it also provided opportunities for joint investment. However, carefully considered protectionist legislation in Malaysia was designed to encourage Japan to engage in more value-added production. Tariffs thus stimulated Japan and other foreign investors to engage in more manufacturing in Malaysia. Particularly significant was the development of the Malayawata Steel Mill which had 39 percent Japanese ownership.

In Singapore, Japan also supplied some small grants, amounting to $8.17 million, in connection with settlement of war claims. It also extended some moderate amounts of yen credit, amounting to $8.17 million, to assist local development plans. In 1969, private export credits amounted to $42 million, and in 1970 registered Japanese investment was $23 million. The Japanese firm Ishikawajima-Harima Industries joined the Singapore Economic Development Board to set up the Jurong Shipyard with 51 percent Japanese ownership, putting it under Japanese control. These large-scale undertakings of Japanese enterprise in the Malayan area together with oil prospecting off nearby Sumatra gave Japan an important economic and strategic stake in the region which was enhanced by the passage of its essential oil shipments through the Straits of Malacca.

Participation in Asian Regional Organizaions
Japan, during Sato's Cabinet, became increasingly active in other aspects of regional development in collaboration with various groups of countries. In this way, it gave a multilateral character to its many policies associated with trade, aid, and investment. Besides extending Japan's economic influence in Asia these collective regional efforts began to bring together the regional states in such a way as to give them a greater voice in their future and to counter somewhat their usual dependence on great powers external to the region. An additional indication of concern was

the establishment of Southeast Asian centers to create more adequate academic expertise in Japan.

One of these regional efforts was the Asian Development Bank, which was created as a result of a meeting of the members of the Economic Commission for Asia and the Far East (ECAFE) held in Bangkok in October 1964. In November 1965, final agreement to establish the bank, with headquarters in Manila, was reached at a meeting of cabinet ministers of the participating countries. Membership was extended to members not in the region, and many developed countries joined the organization as donor countries. By 1966, the bank was joined by thirty-one countries when two-thirds of its initial $1 billion in capital was subscribed, of which $200 million was pledged by Japan. Japan's Foreign Minister Miki emphasized the need to rely upon funds of the other advanced countries for Asian aid in addition to Japan in order to assure a more adequate effort comparable to that in Africa and Latin America.[5] Although the bank was at first severely criticized by American congressman, Otto Passmore, for mismanagement, after five years it had loaned $675 million in eighteen Asian member countries. Indeed, it appeared to be serving the purpose for which it was established.

In April 1966, Japan took the initiative and began an annual conference of Southeast Asian foreign and finance ministers to plan regional economic cooperation. Countries represented at this conference were Japan, Malaysia, Singapore, the Philippines, South Vietnam, Laos, and Thailand with observers from Indonesia and Cambodia. Japan's Foreign Minister Shiina said at that time that Japan's intention in Asia was to see the countries of the Southeast Asian region play a larger role in their own development plans. Japan urged the necessity of investment in agriculture as a basis for industrialization although the less-developed countries feared this approach might continue their reliance upon the role of a supplier of raw materials and obstruct industrialization. Agreement was finally reached on the establishment of an agricultural development conference to be held in December of that year. Despite the economic nature of the meeting, the governments of China and the Soviet Union accused it of planning aggression under the instigation of Japan and the United States in connection with the Vietnam War.

A second Southeast Asian Development Conference was held in April 1967 and it urged plans to broaden the market for processed goods and improvement of transportation and communications facilities. It also urged the Asian Development Bank to provide the agricultural fund and to establish a fisheries center. In the years since the establishment

<hr />

[5] Japan, Ministry of Foreign Affairs, Public Information Bureau, *A Review of World Problems*, Japan Reference Series, No. 9-68, p. 9.

of the conference, annual meetings have continued to be held to advance the development of the region. In 1968, at the third Southeast Asian Development Conference pressure was applied to Japan to increase its aid to the region and for it to agree to the importation of more primary products and processed goods from the Southeast Asian countries. At the fourth conference in 1969, Japan said it would undertake responsibility for part of the post-Vietnam War reconstruction and that it would greatly increase its aid to the region. At the same time it also called for more effort by the Southeast Asian countries for their own development.

South Korea took the initiative in calling the first meeting of the Asian and Pacific Council (ASPAC), which was held in June 1966. At this meeting there were pressures to concentrate the discussion on defense of the region against Communism, particularly by the non-Communist participants in the Vietnam War—South Vietnam, Australia, New Zealand, South Korea, and the Philippines. However, Japan and Malaysia resisted this emphasis. The joint comunique at the close of the meeting urged increasing unity of the countries of the region supporting the solidarity of the nations of Asia and the Pacific. Without naming China, it denounced nuclear testing and supported the United Nations' resolution on the unification of North and South Korea.

Six members of ASPAC were participants in the Manila Conference of the belligerents in the Vietnam War along with the United States. This gave ASPAC the appearance of a regional anti-Communist alliance. To prevent this impression, Japan's Foreign Minister Miki called for peaceful coexistence with China at the meeting held in July 1967. He also warned that, in view of Japan's Peace Constitution, it could not take part in the council if it should prove to be only a group of Vietnam War participants.

At the third ASPAC meeting in 1968, there was general debate of the implications of the planned British withdrawal from Southeast Asia and the possibility of American withdrawal from Vietnam. The divided states, Taiwan, Korea, and Vietnam, along with Thailand emphasized the nuclear threat of China but could not prevail over Japan and Singapore which prevented any anti-Communist denunciations. Foreign Minister Miki urged a flexible, realistic economic and cultural approach to the area with the result that the council agreed to establish a cultural and social center in Seoul, an economic cooperation center in Bangkok, and a roster of technical experts to be maintained in Canberra.

Despite the efforts of Foreign Minister Miki, ASPAC was regarded as an interventionist anti-Communist organization by the opposition forces in Japan. When the 1969 meeting was held at a country resort in Japan, rallies were organized to protest the alleged warmongering character of ASPAC by opposition parties, labor unions, and radical students that resulted in clashes with the police. Miki pressed strongly for international efforts in the establishment of a post-Vietnam War recovery fund for Indochina.

In separate approaches to the advanced countries, Miki also unsuccessfully advocated a combination of Japan's principal trading partners on the Pacific rim, such as Australia, New Zealand, the United States, and Canada, together with its Asian non-Communist neighbors in order to establish a free trade zone and to provide a basis for cooperation in Asian economic development.[6] While such an arrangement would serve Japan's economic interests well, it found relatively little favor with the other potential participants. However, businessmen of the five advanced Pacific countries did form their own Pacific Basin Economic Cooperation Council (PBECC) which became an annual forum for discussion of common interests.

During the Sato prime ministership, Japan more actively participated in the Asian regional development. At the same time, Japan's promotion of its own prosperity was successful through its increased aid, trade, investment, and participation in regional meetings. As well, government grants and credits for development projects for the non-communist neighbors aided those countries and made them more disposed to accept Japanese trade and investment. Private loans and credits stimulated the introduction of Japanese capital goods as did the government aid funds, and together they expanded local markets for Japanese manufacturers. These policies relied upon economic activity and were supported by the avoidance of political pressure through military means. There is also the likelihood that these policies of development assistance may be extended to Japan's Communist neighbors in the near future. Although Japanese investment in Asia previously was concentrated on resource extraction, it is now increasingly entering upon manufacturing and processing in the region. This emphasis may go further towards industrial development of the less-developed neighbors if fear of Japanese economic domination can be shown to be unjustified.

Although the means to regional security for Japan are chiefly economic, security is served by Japan's policies designed to reassure its neighbors, which is especially true in the case of China. Japan's economic activity is also intended to strengthen the regimes and economies of the neighboring states in the anticipation that this will make war and insurrection less likely.

Japan's goal of recognition as a leading power has been served by its greater role in Asian development and the tentative beginnings of

---

[6] Kiyoshi Kojima, *Taiheiyo Keizai Ken to Nihon* (Tokyo: Kunimoto Shobo, 1969). See especially section five, pp. 115–162.

multilateral regional cooperation. Its aid program for Asia, as well as its moderate aid efforts elsewhere, have also provided an opportunity to win global recognition for Japan as a leading OECD country and thereby enhance its global influence and participation in major international political decisions.

Perhaps fortunately, Japan is rivalled in most of its regional activities by the United States so that it cannot aspire to exclusive regional domination. Despite the importance of Asia to Japan and its deepening involvement with it, it still remains even more closely involved with its Pacific rim neighbors, the United States, Australia, New Zealand, and Canada, both in economic and military matters than it is with Asia. Loosening of the military bonds would permit greater independence in Japan's foreign policy but it will also increase economic competition or rivalry with its advanced Pacific rim neighbors. Japan cannot ignore either Asia or its Pacific rim partners, but, as the chief source of tension for Japan, Asia is a region to which it must make a contribution if it is to live in relative peace and prosperity with it.

The role Japan has chosen for itself in Asia is that of a leader in the development of the region in which it has tried to rely on economic means to the exclusion of military power. This role of providing economic leadership has been pursued in a hesitant way which needs to be changed to a more mutually beneficial and better coordinated approach. Its potential for constructive results is enormous if war and disruption can be minimized in the Asian region.

9

Japan as a World Power

JAPAN'S THREE PRINCIPAL GOALS have been to promote its prosperity, to insure its security, and to gain recognition as a leading world power. In the past, the first of these goals has received the greatest emphasis by Japan, and this pursuit of prosperity has been used to move closer to achieving its other two goals. Given the strong internal constraints upon its defense forces, Japan has had no alternative but to rely upon its economic power as a means of achieving its goals and of exercising its influence in the world.

In its economic activities, Japan has increasingly become a global power, and the rather ambitious hope of Prime Minister Ikeda that Japan would be the third pillar of the world economy has been almost realized. Up to the time of the international trade and monetary crises of 1971, Japan's trade and currency were among the most crucial factors creating the economic problems in the world. Until that time, Japan's economic growth was so rapid and its exports were increasing at such a high rate that the pressure of the sales of its manufactured products had an unsettling effect on the other industrialized advanced states. Unfortunately, the Japanese leaders were not sufficiently aware of this fact. At the same time, the United States was suffering from the effects of its ambitious military policies, economic inflation, and internal unrest making the Japanese economic impact particularly difficult for the American economy to bear. The impact of Japan's growth and trade was also experienced by Japan's Asian neighbors, by the countries of the Pacific, by countries in Latin America as their commerce increasingly became oriented towards Japan rather than directed solely towards Europe and the United States.

Japan's foreign policy was resistant to change during the 1960s as internal constraints hindered or rendered attempted changes indecisive. Nowhere was this truer than in the attempt of both Ikeda and Sato to hold their supporting coalition of factions together by minimizing inner-party conflict over foreign policy. The various economic ministries and big business as well as the foreign ministry were often permitted to check one another. The tendency to drift rather than steer a determined course is seen particularly in the comparatively minor problem of textile exports to the United States. Because of his own "southern" electoral strategy, probably no other issue so irritated and angered President Nixon and exemplified the unreliability of the Japanese leaders to him. It may well have precipitated the Nixon economic sanctions of August 1971, when the American administration temporarily adopted an almost openly hostile policy toward Japan for the first time since the Second World War. Significantly, the textile issue was resolved almost immediately as soon as the Japanese had caught their breath after the shock of the Nixon policy. The finance ministry continued to hesitate for two weeks while Japan's foreign exchange reserves shot up from $8 to $12 billion as Japanese banks and trading companies unloaded their dollar holdings. The excessively delayed decision to revalue the yen then brought some temporary relief from the currency crisis.

Since that time large exports have continued to produce large dollar surpluses in Japan and have continued the threat of further revaluations of the yen.

The term "Japan Incorporated" has often been used to characterize the close coordination of Japanese business and government in economic planning, investment, and other aspects which suggest a type of government-directed economy. Although close cooperation has existed for a long time with respect to such matters as allocation of scarce foreign exchange and promotion of exports, it has been far from a tight-knit control such as exists in communist countries. The coordination clearly did not work with respect to the problem of textiles until the government took strong legal measures to compel "voluntary" compliance according to the 1971 agreement with the United States. During the early years of the 1970s, Japan's financial position has become quite different, as foreign exchange is no longer scarce and there is, in fact, an *embarras de richesses*. Exports no longer need to be promoted as they have been in the past. They now need to be curtailed or more carefully controlled whenever there is a possibility that they might arouse hostility abroad. This new situation demands even more effective cooperation between business and government.

For the first time, really large-scale foreign investment is possible for Japan and needs to be carefully allocated in both the advanced and the developing economies of the world. The problem is to find sufficient projects in which to invest rather than any shortage of funds for foreign investment. Capital outflows began to increase as the Japanese government eased the limitations on the foreign investments of Japanese firms and banks in 1971 and 1972. With foreign reserves expected to reach $20 billion by the end of 1972, only massive foreign investment will reduce these reserves sufficiently and this raises the problem of avoiding foreign hostility to sudden and massive movement of Japanese capital. Japan can provide large loans or acquire significant equity in firms abroad but it will need to move cautiously to be sure that it is welcome and that it does not produce fear and resentment of real or suspected Japanese domination.

Global and Regional Economic Objectives

It is evident that Japan has become a great economic power—one which is capable of enormous economic influence in the world. The demands on Japan and its leaders for careful decisions that will not arouse resentment or hostility towards Japan are very great and will not be met easily or quickly. In order to reduce its dependence upon a single supplier, such as the United States and also to reduce its impact on any one country, Japan has diversified its trade and investment policies by seeking supplies and markets throughout the world. However, the sheer volume of its trade and now of its investment capital threaten to be too great in their impact to be simply solved by diversification.

Besides the need for carefully regulated exports and foreign investment, there is a need for increased economic assistance to developing countries. Japan has carried out economic assistance to these countries for some time, but they have been on such a relatively modest scale, or modest in conception, that they now appear rather inadequate. The need to finance programs or projects to meet fully the needs of the recipient country has scarcely been grappled with. But Japan now has the ability to do this if it can find the will. In the past, its terms of economic assistance have not been particularly generous. Unlike China, it gave little in the form of no-interest loans or grants, other than reparations or similar claims. However, a beginning has been made, as in the case of Indonesia, towards more fully considering the needs of recipient countries.

At the same time that Japan's economic assistance is being sought, Japan seems to be suffering from an unusual degree of fear of disruptive economic impact among both its Asian neighbours and the advanced countries. More than most countries, its cultural homogeneity, the uniqueness of its language and culture, as well as its comparative isolation have made it difficult for the Japanese to establish close and intimate ties with foreigners either at home or abroad. This often has made it difficult for the Japanese to fully understand foreign sentiments or attitudes and for the foreigners to perceive the good intentions of the Japanese. As well, the comparative lack of attention abroad to Japanese foreign policies has led to a great deal of ignorance of Japan's actions and intentions, which has made it easy to imagine incorrectly that Japanese attitudes have changed little since its earlier periods of imperialism and traditionalism.

Japan's new status has already aroused much hostility in Western Europe and North America, not because of any intention of the Japanese to injure or take unfair advantage of Western countries, but because of a lack of attention to many abrasive policies whose impact was not fully perceived or given proper weight. Also, even in areas in which it was evident that the United States was agitated by Japan's trade and exchange position, the internal Japanese political situation was simply not responsive to the need for change or capable of making adequate policy response. Such indecisiveness occurred near the end of the Sato regime. It is here that Japan's chief weakness lies rather than in any deliberate callousness or bad faith. This Japanese dilemma will probably continue to be a constraint on Japan's ability to utilize its capability to the full extent conferred by its economic development.

Just as Japan's foreign aid policies have been hampered by relatively short-run or short-sighted objectives of simply promoting Japan's own prosperity, its liberalization policies have been too little and too late. Even though Japan has moved substantially to ease the entry of foreign products and foreign capital into Japan, even in sensitive areas such as automobiles and agricultural products, the effort has been belated and is still too partial to convince American officials and businessmen fully that the United States is not justified in taking protectionist measures against Japan.

Despite the grave difficulties to be perceived in bringing Japan's world economic impact into manageable focus, its global importance clearly will remain great. It is evident that Japan's participation and support is required for any world decisions on the international financial or trade system. Japan is one of the most important members of the group of ten countries that met in Washington in December 1971 to decide upon major shifts in the values of the leading currencies. Similarly, in any major world trade or development decision Japan is an indispensable participant which is further evidence of its role as a great economic power. In terms of the size of its economy measured in the output of goods and services, it ranks after the United States and the Soviet Union. It is economically more powerful than any one member of the European Common Market and may soon equal that of the entire market group.

In aspiring to play a special role in Asia as a leader in economic development, Japan must share the area with the United States which has almost the same stake in terms of trade, aid, and investment that Japan has. This offers the opportunity to Asian neighbors to balance Japanese influence with that of others, and it also compels the leading powers, including Japan, to compete for the favor of the less-developed Asian countries. In consequence, countries such as Thailand, Malaysia, and Singapore do not fear the participation of Japan in their commerce and development to the same extent as countries in which only one leading power is active. Not only does Japan not exclusively dominate the region, but also, despite the growth of Japan's commerce with the region, it is only one area towards which it needs to take more deliberate measures as local economic and political conditions permit. This situation is in contrast to the role of the United States in Latin America where it is the one predominant economic and military power.

Japan's economic foreign policy of commercial penetration and increase of political influence in Asia has been promoted by refraining from any regional military commitments of its own forces, even for convoying and guarding its own shipping. This prevents or minimizes fear of Japanese militarism. The internal constraint from Japanese opposition parties and groups which resist any kind of interventionist policies provides a firm and continuing basis for these policies. The difficulty experienced by the United States in its military objectives in Southeast Asia serves to confirm the wisdom of the Japanese determination to avoid the militarism and imperialism of the past.

Because of its unusually strong foreign exchange position and investment capability, Japan in the 1970s is in a better position than any other power to take the lead in more ambitious development programs if it can make the decision to do so and design a program that expands its welcome rather than increases suspicion or hostility towards it. Such a program is conceivable even if it has not yet been carried out. However, it should probably be multilateral rather than bilateral, as are most present aid plans, and it should be based upon a local Asian grouping in which the recipients would have as much influence as the donor countries among which Japan would be the most important. Ideally, the program would actually fund industrialization projects on a local or regional basis that would fit together and would have some cumulative impact on Asian societies. They might include interest-free loans and substantial grants which would not subject the recipients to unrealistic burdens or obligations to the donor countries.

The Japanese regional development effort could also apply to Communist neighbors, including China and the Soviet Union. Those states are not inclined to depend heavily upon foreign trade and aid and they would stringently control the type of products imported or exported in accord with their social and economic plans which differ from the now prevalent model of the capitalist economies. Despite these important limitations, however, both China and the Soviet Union welcome trade and even some Japanese participation in their development at least in those instances on which they think their own internal development objectives would not be adversely affected. Success and progress would require a lessening of tension and good diplomatic and political relations between these countries and Japan. It might also be possible to combine some of the desirable features of both the Japanese and Chinese models of development for use in the other countries of the region which would be better than the type of programs which at present often lead to unwanted results and inequities that are not desired in a poorer or weaker economy. Japan's goal of promoting its prosperity needs to be expanded and promoted in coordination with the objectives of its neighbors and major trading partners.

Defense Alliance

It is the policies adopted to insure Japan's defense that have always provoked the most profound disagreement in Japan. The controversy has centered upon the defense alliance with the United States. To make Japan more independent of the United States the critics of the alliance would cancel the treaty and eliminate American use of Japanese bases. They would rely, instead, upon a projected joint agreement of Japan, the United States, the Soviet Union, and China to guarantee Japan's neutrality. On the other hand, to make Japan more independent of all countries, some arms makers, military leaders, and conservative politicians would prefer to see Japan arm on a scale of other major powers, and some even favor the acquisition of nuclear weapons.

The nature of the Japan-United States Treaty of Mutual Security has already changed to some extent as a result of the detente or friendlier relations of both Japan and the United States with China and the Soviet Union. The treaty was originally designed to guard against Soviet and Chinese expansion of influence. As the likelihood of conflict between Japan or the United States with China or Russia has declined, the deterrent function of the treaty has grown less necessary. However, other important purposes, such as guaranteeing the friendship and cooperation of Japan and the United States may prove to be even more important.

For Japan the major purpose of the security treaties was to obtain American protection and economic assistance. By the 1970s its purpose became to moderate American reactions over economic competition and clashes. For the United States a major purpose has continued to be to maintain its influence in Asia and prevent any state from dominating the whole region. The right to base its forces in Japan and to utilize the facilities of the richest and most advanced country in Asia is highly prized. In addition, Japanese friendship and logistic support makes it unnecessary for Japan to become a competitor with the United States for military and strategic influence and makes it unlikely that Japan will become a hostile or uncooperative great power. This negative gain for the United States may be the most important gain of all. Nothing would be a greater blow to American influence than a militarily powerful Japan with a Gaullist foreign policy.

Therefore, the current security treaty helps perpetuate friendly relations in both directions. The United States has an incentive to contain its exasperation with Japan over trade and currency. Otherwise, American resentment could result in even more severe blows to Japan's economy than occurred in 1971. Subjected to such economic sanctions, Japan might have an incentive to challenge American influence in Asia or to consider becoming a strong military power. It may have been that the realization of such a possibility sobered President Nixon and his advisor, Professor Henry Kissinger, and inclined them to adopt a more conciliatory attitude toward Japan in 1972.

Both President Nixon and Prime Minister Tanaka in their visits to Peking have found that the defense alliance has strengthened their hands in dealing with Peking. In turn, Peking has even dropped its previous objections to the security treaty and no longer sees it as an instrument of renewed Japanese militarism.[1] To strengthen its position in its conflict with the Soviet Union, China has increased its effort to establish friendly relations with both Japan and the United States. With the demotion of Lin Piao as chief military leader in China, even public denunciations of American and Japanese "imperialisms" have been eliminated. China may regard the existence of the Japan–United States Security Treaty as a welcome counter weight to the Soviet Union.

That cooperation with China could be used to bring pressure on the Soviet Union was shown in late 1971 when China and the United States coordinated their support of Pakistan during the Pakistan–India war over Bangladesh against India. On the other hand, India was aided by the Soviet Union. China and the United States had a common aim in checking expansion of Soviet influence in the subcontinent. By reducing confrontation with each other, China and the United States found they could exert greater leverage against Russia. The Americans, for instance, found they had more time to pursue their aim of checking Soviet influence

[1] Assistant Secretary of State Marshall Green said: "Far from being an obstacle for Japan, they (mutual security relations with the United States) put Japan in a more flexible diplomatic position and made it possible for Japan to have an expanding relationship with others." *Christian Science Monitor*, 14 November 1972, p. 24.

in Europe and in pressing for more Russian concessions in force reduction and disarmament.

Japan's own policy toward Bangladesh was to recognize the new government as soon as Japan felt it could do so without unecessary provocation to Pakistan—especially in view of the $200 million in loans and credits it had outstanding, some of which was spent in East Pakistan before it became a separate country.[2] Foreign Minister Fukuda was willing to send a mission to determine what economic assistance should be given to help in East Bengal's rehabilitation after the war. Until the Sato Cabinet was replaced by the Tanaka Cabinet in July of 1972, Japan was unable to move ahead with normalizing relations with Peking, but, it immediately moved to establish closer relations with other Asian communist states once the United States shifted its attitude on China. Japan, too, thus showed its ability to take advantage of the shifts in Asian politics to strengthen its position with respect to the other three major powers just as they sought through realignment to increase their influence over one another. Its alacrity in recognizing Bangladesh ahead of the United States confirms Japan's new drive to enhance its political influence in Asia, no doubt stimulated by the blows it had received at American hands.

The changes in Japan's international relations in Asia in 1972 indicate that the security treaty was no longer as provocative to the Communist states as it had been. Indeed the treaty might even be viewed by some of them as indirectly beneficial in their own quarrels with each other.

In recent years American forces in Japan have been reduced in numbers. United States bases have been phased out or turned over to Japanese forces. As we have seen, Undersecretary of State U. Alexis Johnson has asserted that the purpose of American bases in Japan is to fulfill American defense commitments in South Korea and to a lesser extent to meet commitments in Taiwan, the Philippines, and Southeast Asia. The naval bases enable the Seventh Fleet of the United States to operate more effectively in the maritime region of East Asia. The Japanese government asserted, as already noted, that, unlike the previous situation, Japan now relies mainly on its own forces, regarding American forces as supplementary. While this undoubtedly is an appeal to national pride, it seems doubtful that it represents any real change in Japanese forces or their mission. The manpower has not been increased significantly for more than a decade and the nature of their armament has not changed.

Also unchanged is the American need for its Japan bases and alliance to sustain its regional influence. The regional influence also relies upon

[2] *Japan Times Weekly*, International Edition, Vol. XII, No. 8, 19 February 1972, p. 2.

a series of bilateral defense treaties with the non-communist states and on American forces in the area and in Japan. Even though tension may be declining because of detente with China and the Soviet Union and the likelihood of conflict may be declining among the major powers, (except for Chinese–Soviet hostility) the maintenance of the treaties and some forces in the region is very valuable for the United States. These strengthen the American negotiating position and influence, which would be seriously eroded if the credibility of these deterrent treaties were to be lessened, or if the treaties were to be abruptly cancelled—even though there is no immediate military need for them.

As has already been seen, as prominent a Liberal Democratic faction leader as Yasuhiro Nakasone, during the 1969 election campaign before he was director-general of the defense agency, advocated eventual replacement of the security treaty with a friendship treaty. As recently as March 1972 Prime Minister Sato indicated in talks with C. L. Sulzberger of the *New York Times* that it would be desirable to limit the use of American forces in Japan to defense of Japan itself, rather than to protection of other states in the region such as Taiwan or South Korea.[3] This represented a volte-face from his affirmation in the joint communique with Nixon in November of 1969 that "the security of the Republic of Korea was essential to Japan's own security" and that "security in the Taiwan area was also a most important factor for the security of Japan." The public affirmation of the responsibility for defense of Korea and Taiwan was necessary to gain American agreement to the return of Okinawa which was effected 15 May 1972.

To propose the repudiation of the Far East clauses in the security treaty, would seem to eliminate the most valuable aspect of it for the United States and to risk snapping the tie that guaranteed its friendship. This would possibly reduce the division within Japan between the government and the opposition over the most provocative aspects of the alliance, and it would be a good time to do so when the military threat was reduced. By the same token, it would also be less necessary when it was less likely to cause antagonism toward Japan, and it would reduce Japanese responsibility for American Asian policies with which Japan collaborated. However, Nixon's visit to Peking seems already, in effect, to have cancelled the Taiwan part of the security treaty.

The American president agreed in the Nixon–Chou communique of February 1972 that:

> The United States acknowledges that all Chinese on either side of the Taiwan Straits maintain that there is but one China and that Taiwan is a part of China. The United States government

[3] *New York Times*, 10 March, 1972, p. 5.

does not challenge that position. It reaffirms its interest in a peaceful settlement of the Taiwan question by the Chinese themselves. With this prospect in mind, it affirms the ultimate objective of the withdrawal of all U.S. forces and military installations from Taiwan.[4]

While the president's adviser, Henry Kissinger, said that the United States still stood by its security treaty with Taiwan to prevent its seizure by force there was good reason to believe the treaty might never be needed for this purpose. Both the Sato and Tanaka Cabinets believed that the effect of the Nixon admissions in Shanghai was to invalidate the Sato statement of 1969 on Taiwan's importance to Japanese security and also the application of the security treaty to Taiwan.[5] The president is reported to have sent Kissinger for a sudden one-day visit to Tokyo to insure that Japan would make no promise to prevent American forces in Japan from being used to defend Taiwan in the course of its negotiations then going on to recognize China diplomatically.[6] But, when the new Japanese prime minister met the president in Hawaii at the end of August no public reference was made to Taiwan, which suggests that the two sides were still in disagreement. However, in the joint statement issued after the meeting, the two leaders did confirm their support of the security treaty in general terms.[7]

The American insistence on the application of the security treaty to Taiwan in spite of its detente with China suggests that the Far East clauses remain for the U.S. the most prized parts of the treaty. This seems especially true in view of the return of Okinawa to Japan and the application to it of restrictions under the security treaty requiring the prior consultation of Japan for dispatch of combat forces from there.

In a rapid and dramatic manner Japan restored diplomatic relations with China when Prime Minister Tanaka went to Peking in September of 1972. Relations were then broken with Taiwan, which has become increasingly isolated diplomatically since it was expelled in favor of the Peking government from the United Nations in October of 1971. The United States remains the only major state still recognizing Taipei. In the circumstances, Japan would be even more reluctant publicly to reaffirm its commitment of 1969 to cooperate in the defense of Taiwan against China. By avoiding open reference to this in the recent summit meetings, Japan has avoided confrontation with the United States over its interpretation of the security treaty.

[4] U.S., Department of State, *Department of State Bulletin*, Vol. LII, No. 1708 (20 March 1972), pp. 435–38.
[5] *Christian Science Monitor*, 25 August 72, p. 9.
[6] *Christian Science Monitor*, 25 August 1972, p. 9 and 31 August 1972, pp. 1, 3.
[7] *Japan Times Weekly*, International Edition, Vol. XII, No. 37, 9 September 1972, p. 2.

Although the defense and diplomatic status of South Korea has not been questioned, the detente of the United States and Japan with China has triggered direct talks between North and South Korea for the first time since the Korean War. In the circumstances, South Korea may view American and Japanese devotion to its defense to be somewhat diminished, although the Japanese government has made no new overtures to North Korea. The Far East clauses of the security treaty probably still hold firm for Korea.

For the United States, the security treaty, and especially its Far East clauses, remains a basis for its role of defender of the weaker states in Asia and thus of its influence there. It believes that the indirect Japanese commitment to this role and consequent cooperation and subordination bolsters it in a way which strengthens the United States in handling its problems in Southeast Asia or dealing with China and the Soviet Union. Especially important is the position of Japan which could still be kept friendly and its acquisition of extensive military power rendered unnecessary by a security treaty without Far East clauses. To repudiate or drop those clauses would be to perhaps accept a much more modest regional role where, the United States could no longer count on a host of small client states to look after and its power would decline.

However, American ability to affect any of the regional states and especially the major states through trade and development is so great that its influence will remain formidable even if the United States reduces its reliance upon military power. Even a more limited security treaty with Japan would be of enormous value to the United States, if it could thus assure its friendship and continue to provide an incentive to resolve the formidable economic clashes that exist with it. Japan is already a powerful rival whose friendship is needed by the United States. Japan's value can be seen by the concern with which it is pursued by both China and the Soviet Union.

A security treaty is no guarantee that two countries will remain friends, as can be seen by the hostility between China and the Soviet Union despite their still unrepudiated 1950 Treaty of Friendship and Alliance. Japan has exercised great tact in normalizing relations with China so as to provide no unpleasant surprises to the United States, which has reciprocated except for its own initiatives toward China in 1971. If the outstanding economic clashes can be solved amicably, the Japanese-American alliance will have done its chief service in maintaining friendly relations between the United States and Japan and in encouraging Japan to follow a policy of peaceful participation in world affairs.

Thus far, Japan's leaders have resolutely opposed the arguments of the bolder nationalists among conservative politicians and businessmen that large-scale armament and even nuclear weapons are essential to recognition of Japan as a great power and to reducing threats against her. The Japanese government, nevertheless, has not ratified the Nuclear Nonproliferation Treaty, and in this has had the support of the opposition parties. In view of the refusal of China, France, and India to participate in the treaty and considering the continued overwhelming American and Soviet arsenals, it may not be altogether unreasonable for Japan to keep the option open to not adhere in future. However, Japan's leadership has little faith in this eventuality. Foreign Minister Takeo Fukuda said: "With development of nuclear weapons it became evident that if they are used mankind will be annihilated. I can't forsee such a Third World War. Consequently, economic strength becomes much more important than military strength. Japan could make nuclear weapons but has no intention of doing so."[8] He then stated that Japan intended to rely on economic strength to make its voice heard in the world.

Internal Constraints

The internal constraints within the Japanese political system continue to inhibit moves toward large-scale rearmament or imperialistic policies despite the burgeoning Japanese ambition to make more use of economic strength to influence the world. The individuals or groups favoring larger armament and a more active military policy remain comparatively few and uninfluential in Japan.[9] Business has not been dominated by the views of the defense industry. The largest makers of military equipment carry on most of their business in the non-military sector of the economy and thus are not depedent upon military spending. More typical of business are the views of Osamu Shimomura of the development bank and former personal economic adviser to Prime Minister Ikeda:

If today the flow into Japan of some 200 million tons of crude oil each year were to be disrupted, the result would be unspeakable confusion, and the whole economy could be brought to a jarring standstill. The security of the Indian and Pacific Oceans, consequently, has become a matter of vital importance for the welfare and existence of our nation. It would be foolish indeed to seek an overcoming of this weakness by means of military strength. Such an approach may have had validity of some sort in the era of the Japanese Empire, when the importation of 4 million tons of oil a year was sufficient for our needs . . . but, that this was no more than a fantasy has been demonstrated by the tragic outcome

---

[8] *New York Times*, 10 March 1972, p. 37.

[9] Frank Langdon, "Attitudes of the Business Community," Chapter 4 in *Forcast for Japan: Security in the 1970s*, edited by James William Morley (Princeton: Princeton University Press, 1972), pp. 111-134.

of the Pacific War. Even in the day of the Japanese Empire, the essential conditions for survival and development could not be established by military might."[10]

The opposition to an enhanced military role for Japan does not stem only from big business. It is the stock in trade of the opposition parties. The trend toward detente between China and the United States gave the opposition added incentive in 1972 to question the rationale of the Fourth Defense Buildup Plan. By an oversight the Sato Cabinet had failed to conform to the legal requirement of attaining formal approval of the plan by the National Defense Council. When the budget was brought down early in 1972, confrontation with the opposition parties forced the cabinet into an unprecedented modification of the budget by freezing funds for new aircraft.

Once the National Defense Council formally approved the Fourth Defense Buildup Plan in October and the new prime minister had successfully concluded his trip to China, the funds for new aircraft were unfrozen in agreement with the Tanaka Cabinet to permit the full plan to go ahead. The three major opposition parties strongly opposed this move on the grounds that establishment of relations with China and the trend toward detente in the region with respect to the United States made the new defense plan unnecessary. To carry it out in the projected form was more than purely defensive.

The Tanaka Cabinet supported the previously planned buildup of its defense forces and also continued support of the security arrangements with the United States despite the welcomed easing of regional tensions. The fourth plan proposes an annual increase in expenditures of about 20 percent which is about on a par with other budget increases. As has already been shown, this rate of spending is not only small in terms of Japan's gross national product but in absolute terms does not fall into the same class as that of other major powers. It would, however, bring Japan to seventh place among the world's states in the absolute amount spent each year and well ahead of the medium- or small-sized states.[11]

Although the opposition parties cannot win elections at present they can oppose the government strongly in Diet debates. Their determined opposition to the Fourth Defense Buildup Plan produced some temporary concessions by the government. Still, their willingness to resort to filibustering, disorder in the Diet, and demonstrations and strikes outside

[10]Osamu Shimomura, "Choices Open to Japan as a Major Economic Power," *Oriental Economist*, Vol. XXXIX, No. 724 (February 1971), p. 16.

[11]International Institute for Strategic Studies, *The Military Balance 1971-1972* (London: International Institute for Strategic Studies, 1971).

is a check on the government which must sustain the parliamentary system to force hotly contested measures through.

The factional competition within the Liberal Democratic party as well as policy rivalry within factions is important. The restoration of relations with China was long prevented by the dominant coalition of factions led by Eisaku Sato, which in turn was dominated by those within the factions who favored Taiwan. Relations were restored or, more accurately, transferred from the Taiwan to Peking government by Prime Minister Tanaka, leading a new dominant coalition within which the pro-Taiwan party faction members were no longer strong. Even though the pro-Taiwan group led by Okinori Kaya included men like Ichiro Nakagawa and Masaaki Nakayama, who had supported Tanaka's presidency of the Liberal Democratic party, it could not deter Tanaka, Ohira, and Kosaka in their determination to normalize relations with the Peking government.

Both Prime Minister Sato and Foreign Minister Fukuda would have been delighted to restore good relations with Peking under conditions like that of the United States which did not severe ties with Taiwan. It was precisely because the Chinese made a break with Taiwan the essential condition that they refused to invite Sato to Peking even when he asked for an invitation after the announcement of the Nixon visit. When Tanaka and his chief supporter, Foreign Minister Ohira, who now leads the former Ikeda faction, indicated they would severe relations with Taiwan, the Peking invitation was forthcoming. Unlike the United States, the Japanese government also went to the full extent of recognizing the Peking regime diplomatically.

The victory of Kakuei Tanaka in the Liberal Democratic party presidential convention in July of 1972 and his consequent prime ministership was attained with the help of the Ohira, Miki, and Nakasone factions, as well as the large part of the Sato faction which supported Tanaka. Former Prime Minister Sato's influence virtually vanished as his other followers supported Takeo Fukuda. Many strongly pro-Taiwan Liberal Democrats were separated from the dominant factional coalition and relegated to the minority group of the party led by Fukuda. Tanaka tried to appease the pro-Taiwan group in the party to some extent by avoiding a too-abject apology for Japan's aggression in the China war and by asking Chou En-lai not to give Chinese support—not likely anyway, at present—to the Japan Communist party. Tanaka also backed the mission to Taiwan of Liberal Democratic party Vice-President Shiina, a former member of the Kishi faction and former foreign minister, with the unpleasant task of explaining Japan's new policy towards Peking. The Liberal Democratic party delegation under former Foreign Minister Zentaro Kosaka, which went to Peking at the same time to negotiate the terms for normalization with China, was summoned suddenly by the Chinese at midnight just before Shiina's return to Japan to explain his statement in Taipei that Japan would like to maintain its relations with Taiwan. Kosaka assured Chou En-lai that it did not represent any lack of good faith on the part of Tanaka but merely represented the feeling of the pro-Taiwan Liberal Democrats as had already been explained to the Chinese prime minister.[12]

The internal constraints upon Japanese foreign policy arising from general support within the governing party for defense cooperation with the United States and friendly resolution of the problems of economic competition still holds true. In this respect the Tanaka Cabinet like its predecessors has not brought about any change. The new dominant coalition within his party led by Tanaka differs from its predecessors by its greater flexibility on Asian relations and willingness to take new initiatives such as severing formal ties with Taiwan and recognizing Peking. This represents a shift toward a more nationalistic and assertive policy in Asia but it does not mean a desire to undertake a more active regional military role or to substantially reduce military cooperation with the United States.

With Foreign Minister Ohira as close confidant and supporter of Prime Minister Tanaka, it is less likely that key issues will be pushed to such extreme points of confrontation as Kishi, Sato, and Fukuda were willing to permit. The new dominant Japanese leaders are likely to go further in conciliating the opposition as well as being closer to them in some of their policy preferences. Even the faction leaders supporting Tanaka are willing to see a looser defense arrangement with the United States if lessening regional tensions permit it and continued support from the United States can be assured. Such a development would further reduce the foreign policy division with the opposition parties and the consequent strain on the political system. Increased influence of the opposition in foreign policy will not incline Japan toward militarism, but will probably strengthen a trend toward less alignment or some sort of neutralism.

In a longer time span, the permanent domination of the Liberal Democrat party appears unlikely. The party has lost popular voting support continually since its organization in 1955, so that the large majorities of seats in recent elections do not represent a popular mandate. Despite Prime Minister Tanaka's popularity his Liberal Democrats lost twenty-six seats in the 10 December 1972 general election. The unexpectedly bad showing of the two center parties in the House of Representatives—the Komei party dropping from forty-seven to twenty-nine and the Democratic Socialists from twenty-nine to nineteen—and the aston-

---

[12] *Asahi Shimbun*, 18 November 1972 and 20 November 1972, morning and evening editions,, p. 1.

ishing increase of the Communists from fourteen to thirty-eight reversed the trend toward moderate multi-party politics. The Japan Socialists gained thirty-one seats to recoup some of their disastrous loss in the previous election.

Should the Liberal Democrats eventually lose their majority of Diet seats, they will have to form some sort of coalition or minority government. This will probably pull government policy more toward the center and possibly even split off the more conservative Liberal Democratic factions. Such a development might permit greater consensus on foreign policy and introduce a greater element of competitiveness into the Japanese political system. Even the Socialists might be able to participate in a governing coalition. Cabinet participation and responsibility for government policy would moderate the extremes of political opposition and might still permit foreign policy stability by depending on a broader political consensus. Insofar as this supported a more independent but also pacific and constructive policy in the Asian region, it would be highly desirable for all countries concerned with Asia.

The internal constraints in international economic policies have much greater complexities when they involve rivalries among ministries and groups outside the government. It has proved almost impossible to liberalize agricultural imports that are viewed by Japanese farmers and their conservative party champions as too competitive. Big business has fought vigorously against liberalizing imports of automobiles or allowing foreign makers to operate within Japan. The relevant ministries have often been even more assiduous in protecting Japanese producers than businessmen themselves. In textiles, business groups effectively organized and resisted government leadership until foreign relations reached a real crisis stage.

The great crisis brought on by Japan's continuing enormous surplus of exports and consequent accumulation of foreign exchange balances seems especially resistant to solution, even after a substantial upward revaluation of its yen has taken place, making exports more expensive. The resistance of the ministry of international trade to imposing an export tax suggests the difficulty which even the Tanaka Cabinet has in coping with this problem.

The difficulty in improving relations with the Soviet Union lies in the economic sphere but not in competition from Japanese business. The question of the Soviet-held northern islands does not seem to be the stumbling block it is often thought to be. Japanese businessmen would like to gain access to the enormous Siberian resources, which would also permit Japan to diversify its sources of raw materials supply. The cost of bringing oil and gas over such vast continental distances, as well as some uncertainties as to the amount of these fuels which can be easily obtained in certain locations, has really been beyond Japanese private business capacity to solve. The improved economic relations between the United States and the Soviet Union has spurred on American companies to attempt to participate in these projects. This has opened the possibility of some three-way cooperation which might spread some of the cost in the global race for shrinking resources. Progress in this sharing of development and trade should enhance friendship with the Soviet Union. It also illustrates the enormous potential influence available to both the United States and Japan, an influence which is not dependent upon military force. It is likely that Japan's own Asian influence will increase enormously in the coming years if the prospects of increased access to raw materials and markets continues to be good. Japan has scarcely scratched the surface of the potential value of an active policy of leadership in development assistance, especially with respect to its two major communist neighbors.

Japan is well on its way to becoming a more influential world and regional power without becoming a great military power. In a period when economic strength may prove to be more important than military strength, there is almost no limit to its ambition provided its strength is not permitted to damage, or compete in a harmful way with either the developing countries or the major developed countries. This will not be easy to assure, particularly because of the enormous internal political difficulties Japan is encountering at the moment. If it is successful in containing the trade crisis of the early 1970s by the necessary self-restraint and successful in resolving the sharp economic clash with the United States, there is no reason it cannot surmount the challenge of development in the second and third worlds which awaits it.

Even if the major powers reduce some of their tensions and are able to prevent war among themselves, it is perhaps too much to expect that regional and smaller wars and uprisings will disappear in Asia or the Middle East. Still, it is unlikely that Japan will become involved in view of its limited defense policies and the built-in internal constraints against foreign interventionist policies. Despite the exaggerated fears of its own opposition parties, Japan's immediate and likely future buildup of its own defense forces is comparatively modest for a country of its capability and should do no more than permit it to take limited defensive actions. Japan's future world role is surely as a major economic power devoted to international economic development, not that of a new armed superpower bent on the traditional obsession with arms races and domination of smaller countries.

SELECTED BIBLIOGRAPHY

English Language Material

I. GOVERMENT PUBLICATIONS

China. Chinese People's Institute of Foreign Affairs. *Oppose the Revival of Japanese Militarism.* Peking: Foreign Languages Press, 1960. "Foreign Minister Chou En-lai's Statement on the Announcement by the United States of America of the Coming into Effect of the Illegal Separate Peace Treaty with Japan."

China. Chinese People's Institute of Foreign Affairs. *Oppose the Revival of Japanese Militarism.* Peking: Foreign Language Press, 1960. "Treaty of Friendship, Alliance and Mutual Assistance between the People's Republic of China and the Union of Soviet Socialist Republics, February 14, 1950."

Japan. Defense Agency. *Defense of Japan.* 1969.

Japan. Japan External Trade Organization. *Trade and Industry of Japan: Economic Cooperation of Japan,* Extra Edition. 1970.

Japan. Ministry of Finance. *Summary Report of Trade of Japan.* 1971.

Japan. Ministry of Foreign Affairs. *Highlights of Japan's Foreign Aid.* 1969.

Japan. Ministry of Foreign Affairs. *Japan's Economic Cooperation.* 1971.

Japan. Ministry of Foreign Affairs. Public Information Bureau. *Addresses and Speeches by H. E. Nobuhiko Ushiba, Ambassador to the United States.* 1971.

Japan. Ministry of Foreign Affairs. Public Information Bureau. *Foreign Investment in Japan.* Japan Reference Series, No. 6-68, 1968.

Japan. Ministry of Foreign Affairs. Public Information Bureau. *Foreign Relations and Mutual Respect: Two Speeches by Mr. Takeo Miki, Foreign Minister of Japan.* Japan Reference Series, No. 4-68, 1968.

Japan. Ministry of Foreign Affairs. Public Information Bureau. *Foreign Relations, A Year in Review,* Excerpts from Diplomatic Bluebook, April 1970–March 1971. Japan Reference Series, No. 3-71, 1971.

Japan. Ministry of Foreign Affairs. Public Information Bureau. *For World Peace and Prosperity: Foreign Policy Speech by Foreign Minister Takeo Miki at the 55th Extraordinary Session of the Diet, 14 March 1967.* Japan Reference Series, No. 3-67, 1967.

Japan. Ministry of Foreign Affairs. Public Information Bureau. *Japan's Foreign Aid.* Japan Reference Series, No. 2-67, 1967.

Japan. Ministry of Foreign Affairs. Public Information Bureau. *Japan's Foreign Policy: Speech by Foreign Minister Takeo Miki at Australian National University, 29 July 1968.* Japan Reference Series, 8-68, 1968.

Japan. Ministry of Foreign Affairs. Public Information Bureau. *New Tasks for Japan: Two Speeches by Mr. Eisaku Sato, Prime Minister of Japan, June 1969.* Japan Reference Series, No. 3-69, 1969.

Japan. Ministry of Foreign Affairs. Public Information Bureau. *The Northern Territorial Issue, Japan's Position on Unsettled Question between Japan and the Soviet Union.* Japan Reference Series, No. 5-68, 1968.

Japan. Ministry of Foreign Affairs. *The Northern Territorial Issue.* 1970.

Japan. Ministry of Foreign Affairs. Public Information Bureau. *Okinawa, Some Basic Facts.* Japan Reference Series, No. 2-69, 1969.

Japan. Ministry of Foreign Affairs. Public Information Bureau. *Roads to Human Development: Administrative Policy Speech by Prime Minister Eisaku Sato at the 55th Extraordinary Session of the Diet, 14 March 1967.* Japan Reference Series, No. 1-67, 1967.

Japan. Ministry of Foreign Affairs. Public Information Bureau. *A Review of World Problems; Speech by Foreign Minister Takeo Miki at the Twenty-third Session of the General Assembly of the United Nations, 4 October 1968.* Japan Reference Series, No. 9-68, 1968.

Japan. Ministry of Foreign Affairs. Public Information Bureau. *The Search for National Security: Two Articles by Mr. Kiichi Aichi, Foreign Minister of Japan.* Japan Reference Series, No. 4-69, 1969.

Japan. Ministry of Foreign Affairs. Public Information Bureau. *Some Thoughts on the 1970's: Article by Mr. Nobuhiko Ushiba, Vice Minister for Foreign Affairs.* Japan Reference Series, No. 5-69, 1969.

Japan. Ministry of Foreign Affairs. Public Information Bureau. *Toward Greater Responsibility: Two Speeches by Mr. Eisaku Sato, Prime Minister of Japan, December 1967.* Japan Reference Series, No. 6-67, 1967.

Japan. Overseas Technical Cooperation Agency. *Technical Cooperation of the Japanese Government, '68 Annual Report.* 1968.

Organization of Economic Cooperation and Development. *Development Assistance, 1971 Review.*

United Nations. Treaty Series. *Treaties and International Agreements Registered or Filed and Reported with the Secretariat of the United Nations,* Vol. CXXXVIII, No. 1858 (1952). "Treaty of Peace Between the Republic of China and Japan, with Protocol, Exchange of Notes, and Agreed Minutes," 28 April 1952.

U. S. Congress. Senate. Committee on Foreign Relations. *Asian Development Bank Special Funds. Hearings before the committee on foreign relations, Senate to authorize the appropriation of $200,000,000 for a U.S. contribution to multilateral special funds of the Asian Development Bank on S. 2479,* 90th Cong., 1st sess., Oct. 3, 1967.

U.S. Congress. Senate. Committee on Foreign Relations. *Asia, the Pacific and the United States. Hearings before the committee on foreign relations, Senate with former Ambassador to Japan, Edwin O. Reischauer,* 90th Cong., 1st sess., January 1967.

U.S. Congress. Senate. Committee on Foreign Relations. *The Rim of Asia, Report of Senator Mike Mansfield on a Study Mission to the Western Pacific.* 90th Cong., 1st sess., September 1967. Washington, D.C.: Government Printing Office, 1967.

U.S. Congress. Senate. Committee on Foreign Relations. *United States Foreign Policy: Asia,* by Conlon Associates, Study No. 5, November 1, 1959, 86th Cong., 1st sess., 1959. Washington, D.C.: Government Printing Office, 1959. "U.S. Foreign Policy in Northeast Asia," by Robert A. Scalapino.

U.S. Department of State. American Embassy, Tokyo. *Daily Summary of the Japanese Press,* 15 August 1969. "JDA (Japanese Defense Agency) Having Difficulty in Expression of Threat in Preparing Defense White Paper."

U.S. Department of State. American Embassy, Tokyo. *Summaries of Selected Japanese Magazines, 6-20 October 1969.* "Strategic Concept of Autonomous Defense."

U.S. Department of State. *Department of State Bulletin,* Vol. XLII, No. 1076 (8 February 1960). "Eisenhower-Kishi Joint Communique, January 19, 1960."

U.S. Department of State. *Department of State Bulletin,* Vol. LXI, No. 1578 (22 September 1969). "The Message the President carried to the nations of Asia."

U.S. Department of State. *Department of State Bulletin,* Vol. LXI, No. 1547 (25 August 1969), "President Nixon's Round-the-World Trip."

U.S. Department of State. *Department of State Bulletin,* Vol. LII, No. 1536 (1 February 1965). "Sato-Johnson Communique of January 1965."

U.S. Department of State. *Department of State Bulletin,* Vol. LXI, No. 1590 (5 December 1969). "Sato-Nixon Joint Communique of 21 November 1969."

U.S. Department of State. *Department of State Bulletin,* Vol. XXX, No. 771 (5 April 1954). "Statement by Ambassador to Japan Allison on Signing the Mutual Defense Assistance Agreement."

U.S. Department of State. *Department of State Bulletin,* Vol. XXXVII, No. 941 (8 July 1957). "Visit of Prime Minister Nobusuke Kishi of Japan: Joint Communique."

U.S. Department of State. *United States Treaties and Other International Agreements,* Vol. XI, pt. 2. "First Exchange of Notes to Treaty of Mutual Cooperation and Security Between the United States of America and Japan," TIAS 4509, 19 January 1960.

U.S. Department of State. *United States Treaties and Other International Agreements,* Vol. XI, pt. 2. "Third Exchange of Notes to the Treaty of Mutual Cooperation and Security Between the United States of America and Japan," TIAS 4509, 19 January 1960.

U.S. Department of State. *United States Treaties and Other International Agreements,* Vol. V, pt. 1. "Mutual Defense Assistance Agreement, with Annexes, Between the United States of America and Japan," TIAS 2957, 8 March 1954.

U.S. Department of State. *United States Treaties and Other International Agreements,* Vol. III, pt. 3. "Security Treaty Between the United States of America and Japan," TIAS 2491, 8 September 1951.

U.S. Department of State. *United States Treaties and Other International Agreements,* Vol. IX, pt. 2. "Treaty of Mutual Cooperation and Security Between the United States of America and Japan," TIAS 4509, 19 January 1960.

U.S. Department of State. *United States Treaties and Other International Agreements,* Vol. III, pt. 3. "Treaty of Peace with Japan, Declarations by Japan, and Exchanges of Notes," TIAS 2490, 8 September 1951.

II. Books

Brezezinski, Zbigniew. *The Fragile Blossom, Crisis and Change in Japan.* New York: Harper & Row, 1972.

Center for Strategic Studies. *United States-Japanese Political Relations, The Critical Issues Affecting Asia's Future.* Washington, D.C.: Georgetown University, 1968.

Curtis, Gerald L., ed. *Japanese-American Relations in the 1970's.* Washington, D.C.: Columbia Books, 1970.

Dunn, Frederick S. *Peace-Making and the Settlement with Japan*. Princeton: Princeton University Press, 1963.

Emmerson, John K. *Arms, Yen & Power, The Japanese Dilemma*. New York: Dunellen, 1971.

Fukui, Haruhiro. *Party in Power, The Japanese Liberal-Democrats and Policy-Making*. Berkeley and Los Angeles: University of California Press, 1970.

Glazer, Herbert. *The International Businessman in Japan*. Tokyo: Charles E. Tuttle, 1968.

Greene, Fred. *U.S. Policy and the Security of Asia*. New York: McGraw-Hill, 1968.

Hellmann, Donald C. *Japan and East Asia: The New International Order*. New York: Frederick A. Praeger, 1972.

_____. *Japanese Domestic Politics and Foreign Policy, The Peace Agreement with the Soviet Union*. Berkeley and Los Angeles: University of California Press, 1969.

_____. *Japan in the Postwar East Asian International System*. McLean, Va.: Research Analysis Corporation, 1969.

Higa, Mikio. *Politics and Parties in Postwar Okinawa*. Vancouver: University of British Columbia Publications Centre, 1963.

Hilsman, Roger. *To Move A Nation: The Politics of Foreign Policy in the Administration of John F. Kennedy*. New York: Dell Publishing, 1967.

Hunsberger, Warren S. *Japan and the United States in World Trade*. New York: Harper and Row, 1964.

International Institute for Strategic Studies. *The Military Balance, 1971-1972*. London: International Institute for Strategic Studies, 1972.

Kajima Institute of International Peace. *Japan in Current World Affairs*. Tokyo: The Japan Times, 1971.

Kajima, Morinosuke. *A Brief Diplomatic History of Modern Japan*. Tokyo: Charles E. Tuttle, 1965.

_____. *Modern Japan's Foreign Policy*. Tokyo: Charles E. Tuttle, 1969.

Kim, Young C. *Major Issues in Japan's Security Policy Debate*. McLean Va.: Research Analysis Corporation, 1969.

Kim, Young Hum. *East Asia's Turbulent Century, with American Diplomatic Documents*. New York: Appleton-Century-Crofts, 1966.

Kitamura, Hiroshi. *Psychological Dimensions of U.S.-Japanese Relations*. Cambridge, Mass.: Center for International Affairs, Harvard University, 1971.

Kohler, Beate. *Der Vertrag ueber die Nichtverbreitung von Kernwaffen und das Problem der Sicherheitsgarantien*. Frankfurt: Alfred Metzner Verlag, 1972. Chapter 7, "Der Fall Japan."

Maddison, Angus. *Economic Growth in Japan and the U.S.S.R.* New York: W.W. Norton & Co., 1969.

McNelly, Theodore, ed. *Sources in Modern East Asian History and Politics*. New York: Appleton-Century-Crofts, 1967.

Mendel, Douglas H., Jr. *The Japanese People and Foreign Policy*. Berkeley and Los Angeles: University of California Press, 1961.

Millar, T. B. *The Indian and Pacific Oceans: Some Strategic Considerations*. Adelphi Papers, No. 57. London: Institute for Strategic Studies, 1969.

Miller, J. D. B., ed. *India, Japan, Australia: Partners in Asia?* Canberra: Australian National University Press, 1968.

Morley, James William, ed. *Forecast for Japan, Security in the 1970's*. Princeton: Princeton University Press, 1972.

————. *Japan and Korea, America's Allies in the Pacific.* New York: Walker, 1965.

Olson, Lawrence. *Dimensions of Japan: A Collection of Reports Written for the American Universities Field Staff.* New York: American Universities Field Staff, Inc., 1963.

————. *Japan in Postwar Asia.* New York: Praeger, 1970.

Osgood, Robert E., George R. Packard, John H. Badgley. *Japan and the United States in Asia.* Baltimore, Md.: John Hopkins Press, 1968.

Packard, George R. *Protest in Tokyo, The Security Treaty Crisis of 1960.* Princeton: Princeton University Press, 1966.

Passin, Herbert, ed. *The United States and Japan.* Englewood Cliffs, N.J.: Prentice-Hall, 1966.

Rosecrance, R. N. *Australian Diplomacy and Japan 1945-1951.* Melbourne: Melbourne University Press, 1962.

Royama, Michio. *The Asian Balance of Power.* Adelphi Papers, No. 42. London: Institute for Strategic Studies, 1967.

Stockwin, J. A. A. *The Japanese Socialist Party and Neutralism, A Study of a Political Party and Its Foreign Policy.* Melbourne: Melbourne University Press, 1968.

Support the Just Struggle of the Japanese People against the Japan-U.S. Treaty of Military Alliance. Peking: Foreign Languages Press, 1960.

Thomson, George G. *Problems of Strategy in the Pacific and Indian Oceans.* New York: National Strategy Information Center, 1970.

Uemura, Kogoro. *Challenge for Responsible Partnership.* Washington, D.C.: United States-Japan Trade Council, 1971.

United States-Japan Trade Council. *United States and Japan: A Comparison of Trade and Economic Data.* Washington, D.C.: United States-Japan Trade Council, 1971.

Weinstein, Martin E. *Japan's Postwar Defense Policy, 1947-1968.* New York: Columbia University Press, 1971.

————. *Japan, The Risen Sun.* Foreign Policy Association Headline Series, No. 202, 1970.

Welfield, John. *Japan and Nuclear China, Japanese Reactions to China's Nuclear Weapons.* Strategic and Defence Studies Centre. Canberra Papers on Strategy and Defence, No. 9. Canberra: Australian National University Press, 1970.

White, John. *Japanese Aid.* London: Overseas Development Institute, 1964.

Wilcox, Wayne Ayres. *Asia and United States Policy.* Englewood Cliffs, N.J.: Prentice-Hall, 1967.

Williams, Shelton L. *Nuclear Nonproliferation in International Politics, The Japanese Case.* The Social Science Foundation and Graduate School of International Studies Monograph Series in World Affairs. Volume 9, Monograph 3—1971-72. Denver: University of Denver, 1972.

Yoshida, Shigeru. *The Yoshida Memoirs, The Story of Japan in Crisis.* London: Heinemann, 1961.

III. Articles

Adachi, Tadashi. "Japan in International Trade." *Contemporary Japan,* Vol. XXVIII, No. 3 (May 1966).

Aichi, Kiichi. "Japan's Legacy and Destiny of Change." *Foreign Affairs,* Vol. XLVIII, No. 1 (October 1969).

Allen, G. C. "Japan's Place in Trade Strategy." *Trade Strategy and the Asian-Pacific Region.* Edited by Hugh Corbet. Toronto: University of Toronto Press, 1970.

Baerwald, Hans H. "Nikkan Kokkai: The Japan-Korea Treaty Diet." *Cases in Comparative Politics, Asia.* Edited by Lucian W. Pye. Boston: Little, Brown, 1970.

_____ "Strategic Policy and International Relations, A Preliminary View from Japan." Paper for the Conference on Comparative Strategic Policy and International Relations Theory, University of Virginia, 7–8 March 1969.

Bellamy, Ian. "Japan and the Nuclear Non-Proliferation Treaty." *Australia's Neighbours,* Fourth Series, No. 68 (January–February 1970).

Bryant, William. "Japanese Businessmen and Private Economic Diplomacy." *Japan Interpreter,* Vol. VI, No. 2 (Summer 1970).

Buck, James H. "The Japanese Self-Defense Forces." *Asian Survey,* Vol. VII, No. 9 (September 1967).

Cho, Sung Yoon. "South Korea's Relations with Japan as Seen in the Normalization Treaty-Making Process 1964–1965." In *Japan in World Politics.* Edited by Young C. Kim. Washington, D.C.: Institute for Asian Studies, 1972.

Clemens, Walter C. "SALT, The NPT, and U.S.-Japanese Security Relations." *Asian Survey,* Vol. X, No. 12 (December 1970).

D'Cruz, V. D. "Japanese Foreign Policy and the Cold War." *Australian Quarterly,* Vol. XXXVII, No. 3 (September 1965).

Emmerson, John K. "Japan, Eye on 1970." *Foreign Affairs,* Vol. XLVII, No. 2 (January 1969).

Fukushi, Jiro. "Economic Cooperation with Southeast Asia." *Japan Quarterly,* Vol. X No. 2 (April–June 1963).

Gallois, Pierre. "Letters to the Editor." *Journal of Social and Political Ideas in Japan,* Vol. IV, No. 2 (August 1966).

Goto, Motoo. "Japan in Asia." *Japan Quarterly,* Vol. XVI, No. 4 (October–December 1969).

Hatano, Hirokazu. "Sino-Japanese Relations Today." *Japan Quarterly,* Vol. XV, No. 3 (July–September 1968).

Hellmann, Donald C. "The Emergence of an East Asian International Sub-System." *International Studies Quarterly,* Vol. XIII, No. 4 (December 1969).

_____. "Japan's Relations with Communist China." *Asian Survey,* Vol. IV, No. 10 (October 1964).

Higa, Mikio. "Okinawa: Recent Political Developments." *Asian Survey,* Vol. III, No. 9 (September 1963).

_____."The Reversion Theme in Current Okinawan Politics." *Asian Survey,* Vol. VII, No. 3 (March 1967).

Hosoya, Chihiro. "Japan and the United Nations." *Japan Institute of International Affairs Annual Review,* Vol. IV, 1965-68.

Hsiao, Gene T. "Communist China's Trade Treaties and Agreements (1949–1964)." *Vanderbilt Law Review,* Vol. XXI, No. 5 (October 1968).

_____. "The Role of Trade in China's Diplomacy with Japan." *The Dynamics of China's Foreign Relations.* Edited by Jerome Alan Cohen. Cambridge, Mass.: Harvard University Press, 1970.

Huh, Kyung-Mo. *Japan's Trade in Asia, Developments Since 1926—Prospects for 1970.* New York: Frederick A. Praeger, 1966.

Ikematsu, Fumio. "The ROK-Japan Treaty and Political Parties." *Contemporary Japan,* Vol. XXVIII, No. 3 (May 1966).

Imai, Ryukichi. "The Non-Proliferation Treaty and Japan." *Bulletin of the Atomic Scientists*, Vol. XXV, No. 5 (May 1969).

Ishida, Takeshi. "Japanese Public Opinion and Foreign Policy—Present Aspects and Future Outlook." *Annals of the Institute of Social Science*. (University of Tokyo), No. 9, 1968.

Ishikawa, Tadao. "Outlook on Sino-Japanese Relations." *Japan in World Politics*. Edited by Young C. Kim. Washington, D.C.: Institute for Asian Studies, 1972.

Ishimoto, Yasuo. "The Northern Territories and a Peace Treaty with the U.S.S.R." *Japan Institute of International Affairs Annual Review*, Vol. IV, 1965–68.

Ito, Kobun. "Japan's Security in the 1970's." *Asian Survey*, Vol. X, No. 12 (December 1970).

Kato, Shunsaku. "Postwar Japanese Security and Rearmament." *Papers on Modern Japan, 1968*. Canberra: Australian National University Press, 1968.

Kawai, Kazuo. "The Formulation and Recent Character of Japanese Foreign Policy." *Control of Foreign Relations in Modern Nations*. Edited by Philip W. Buck and Martin W. Travis. New York: Norton & Co., 1957.

Kennen, George F. "Japanese Security and American Policy." *Foreign Affairs*, Vol. XLIII, No. 1 (October 1964).

Kim, Young C. "Japan's Security Policy Debate." *Japan in World Politics*. Edited by Young C. Kim. Washington, D.C.: Institute for Asian Studies, 1972.

––––––. "Okinawa Reversion as an Issue in Japanese Politics." *Orbis*, Vol. XII, No. 4 (Winter 1969).

Kishi, Nobusuke. "Political Movements in Japan." *Foreign Affairs*, Vol. XLIV, No. 1 (October 1965).

Kishida, Junnosuke. "Chinese Nuclear Development." *Japan Quarterly*, Vol. XIV, No. 2 (April–June 1967).

Kobayashi, Noritake. "Some Organization Problems." *Joint Ventures and Japan*. Edited by Robert J. Ballon. Tokyo: Charles E. Tuttle, 1967.

––––––. "Through Japanese Eyes." *The World of Japanese Business*. Edited by T. F. M. Adams and N. Kobayashi. Tokyo: Kodansha International, 1969.

Kojima, Kiyoshi. "Japan's Foreign Aid Policy." *Papers on Modern Japan, 1965*. Edited by D. C. S. Sissons. Canberra: Australian National University, 1965.

––––––. "Japan's Role In Asian Agriculture." *Japan Quarterly*, Vol. XIV, No. 2 (April–June 1967).

––––––. "A Proposal for International Aid." *The Developing Economies*, Vol. II, No. 4 (December 1964).

Kosaka, Masataka. "Japan's Postwar Foreign Policy." *Papers on Modern Japan, 1968*. Edited by D. C. S. Sissons. Canberra: Australian National University, 1968.

Langdon, Frank C. "The Attitudes of the Big Business Community." *Forecast for Japan: Security in the 1970s*. Edited by James William Morley. Princeton: Princeton University Press, 1972.

––––––. "Japanese Liberal Democratic Factional Discord on China Policy." *Pacific Affairs*, Vol. XLI, No. 3 (Fall 1968).

––––––. "Japan: Multi-Party Drift and Okinawa Reversion." *Asian Survey*, Vol. IX, No. 1 (January 1969).

––––––. "Japan's Foreign Policy-Making Process." *Japan in World Politics*.

Edited by Young C. Kim. Washington, D.C.: Institute for Asian Studies, 1972.

_____. "Strains in Current Japanese-American Defense Cooperation." *Asian Survey*, Vol. IX, No. 9 (September 1969).

Lee, Chae-Jin. "The Politics of Sino-Japanese Trade Relations, 1963-1968." *Pacific Affairs*, Vol. XLII, No. 2 (Summer 1969).

Maruyama, Shizuo. "Asian Regionalism." *Japan Quarterly*, Vol. XV, No. 1 (January-March 1968).

Matsueda, Tsukasa and George Moore. "Japan's Shifting Attitudes toward the Military: Mitsuya Kenkyu and the Self-Defense Force." *Asian Survey*, Vol. VII, No. 9 (September 1967).

Matsumoto, Shigeharu. "The Future of U.S.-Japanese Relations." *Japan Quarterly*, Vol. XIII, No. 1 (January-March 1966).

_____. "Japan and China: Domestic and Foreign Influences on Japan's Policy." *Policies toward China: Views from Six Continents*. Edited by A. M. Halpern. New York: McGraw-Hill for Council on Foreign Relations, 1965.

Mendel, Douglas H., Jr. "Japan Reviews Her American Alliance." *Public Opinion Quarterly*, Vol. XXX, No. 1 (Spring 1966).

_____. "Japanese Views of Sato's Foreign Policy, The Credibility Gap." *Asian Studies*, Vol. VII, No. 7 (July 1967).

_____. "Japan's Taiwan Tangle." *Asian Survey*, Vol. IV, No. 10 (October 1964).

_____. "Security Without Arms." *Far Eastern Economic Review*, Vol. LXIII, No. 3 (16 January 1969).

Mobius, Mark J. "The Japan-Korea Normalization Process and Korean Anti-Americanism." *Asian Survey*, Vol. VI, No. 4 (April 1966).

Moorthy, K. Krishna. "Japan's Foreign Aid: Why the Tempo Is So Slow." *Far Eastern Economic Review*, Vol. XXXVI, No. 3 (3 May 1962).

Morley, James W. "Japan's Position in Asia." *Journal of International Affairs*, Vol. XVII, No. 2 (1963).

_____. "Japan's Security Policy in Transition." *Current History*, April 1964.

_____. "The Soviet-Japanese Peace Declaration." *Political Science Quarterly*, Vol. LXXII, No. 3 (September 1957).

Mostby, P. A. "Japan and the Bomb." *Foreign Affairs Reports*, December 1964.

Nixon, Richard M. "Asia after Vietnam." *Foreign Affairs*, Vol. XLVI, No. 1 (October 1967).

Ogata, Sadako. "The Japanese Attitude toward China." *Asian Survey*, Vol. V, No. 8 (August 1965).

Oi, Atsushi. "Rearmament and Japan." *Asian Survey*, Vol. I, No. 7 (September 1961).

Okita, Saburo. "Japan in South and Southeast Asia: Trade and Aid." *India, Japan, and Australia: Partners in Asia?* Edited by J. D. B. Miller. Canberra: Australian National University, 1968.

Okumiya, Masatake. "Japan's Defense Forces." *United States Naval Institute Proceedings*, Vol. XCI, No. 12, Whole No. 751 (December 1965).

Olson, Lawrence. "The Politics of Flower Arrangement, Aspects of Japanese-Philippine Relations." *American Universities Field Staff Reports Services*, East Asia Series, Vol. IX, No. 12 (Japan), (30 November 1961).

Ozaki, Robert S. "Japanese Views on Foreign Capital." *Asian Survey*, Vol. XI, No. 11 (November 1971).

_____. "Japan's Role in Asian Economic Development." *Asian Survey*, Vol. VII, No. 4 (April 1967).

Reischauer, Edwin O. "The Broken Dialogue with Japan." *Foreign Affairs*, Vol. XXXIX, No. 1 (October 1960).

_____. "Our Dialogue with Japan." *Foreign Affairs*, Vol. XLV, No. 2 (January 1967).

_____. "Transpacific Relations." *Agenda for the Nation*. Edited by Kermit Gordon. Washington, D.C.: The Brookings Institution, 1968.

Royama, Michio. "The Domestic Factors Affecting Japanese Foreign Policy." *Japan Institute of International Affairs. Annual Review*, Vol. IV, 1965–68.

Saeki, Kiichi. "Collective Defense, A Realistic Guarantee of Japan's Security." *Journal of Social and Political Ideas in Japan*, Vol. IV, No. 1 (April 1966).

Sato, Eisaku. "Japan's Role in Asia." *Contemporary Japan*, Vol. XXVIII, No. 4 (May 1967).

Scalapino, Robert A. "Foreign Policy of Modern Japan." *Foreign Policy in World Politics*. Edited by Roy C. Macridis. 2d ed. Englewood Cliffs, N.J.: Prentice-Hall, 1962.

Seki, Hiroharu. "International Environment and the Postwar Japanese Diplomacy." *The Developing Economies*, Vol. VI, No. 4 (December 1968).

Seki, Yoshihiko. "The Foreign Policy of Japan." *Foreign Policies in a World of Change*. Edited by Joseph E. Black and Kenneth W. Thompson. New York: Harper & Row, 1963.

Shimomura, Osamu. "Choices Open to Japan as a Major Economic Power." *Oriental Economist*, Vol. XXXIX, No. 724, (February 1971).

Simon, Sheldon W. "China and Japan, Approach-Avoidance Relations." *Current Scene, Developments in Mainland China*, Vol. X, No. 1 (7 January 1972).

_____. "New Soviet Approaches to the Japanese Left." *Asian Survey*, Vol. VI (June 1966).

_____. "The *Pueblo* Incident and the South Korean *Revolution* in North Korea's Foreign Policy, A Propaganda Analysis." *Asian Forum*, July–September 1970.

_____. "Sino-Japanese Relations in China's Asian Policy." *Current Scene, Developments in Mainland China*, Vol. VII, No. 22 (15 November 1969).

_____. "A Systems Approach to Security in the Indian Ocean Arc." *Orbis*, Vol. XIV, No. 2 (Summer 1970).

Sissons, D. C. S. "The Pacifist Clause of the Japanese Constitution, Legal and Political Problems of Rearmament." *International Affairs*, Vol. XXXVII, No. 1 (January 1961).

Soukup, James R. "Japanese-African Relations: Problems and Prospects." *Asian Survey*, Vol. V, No. 7 (July 1965).

Stockwin, J. A. A. "Domestic Political Restraints and Japanese Foreign Policy." *Australian Outlook*, Vol. XXII, No. 2 (August 1968).

_____. "Foreign Policy Perspectives of the Japanese Left, Confrontation or Consensus?" *Pacific Affairs*, Vol. XLII, No. 4 (Winter 1969–70).

_____. "Japan and Asia." *Current Affairs Bulletin*, Vol. 47, No. 7 (22 February 1971).

_____. "Japanese Foreign Policy and Australia." *Australia's Neighbours*, Fourth Series, No. 74 (March–April 1971).

_____. "Japanese Foreign Policy: Or How to Be a Non-Imperialist and Still Win." *Australian Quarterly*, Vol. XL, No. 1 (March 1968).

Sulzberger. C. L. "Japan's Sun Also Rises." *New York Times*, 10 March 1972.

Sugiyama, Shigeo. "Diplomatic Relations Between Japan and the Soviet Union with Particular Emphasis on Territorial Questions." *Japan in World Politics.* Edited by Young C. Kim. Washington, D.C.: Institute for Asian Studies, 1972.

Takita, Kazuo. "Positive Aid." *Far Eastern Economic Review,* Vol. LV, No. 8 (23 February 1967).

Van Cleave, William R. and Rood, Harold W. "A Technological Comparison of Two Potential Nuclear Powers, India and Japan." *Asian Survey,* Vol. VII, No. 7 (July 1967).

Vellut, J. L. "Japanese Reparations to the Philippines." *Asian Survey,* Vol. III, No. 10 (October 1963).

Vreeland, Mildred C. "Communist China and Japan: A Study of Chinese Perceptions and Policies." *Japan in World Politics.* Washington, D.C.: Institute for Asian Studies, 1972.

Wakaizumi, Kei, "Japan and Southeast Asia in the 1970's." *Current History,* April 1971.

_____. "Japan Beyond 1970." *Foreign Affairs,* Vol. XLVII, No. 3 (April 1969).

_____. "The Problem for Japan." *A World of Nuclear Powers?* Edited by Alistair Buchan. Englewood Cliffs, N.J.: Prentice-Hall, 1966.

Watanabe, Takeshi. "The Asian Development Bank Starts Functioning." *Contemporary Japan,* Vol. XXVIII, No. 4 (May 1967).

Weinstein, Martin E. "Defending Postwar Japan." *The New Leader,* Vol. L, No. 14 (3 July 1967).

_____. "Defense Policy and the Self-Defense Forces." *Japan Interpreter,* Vol. VI, No. 2 (Summer 1970).

_____. "Japan and the Continental Giants." *Current History,* April 1971.

Yoshida, Shigeru. "Japan and the Crisis in Asia." *Foreign Affairs,* Vol. XXIX, No. 2 (January 1951).

Japanese Language Material

I. GOVERNMENT PUBLICATIONS

Japan. Boei Cho. *Nihon no Boei, Boei Hakusho.* Tokyo: Okura Sho Insatsu Kyoku, 1970.

Japan. Gaimu Sho. *Waga Gaiko no Kinkyo.* No. 10, Shiryo. Sato Naikaku Sori Daijin Shisei Hoshin Enzetsu.

Japan. Gaimu Sho. *Waga Gaiko no Kinkyo.* No. 12. Sato Naikaku Sori Daijin Shoshin Hyomei Enzetsu.

Japan. Kokkai. Shugi In. Fujiyama Gaimu Daijin no Nichi-Bei Anzen Hosho Joyaku Kaitei ni Kan Suru Kosho no Keii ni Tsuite no Enzetsu ni Tai Suru Tokano Hisako no Shitsugi. *Kampo Gogai, Shugi In Kaigiroku,* 33rd Diet, 10 December 1956.

Japan. Kokkai. Shugi In. Ikeda Naikaku Sori Daijin no Shisei Hoshin ni Kan Suru Enzetsu (Gaiko ni Kan Suru Bubun). *Kampo Gogai, Shugi In Kaigiroku,* 36th Diet, No. 3, 21 October 1960.

Japan. Kokkai. Shugi In. Mitsuya Kenkyu Jiken. *Yosan Iin Kai Giroku,* 48th Diet, No. 10, 10 February 1965.

Japan. Minshu Shugi Kenkyu Kai. *Nihon Gaiko no Hoshin Kettei ni Kan Suru Kenkyu.* (Tokyo: Naikaku Chosa Shitsu, n.d.).

Japan. Naikaku. Naikaku Kambo. Naikaku Chosa Shitsu. "Beikoku no Ajia Seisaku to Nichi-Bei Kankei." *Chosa Geppo,* 161, Vol. XIV, No. 5 (May 1969).

Japan. Naikaku. Naikaku Kambo. Naikaku Chosa Shitsu. "Chosen Hanto o Meguru Kokusai Josei." *Chosa Geppo,* 165, Vol. XIV, No. 9 (September 1969).

Japan. Naikaku Kambo. Naikaku Chosa Shitsu. "Nihon no Kaku Seisaku to Gaiko." *Chosa Geppo,* 150, Vol. XIII, No. 6 (June 1968).

Japan. Sori Fu. *Nihon no Anzen o Mamoru ni wa Anzen Hosho ni Tsuite no Seifu no Kangaekata,* 1969.

Japan. Tsusho Sangyo Sho. Boeki Shinko Kyoku. *Keizai Kyoryoku no Genjo to Mondaiten,* 1968. Tokyo: Tsusho Sangyo Chosa Kai, 1968.

Japan. Tsusho Sangyo Sho. Tsusho Kyoku. "Shiryo Shu." Tokyo: Tsusho Sangyo Sho, 1 February 1972.

II. Books

Akeno, Yoshio and Susumu Kobayashi. *Hirakeyuku Chugoku Keizai.* Tokyo: Tsusho Sangyo Chosa Kai, 1971.

Anzen Hosho Chosa Kai. *Nihon no Anzen Hosho, 1970-nen e no Hembo.* Tokyo: Anzen Hosho Chosa Kai, 1967.

Asahi Shimbun Anzen Hosho Mondai Chosa Kai. *Anzen Hosho to wa Nani Ka.* Vol. I of *Nihon no Anzen Hosho.* Tokyo: Asahi Shimbun Sha, 1967.

_____. *1970-nen no Seiji Kadai.* Vol. II of *Nihon no Anzen Hosho.* Tokyo: Asahi Shimbun Sha, 1967.

_____. *Chugoku no Kaku Senryaku.* Vol. III of *Nihon no Anzen Hosho.* Tokyo: Asahi Shimbun Sha, 1967.

_____. *Chugoku Jimmin Kaiho Gun.* Vol. IV of *Nihon no Anzen Hosho.* Tokyo: Asahi Shimbun Sha, 1967.

_____. *Amerika no Kyokuto Senryaku.* Vol. V of *Nihon no Anzen Hosho.* Tokyo: Asahi Shimbun Sha, 1967.

_____. *Amerika Senryaku Ka no Okinawa.* Vol. VI of *Nihon no Anzen Hosho.* Tokyo: Asahi Shimbun Sha, 1967.

_____. *Soren Gaiko to Ajia* Vol. VII of *Nihon no Anzen Hosho.* Tokyo: Asahi Shimbun Sha, 1967.

_____. *Nihon no Jieiryoku.* Vol. VIII of *Nihon no Anzen Hosho.* Tokyo: Asahi Shimbun Sha, 1967.

_____. *Nihon no Boei to Keizai.* Vol. IX of *Nihon no Anzen Hosho.* Tokyo: Asahi Shimbun Sha, 1967.

_____. *Nichi-Bei Ampo Joyaku no Shoten.* Vol. X of *Nihon no Anzen Hosho.* Tokyo: Asahi Shimbun Sha, 1967.

_____. *Gendai no Gunshuku.* Vol. XI of *Nihon no Anzen Hosho.* Tokyo: Asahi Shimbun Sha, 1967.

_____. *Shorai no Anzen Taisei to Nihon.* Vol. XII of *Nihon no Anzen Hosho.* Tokyo: Asahi Shimbun Sha, 1967.

_____. *Ampo Mondai Yogo: Shiryo Shu.* First Supplement to *Nihon no Anzen Hosho.* Tokyo: Asahi Shimbun Sha, 1967.

_____. *Okinawa Henkan: Tsuki Asahi Shimbun Yoron Chosa.* Second Supplement to *Nihon no Anzen Hosho.* Tokyo: Asahi Shimbun Sha, 1968.

Daigokai Ampo Kenshu Kai. *Kaiyo Kokka Nihon no Boei to Shi Pawa to no Shomondai.* Tokyo: Ampo Kenshu Kai, 1969.

Dai Rokkai Nichi-Bei Zaikaijin Kaigi Nihongawa Daihyo Dan. *Dai Rokkai Nichi-Bei Zaikaijin Kaigi Hokokusho.* Tokyo: Keizai Dantai Rengo Kai, 1969.

Doba, Hajime. *Nihon no Gunjiryoku, Jiei Tai no Uchimaku.* Tokyo: Yomiuri Shimbun Sha, 1963.

Eto, Shinkichi and Yonosuke Nagai, eds. *Sekai no Naka no Nihon.* Tokyo: Ushio Shuppan Sha, 1969.

Fukushima, Shingo. *Hibuso no Tsuikyu.* Tokyo: Saimaru Shuppan Kai, 1969.

Gekkan Jiji Henshu Bu. *Kaku Jidai no Nihon o Kangaeru.* Tokyo: Gekkan Jiji Sha, 1968.

Haji, Fumio. *Ningen Ikeda Hayato.* Tokyo: Kodan Sha, 1967.

Hani, Goro. *Nihon Gunkoku Shugi no Fukkatsu.* Tokyo: Gendai Hyoron Sha, 1971.

Hoso Keizai Shisetsu Dan. *Seifu Haken Hoso Keizai Shisetsu Dan Kokokusho.* Tokyo: Keizai Dantai Rengo Kai, 1966.

Inumaru, Hideo, ed. *Kokubo to Gendai.* Tokyo: Kiyu Ajia Sha, 1969.

Ito, Masaya. *Ikeda Hayato, Sono Sei to Shi.* Tokyo: Shiseido, 1966.

Jiji Mondai Kenkyujo. *Bei-Gun Kichi, Dare no Tame no Mono Ka.* Tokyo: Jiji Mondai Kenkyujo, 1968.

Jiminto Anzen Hosho Chosa Kai. *Nihon no Anzen to Boei.* Tokyo: Hara Shobo, 1966.

Kajima, Morinosuke. *Nihon no Gaiko, Kako to Genzai.* Tokyo: Kajima Kenkyujo Shuppan Kai, 1967.

_____. *Nihon no Gaiko Seisaku.* Tokyo: Kajima Kenkyujo Shuppan Kai, 1966.

_____. *Nihon no Heiwa to Anzen.* Tokyo: Kajima Kenkyujo Shuppan Kai, 1969.

_____. *Nihon to Nishi Doitsu no Anzen Hosho.* Tokyo: Kajima Kenkyujo Shuppan Kai, 1967.

Kameoka, Taro. *Jidosha Senso, BIG-3 Tai Nihon.* Tokyo: Kodan Sha, 1968.

Kamiya, Fuji. *Amerika no Ajia Seisaku no Tembo.* 1970-nendai no Nichi-Bei Kankei. August 1969 Symposium. Shiryo No. 2-1. Tokyo: [Naikaku Chosa Shitsu], 1969.

_____. *Shichiju-nendai no Chosen Hanto.* 1970-nendai no Nichi-Bei Kankei. August 1969 Symposium. Shiryo No. 3-2. Tokyo: [Naikaku Chosa Shitsu], 1969.

Kanamori, Hisao. *1970-nendai no Nichi-Bei Boeki Kankei.* 1970-nendai no Nichi-Bei Kankei. August 1969 Symposium. Shiryo No. 5. Tokyo: [Naikaku Chosa Shitsu], 1969.

Keizai Dantai Rengo Kai. Boei Seisan Iin Kai. *Boei Seisan Iin Kai Junen Shi.* Tokyo: Keizai Dantai Rengo Kai Boei Seisan Iin Kai, 1964.

_____. *Nichi-Bei Keizai Kankei no Shomondai.* Tokyo: Keizai Dantai Rengo Kai, 1969.

Keizai Doyu Kai. *Tagenka Jidai to Kigyo Keiei.* Tokyo: Kajima Kenkyujo Shuppan Kai, 1972.

Kishi, Nobusuke. *Ampo Joyaku Kaitei no Ikisatsu to Sono Haikei.* Tokyo: Jiyu Minshu To, 1969.

Kojima, Kiyoshi. *Taiheiyo Keizaiken to Nihon.* Tokyo: Kunimoto Shobo, 1969.

_____. *Teikaihatsukoku no Boeki.* Tokyo: Kunimoto Shobo, 1964.

Kosaka, Masataka. *Saisho Yoshida Shigeru.* Tokyo: Chuo Koron Sha, 1968.

_____. *1970-nendai no Nihon no Kadai*. 1970-nendai no Nichi-Bei Kankei. August 1969 Symposium. Shiryo No. 7. Tokyo: [Naikaku Chosa Shitsu], 1969.

Mainichi Shimbun Sha. *Ampo to Boei Seisan, Nihon no Heiwa to Anzen*. Tokyo: Mainichi Shimbun Sha, 1969.

_____. *Jiminto Seiken no Anzen Hosho, Kokkai Hoshi 70-nen e no Shitsumonsen*. Tokyo: Mainichi Shimbun Sha, 1969.

Maruyama, Shizuo. *Tonan Ajia to Nihon*. Tokyo: Ajia Keizai Kenkyujo, 1968.

Miyako no Mori Shuppan Sha Henshu Bu. *Nihon no Gunkoku Shugi o Kangaeru*. Tokyo: Miyako no Mori Shuppan Sha, 1972.

Miyamoto, Yoshio. *Shin Hoshu To Shi*. Tokyo: Jiji Tsushin Sha, 1962.

Miyazato, Seigen. *Amerika no Okinawa Tochi*. Tokyo: Iwanami Shoten, 1966.

Miyazawa, Kiichi. *Tokyo-Washinton no Mitsudan*. Tokyo: Jitsugyo no Nihon Sha, 1956.

Nagai, Yonosuke. *Heiwa no Daisho*. Tokyo: Chuo Koron Sha, 1967.

_____. *Nihon Gaiko no Sentaku*. 1970-nendai no Nichi-Bei Kankei. August 1969 Symposium. Shiryo No. 1. Tokyo: [Naikaku Chosa Shitsu], 1969.

Nakamura, Kikuo, ed. *Nichi-Bei Ampo Kotei Ron*. Tokyo: Yushindo, 1967.

Nihon Heiwa Iin Kai. *Kono Ampo Joyaku, 70-nen Mondai no Shoten*. Tokyo: Heiwa Shobo, 1968.

Nihon Kokusai Kenkyujo. *Nichi-Bei Kankei to Chugoku Mondai*. Tokyo: Nihon Kokusai Kenkyujo, 1971.

Nihon Kokusai Mondai Kenkyujo. *Nihon no Anzen Hosho*. Tokyo: Kajima Kenkyujo Shuppan Kai, 1964.

Nishi, Haruhiko. *Kaiso no Nihon Gaiko*. Tokyo: Iwanami Shoten, 1965.

_____. *Watakushi no Gaiko Hakusho, Taiken-teki Kokusai Kankei Ron*. Tokyo: Bungei Shunju Shinsha, 1963.

Nitchu Boeki Sokushin Giin Remmei, ed. *Nitchu Kankei Shiryo Shu, 1945-1966*. (Tokyo: Nitchu Boeki Sokushin Giin Remmei, 1967.)

Ohira, Masayoshi. *Nihon Gaiko no Zahyo*. Shin Zaisei Kenkyu Kai, 1966.

_____. *Shimpu Shuu*. Tokyo: Kajima Kenkyujo Shuppan Kai, 1966.

Okamoto, Fumio. *Sato Seiken*. Tokyo: Shirouma Shuppan Kabushiki Kaisha, 1972.

Okazaki, Kaheita. *Watakushi wa Omou, Nihon no Kadai*. Tokyo: Yomiuri Shimbun Sha, 1972.

Okita, Saburo. *Ajia no Naka no Nihon Keizai*. Tokyo: Daiyamondo Sha, 1966.

Oto, Motonaga. *Tonan Ajia no Nogyo Kaihatsu*. Tokyo: Nihon Kokusai Kenkyujo, 1968.

Royama, Masamichi. *Kokusai Seiji to Nihon Gaiko*. Tokyo: Chuo Koron Sha, 1959.

Saeki, Kiichi. *Nichi-Bei Kankei ni Okeru Tairitsu to Kyoroku*. 1970-nendai no Nichi-Bei Kankei. August 1969 Symposium. Shiryo No. 6. Tokyo: [Naikaku Chosa Shitsu], 1969.

Takahashi, Shogoro and Shujiro Tanaka. *Nitchu Boeki Kyoshitsu*. Tokyo: Seinen Shuppan Sha, 1968.

Takeyama, Yasuo. *Fukurodataki no Nihon, Amakunai Heiwa Kokka no Michi*. Tokyo: Saimaru Shuppan Kai, 1972.

Tanaka, Naokichi. *Kaku Jidai no Nashonaru Intaresuto*. Tokyo: Minshu Shugi Kenkyu Kai [Naikaku Chosa Shitsu], 1969.

_____. *Kaku Jidai no Nihon no Anzen Hosho*. Tokyo: Kajima Kenkyujo Shuppan Kai, 1966.

Tsuji, Kiyoaki, ed. *Seiji*. Vol. I of *Shiryo Sengo Nijunen Shi*. Tokyo: Nihon

Hyoron Sha, 1966.
Utsunomiya, Tokuma. *Ajia Mondai to Watakushi no Tachiba, Gakusei e no Koen.* Tokyo: Kobunso, 1966.
Watanabe, Toshio. *Teikaihatsukoku Keizai Enjo Ron.* Tokyo: Ajia Keizai Kenkyujo, 1969.
Watanabe, Yozo and Kojiro Okakura, eds. *Nichi-Bei Ampo Joyaku, Sono Keisetsu to Shiryo.* Tokyo: Rodo Jumpo Sha, 1968.
Yashiki, Hiroshi. *Nitchu Boeki Annai.* Tokyo: Nihon Keizai Shimbun Sha, 1964.
Yomiuri Shimbun Sha Seiji Bu. *Kiroku Kokkai Ampo Ronso, Sokkiroku to Yoten Kaisetsu.* Tokyo: Yomiuri Shimbun Sha, 1968. 2 vols.
Yoshida, Shigeru. *Kaiso Junen.* Tokyo: Shincho Sha, 1957. 4 vols.
Yoshino, Toshihiko. *Shihon no Jiyuka to Kinyu.* Tokyo: Iwanami Shoten, 1969.

III. ARTICLES

Aichi, Kiichi. "Nikuson Seiken to Nichi-Bei Kankei." Kokumin Seiji Kenkyu Kai *Getsuyo Kai Repoto* 416, 25 November 1968.
Aoki, Kazuo. "Boei Ronso to Sono Shiso-teki Naikei." Kokumin Seiji Kenkyu Kai *Getsuyo Kai Repoto* 376, 19 February 1968.
Ariyoshi, Hisao. "Sanjibo to Nihon no Boei." Kokumin Seiji Kenkyu Kai *Getsuyo Kai Repoto* 333, 3 April 1967.
Boeki Kiki Sangyo Jittai Chosa Iin Kai. "Boei Kiki Sangyo Jittai Chosa." [Tokyo: Keizai Dantai Rengo Kai], 1968.
Esaki, Masumi. "Waga Kuni no Anzen Hoshosaku." Kokumin Seiji Kenkyu Kai *Getsuyo Kai Repoto* 430, Ampo Shirizu No. 3, 25 March 1969.
Fujishima, Udai. "Jishu Boei o Meguru Sei-Zaikai no Omowaku." *Bessatsu Chuo Koron, Keiei Mondai,* Autumn 1969.
Fujiyama, Aiichiro. "Nichi-Bei Giin Chugoku Mondai Kondan Kai ni Shusseki Shite." Kokumin Seiji Kenkyu Kai *Getsuyo Kai Repoto* 424, 10 February 1969.
Funada, Naka. "Waga Kuni no Anzen Hosho Seisaku." Kokumin Seiji Kenkyu Kai *Getsuyo Kai Repoto* 364, 13 November 1967.
Fuwa, Tetsuzo. "Kyosanto no Anzen Hosho Seisaku." Kokumin Seij Kenkyu Kai *Getsuyo Kai Repoto* 432, Ampo Shirizu, No. 4, 7 April 1969.
Horii, Toshikatsu. "Shunto to Ampo Toso." Kokumin Seiji Kenkyu Kai *Getsuyo Kai Repoto* 431, Ampo Shirizu No. 4, 31 March 1969.
Hoshino, Yasusaburo. "Kokkai Ronso kara Kyokuto, Jizen Kyogi, Kempo." *Sekai,* No. 172 (April 1960).
Imai, Hisao. "Asuppaku no Seiji Domei-teki Seikaku." *Gendai Seiji,* No 18 (August 1969).
Imamatsu, Jiro. "Genchi de Mita Taiwan Jijo." Kokumin Seiji Kenkyu Kai *Getsuyo Kai Repoto* 294, 11 July 1966.
Ishibashi, Masashi, "Daisanji Boeiryoku Seibi Keikaku Hihan." Kokumin Seiji Kenkyu Kai *Getsuyo Kai Repoto* 338, 15 May 1967.
_____. "Shakaito no Anzen Hosho Seisaku." Kokumin Seiji Kenkyu Kai *Getsuyo Kai Repoto* 426, Ampo Shirizu No. 1, 24 February 1969.
Kawamata, Katsuji. "Intabyu, Jidosha Jiyuka Ron ni Hantai Suru; Shokuminchi ni Sarete Ii Ka . . ." *Asahi Janaru,* Vol. X, No. 30 (21 July 1968).
Kawamoto, Yoshinobu. "Kokubo Shiso no Shin Dankai." *Sekai,* November 1969.
Kawasaki, Hideji. "Nihon Gaiko no Susumubeki Michi." Kokumin Seiji Kenkyu Kai *Getsuyo Kai Repoto* 288, 23 May 1966.

_____. "Sato Seisaku e no Hihan." Kokumin Seiji Kenkyu *Getsuyo Kai Repoto* 377, 26 February 1968.

Kaya, Okinori. "Waga Kuni no Anzen Hoshosaku." Kokumin Seiji Kenkyu Kai *Getsuyo Kai Repoto* 428, Ampo Shirizu No. 2, 10 March 1969.

Kokusai Josei Kenkyu Kai. "Beikoku no Ajia Seisaku to Nichi-Bei Kankei." Tokyo: [Naikaku Chosa Shitsu], 1969.

Mabuchi, Yoshitaka. "Fukureagaru Boei Sangyo, Gunkoku Shugi Hihan no Takamaru Naka de." *Bessatsu Chuo Koron Keiei Mondai*, Spring 1971.

"Mitsuya Kenkyu Kokkai Gijiroku Shugi In Yosan Iin Kai Zembun, 10 February 1965." *Chuo Koron*, April 1965.

Naka, Akira. "Amerika wa Betonamu o Do Suru Ka." Kokumin Seiji Kenkyu Kai *Getsuyo Kai Repoto* 386, 6 May 1968.

Nakabo, Yosaku. "Ajia ni Yuragu Nikkan Kankei." Kokumin Seiji Kenkyu Kai *Getsuyo Kai Repoto* 346, 10 July 1967.

_____. "Nikkan Hijun o Meguru Kankoku Josei." Kokumin Seiji Kenkyu Kai *Getsuyo Kai Repoto* 251, 23 August 1965.

Nakamura, Mitsugu. "Jonson to Sono Ajia Seisaku." Kokumin Seiji Kenkyu Kai *Getsuyo Kai Repoto* 306, 3 October 1966.

Narasaki, Yanosuke. "Bori Taisei no Jittai o Tsuku." Kokumin Seiji Kenkyu Kai *Getsuyo Kai Repoto* 379, 11 March 1968.

Ohira, Masayoshi. "Chokumen Suru Gaiko Mondai." Kokumin Seiji Kenkyu Kai *Getsuyo Kai Repoto* 177, 3 February 1964.

Okada, Haruo. "Mitsuya Keikaku no Honshitsu to Sono Haikei." Kokumin Seiji Kenkyu Kai *Getsuyo Kai Repoto* 235, 5 April 1965.

Okada, Soji. "Nikkan Hijun Kokkai ni Kaku Nozomu." Kokumin Seiji Kenkyu Kai *Getsuyo Kai Repoto* 254, 13 September 1965.

_____. "Sato Gaiko Hihan." Kokumin Seiji Kenkyu Kai *Getsuyo Kai Repoto* 360, 23 October 1967.

Okasaki, Kaheita. "Chugoku kara Kaette." Kokumin Seiji Kenkyu Kai *Getsuyo Kai Repoto* 380, 19 March 1968.

_____. "Nitchu Boeki Kosho o Kaerimite." Kokumin Seiji Kenkyu Kai *Getsuyo Kai Repoto* 260, 25 October 1965.

Royama, Masamichi. "Kiki no Ajia-teki Tokushitsu, Sono Rekishiteki Haikei." *Sekai no Naka no Nihon*. Edited by Shinkichi Eto and Yonosuke Nagai. Tokyo: Ushio Shuppan Sha, 1969.

Saeki, Kiichi. "Betonamu Senso wa Do Naru." Kokumin Seiji Kenkyu Kai *Getsuyo Kai Repoto* 238, 26 April 1965.

Sakanaka, Tomohisa. "Boeiryoku Seibi no Hoko to Mondaiten." Asahi Shimbun Anzen Hosho Mondai Chosa Kai. *Nihon no Jieiryoku*. Vol. XIII of *Nihon no Anzen Hosho*. Tokyo: Asahi Shimbun Sha, 1967.

Senga, Tetsuya. "Jishu Boeiryoku to Nihon Keizai." Kokumin Seiji Kenkyu Kai *Getsuyo Kai Repoto* 445, Ampo Shirizu No. 9, 14 July 1969.

Sone, Eki. "Minshato no Gaiko Boei Seisaku." Kokumin Seiji Kenkyu kai *Getsuyo Kai Repoto* 434, Ampo Shirizu No. 6, 21 April 1969.

Suzuki, Kazuhiro. "Komeito no Gaiko Boei Seisaku." Kokumin Seiji Kenkyu Kai *Getsuyo Kai Repoto* 435, Ampo Shirizu No. 7, 6 May 1969.

Tagawa. Seiichi. "Nitchu Oboegaki Boeki Kosho no Seiritsu." Kokumin Seiji Kenkyu Kai *Getsuyo Kai Repoto* 433, 14 April 1969.

Takasaki, Tatsunosuke. "Shu On-rai to Kaidan Shite." *Chuo Koron*, February 1961.

Tsuchiya, Rokuro. "Okinawa Go to Betonamu Go no Setten." *Gendai Seiji*, No. 18, August 1969.

Utsunomiya, Tokuma. "Amerika Seikai no Atarashii Choryu." Kokumin Seiji Kenkyu Kai *Getsuyo Kai Repoto* 402, 19 August 1968.

_____. "Bunka Kakumei Ka no Chugoku o Kaku Kangaeru." Kokumin Seiji Kenkyu Kai *Getsuyo Kai Repoto* 347, 17 July 1967.

_____. "Chugoku, Kita Betonamu Kambojia o Otozurete." Kokumin Seiji Kenkyu Kai *Getsuyo Kai Repoto* 226, 1 February 1964.

Yi, Yong-gun. "Chosen Toitsu Mondai to Nihon." Kokumin Seiji Kenkyu Kai *Getsuyo Kai Repoto* 391, 6 June 1968.

Index